D0590442

CONFESSIONS of a SHOWMAN

My Life in the Circus

GERRY COTTLE

with Helen Batten

First published in 2006 by Vision,
a division of Satin Publications Ltd
101 Southwark Street
London SE1 0JF
UK
info@visionpaperbacks.co.uk
www.visionpaperbacks.co.uk
Publisher: Sheena Dewan

Back flap author photo: Fin Costello
Photo of Gerry in front of circus tent: Conrad Blakemore
Photo of Chinese State Circus on back jacket: Linda Rich

ISBN-13: 978-1-904132-85-1
ISBN-10: 1-904132-85-5

2 4 6 8 10 9 7 5 3 1

Cover and text design by ok?design
Printed and bound in the UK by Mackays of Chatham Ltd,
Chatham, Kent

To my family, who have always been loyal

Contents

Chapter One

What Will the Neighbours Think?
1945-65

I ran away to join the circus when I was fifteen.

> Please do not under any circumstances try to find me. I have gone forever.
> I have joined the circus. You do not understand me. You are not listening
> to me. I do not need O levels where I am going. I am going to join the
> circus. I have gone.

So ran the tape my school friend played from a telephone box down
the line to my parents. Poor Mother and Father. It was not the done
thing in those days for a Surrey stockbroker's son attending a
prestigious grammar school to run away and join the circus. It must
have been a bit of a shock.

   Don't think this was an act of impulse. I had been planning my exit
for months. I had cultivated a friendship with the Roberts brothers,
the owners of one of the biggest circuses in the country, and I knew
exactly where they were touring. One morning in March 1961 I set off
as usual on my bike, but instead of going to school I went to Cheam
station, where I abandoned my bike and jumped on the 9.15 to
London and from there caught a train up to Newcastle. (I had already
given my younger sister, Jane, half a crown to collect the bike from the
station, take my uniform from the saddle bag and hang it up in my
wardrobe, that's how organised I was.) I walked from Newcastle station

to Roberts Brothers Circus. As I got closer and caught my first glimpse of the Big Top with its jaunty flags flapping in the wind, my stomach turned somersaults. I was totally excited and petrified at the same time. I had half a mind to turn around and get straight back on the train to London, but I knew if I went back now I would have serious egg on my face and – horror of horrors – still have to sit my O levels. I took a deep breath and holding my head as high as possible strode on to the ground. People I knew saluted me on all sides, 'Hello Gerry.' Nobody seemed surprised to see this rather intense posh Surrey schoolboy turn up in Newcastle, but then people turn up all the time on the circus and then leave just as quickly. I could see Mr Bobby Roberts supervising the tent men:

'Hello Gerry. You come to see the show?'

'No sir. I have run away from home and I want to join the circus.'

'Ah. I see.'

Bobby grinned. As the owner of a circus, it was a request he received almost every day from people of all walks of life. Usually it was men running away from something – pregnant girlfriends, nagging wives, the law. But sometimes it could be ordinary people who had fallen in love with the romance of circus and finally got the courage to walk away from normal life, or men who for one reason or another were just down on their luck and had nowhere else to go. Some took to it like ducks to water, others left as quickly as they had arrived. I think I was probably the first stockbroker's son who had stepped into his wagon though.

'Look, Gerry, I'd love to have you come and join us. But you're still very young and I really think I need your parents' permission before you can travel with us.'

My heart sank. I was going to have to ring them up. I just couldn't face my mother's displeasure, my father's silent disgust. Disappointment must have been written all over my face.

'Look, Gerry. We're going to be here in Newcastle for another week. You're welcome to stay with us as long as we're here. Muck in with the tent men. You can sleep in the stables and when you feel ready ring your parents. See what they say and then come back and talk to me again.'

What Will the Neighbours Think?

Fair enough, I thought.

It took me five days to pluck up courage to ring home. I had made the tape recording precisely because I couldn't face them. My parents, particularly my mum, had high hopes for me and were very conservative. She always called me Gerald. One day she asked me what I wanted to do. I said I wanted to work outside and travel. 'Why don't you become a civil engineer?' she said brightly. Just think, if Mum had had her way, I could be laying pipes in Zimbabwe now or building the M25 forever. But after five days, the circus was packing up and I had to make the call. With trepidation I went to the nearest phone box and after several false starts dialled the number, Melville 1535. Mum answered, sounding completely normal, bright and posh.

'Mum, it's Gerry.' There was silence.

'Oh. I think you had better speak to your father.' There was the sound of my dad coming on to the line.

'I'm sorry Dad, but you left me with no choice. I have to join the circus. There's nothing else I want to do. I would rather die than leave the circus.' There was silence. No screaming or shouting. Very cunning. If they had done that I would have disappeared for ever.

'Gerry, if you come home we will let you leave school on one condition – that Mr Blenkinsop thinks it's a good idea.'

They had obviously already worked out a plan. Blenkinsop was my headmaster. On the surface this would seem like a clever move. No headmaster would recommend a child leaving school just a month before they sat their O levels. But what I knew and Blenkinsop knew was that it would be best for everyone concerned if I never went near an exam paper. Despite going to one of the country's best grammar schools, I was about to fail them spectacularly. Since arriving at Rutlish at the age of eleven I had done as little work as possible, bluffed my way through every test and bunked a day's school wherever I could in order to work on my circus skills. Instead of geometric tables and Latin primers, I had dedicated myself to learning the arts of juggling, clowning and walking the tightrope. My Latin master said I was the most hopeless pupil he had ever come across. I had managed to get through undetected by being crafty and deploying that time-old trick of writing facts up my arms and between my fingers when sitting exams. But now the day of reckoning was nigh, there was nowhere left to hide. This was the real reason I had to run away to join the circus. I had already learned one of life's lessons – that it's much better to jump than be pushed. Much more romantic to run away and join the circus than be forced to because, I had failed so badly, nowhere else would have me. I agreed to come home.

We sat outside the headmaster's office. Me back in the uniform, still neat and pressed thanks to sister Jane. Mum looking fabulous as always in her best twin-set hat and gloves (she used to be an air stewardess for BOAC in those very glamorous early days of flight). Dad in his pin-stripe suit, totally respectable city jobber. We were ushered in. Blenkinsop did not fail me.

'I think Gerald is completely right. It would be best if he left school right away.'

My parents' jaws hit the floor.

'But surely his O levels?' my father spluttered.

'I don't think there is much to be gained by Gerald sitting them. He has shown absolutely no sign of achieving anything worth having.'

'But surely he might surprise us on the day.'

'Well, Mr Cottle. That may be, but there is another matter. While Gerald was away I received an official complaint against him from the parents of another pupil in his class. It seems he pushed a boy off his bike causing damage to his uniform and some quite nasty bruising.'

Well, the little rotter had been rude, hadn't he? Anyway, he did me a favour because there was not much my parents could say after that. I had been dismissed. Mum and Dad had no alternative but to put me on the next train back to the circus. I had managed to take my first step towards my ultimate ambition – to own the biggest circus Britain had ever seen.

What Will the Neighbours Think?

I decided I was going to own Britain's biggest ever circus the day my parents took me to see Jack Hilton's Circus in Earl's Court in 1953. It was a Christmas treat and I was just eight years old. It was the polar bears that got me. A tiny East German lady in a saucy costume had these huge white beasts jumping through hoops and sliding down slides. It seemed impossibly glamorous and dangerous and exciting. The women were beautiful and sexy, the men rough and macho. They did not look like my parents. The next day I announced my ultimate ambition was to be the circus boss and proceeded to bully my little sister and cousin to form the first ever Gerry Cottle's Circus, performing to my rather bemused parents. From then on I never ever doubted that this was what I was going to do and devoted all my time and energy to achieving it.

As I've said, most outsiders who join the circus are running away from something. Well, in the short term I was running away from my O levels, but in the long term I was running away from the dull boring world that was British suburbia in the 1950s. It's difficult to imagine now just how boring life was in those days. It was a much quieter, slower society. The roads were empty. Nothing was open on Sundays. Food was frozen or came out of tins – Batchelor's soup, Bird's custard, Robinson's orange squash, Rowntree's jelly, and Birds Eye fish fingers and peas. Holidays were at Broadstairs, Weston-super-Mare, Butlin's. Television only came on at six in the evening. The most exciting thing in my life was *Highway Patrol*. Later on I would spend hours trying to tune in to the pirate station Radio Luxembourg, desperate to catch a little Tommy Steele or Elvis through the crackly airwaves. Just wearing a pair of jeans was seen as some form of radical statement. Middle-class boys didn't do it. I had to leave the house in grey slacks and get changed into my jeans in the garage.

I never did feel right in the comfortable middle-class world my parents had worked so hard to create for me. My overwhelming memory of childhood is frustration at having to wear grey. My mother just didn't see the point in colours. She thought they were common. I remember having a terrible argument in an Epsom department store over jumpers. She wanted me to have a grey one. I wanted a coloured one. In the end we compromised and bought a grey jumper with a red stripe, but the whole way home she was going on about it. She was worried about what the neighbours might think.

She was terribly ambitious (I guess it's something I've inherited). Her mother had done better than her mother and Mum was determined to carry on the trend. In those days people from council houses rarely had puddings, so we were the sort of family that always had to have one – bananas and custard or apples and custard (which is why I'm so fat now). It was always about which knife and fork to use and we were never ever allowed tomato sauce. I used to love going round to my old nan's because she'd give me egg and chips and the evil tomato sauce. At a young age Mum took me off to elocution lessons with an old man in a smelly dark house. I really hated it. She called me Gerald, I felt like Gerry. I was actually terribly spoilt. I was the darling son of a clever, pretty mother. But Mum was also pushing me to do better all the time and I started to rebel.

Dad was a very meticulous, very organised man. He left home for the city at exactly the same time every day, bowler hat on head, umbrella on arm and *Financial Times* in briefcase. He took pride in his marrows and wiped his car dry when it got wet in the rain. Their lives revolved around a small circle of friends. There was Joan and John, Joan and Dudley, Joan and Bunny and my parents Joan and Reg. Life was one long round of keeping up with the Joanses. They would go round to each other's houses at least twice a week, have a Dubonnet, eat crisps and flirt a bit, then go home at half past eight for their dinner. I think they were having a good time, but it was all rather proper and correct and certainly not the sort of fun I was looking for when I grew up.

Instead I used a more distant relation as a role model. My uncle Sid was a bit wide, a rogue who bought a brand-new big American car out of the motor show every year. He lived in a big house in Finchley with an aquarium – very alternative in those days I can tell you. In the 1950s if you had a job you kept it all your life. In the two years after he left school, Uncle Sid had twenty-six jobs. In the end he went personally bankrupt. In order to survive he travelled across the country staying in B & Bs with a whole load of vacuums in the back of his car covered by a blanket. He put adverts in local papers offering a new vacuum for sale. People would ring up and he would say it was an unwanted wedding gift or something. Then he'd go round to their house, show them the cleaner, say he was desperate for money and could they help him. People would fall for it all the time. To be fair, Uncle Sid was a hard-working survivor. I have been likened to my uncle Sid. I was particularly impressed with his stamina when it came to women. He ran away with a barmaid in his sixties. She left him twenty-six years later when he was in his late eighties. I went to see him sometime after. He was all on his own, practically penniless, in a bedsit:

'How are you coping, Uncle?'

'Never been better, Gerry. All my life I've been bothered by women. Now it's so wonderfully peaceful. I've decided I'm not going near another woman again.'

At the tender age of ninety-three!

So there are some rogue genes flying around the Cottle family. And I think it must be that bit of me that was drawn to the exotic world of the Big Top. I was lucky, the years after the war were the heyday of circus in this country. In a world where there was very little entertainment, the circus coming to town was a very big event. In fact there was always a big circus show on TV straight after the Queen's speech. It would be Billy Smart's on the BBC versus Chipperfield's on ITV. And like pantomime today, Christmas wouldn't be Christmas without a visit to the circus. There were three really big circuses which set the standard – Bertram Mills', the Chipperfield's and Smart's. It's hard to imagine now, but Bertram Mills' Christmas season at Olympia was by royal appointment. The Queen would attend the opening night and the audience would be made up of all the diplomats and their wives. Their 6,000 seats were full night after night. London was entertained by the best acts from all over the world and a full orchestra.

Being rather spoilt, my parents treated this sudden fascination for the Big Top as an eccentric hobby Gerald would soon grow out of, and indulged me. Dad bought the promotional programme for the

Bertram Mills' Christmas Circus in September and I would study it over and over, getting more and more excited about my Christmas visit. I still remember the acts – Lily Yokoi, the Japanese girl on her trick bike, Coco the clown, wearing the biggest pair of boots ever made. Borra King of the Pickpockets was amazing. He'd get the Lord Mayor of London into the ring and while talking to him would say, 'I think you've forgotten something, Sir,' and hand him his tie. Rudy Horn would juggle while riding a unicycle. He would balance six cups of tea on his head and flick in the sugar cubes using his foot. The finale was flicking the teaspoon into the top cup. Tagora would get his tigers to lie down and then jump on them. Koringa hypnotised crocodiles, then lifted them up.

Compared with my life the circus was bursting with colour. I wanted all of it. Not just the performing, but the tent, the posters, the caravans – life on the open road.

But my ambition to own my own circus seemed an impossible dream until two chance holiday encounters. After the war there were about forty circuses travelling round the country. Most of them were small family circuses who lived hand to mouth, moving from field to field. They were centred around one family – the parents, the children, and their spouses and children, with maybe a couple of loyal retainers. There were often not more than ten people in the circus doing everything from putting up the tent and posters to walking the tightrope. It was a really hard existence and the sort of places they turned up at often had three or four other circuses visit in the same year, so it was really difficult to get a decent-sized audience. When I was ten years old we spent a week on holiday in a little village called Camelford in Cornwall. In a field was this little circus called Buffalo Bill's Wild West Circus. All they had was a bus and a small caravan and it was run by a man who called himself Count Lazard, dressed up as a cowboy. They had dogs, monkeys, a pony, a boa constrictor, a bear and a lion all living in the back of a single-decker bus while the family had exclusive use of the front. The show itself consisted of some knife throwing and a bit of whip cracking interspersed with some animals walking around the ring. But the highlight was a lady dancing in the lion's cage. The lion didn't actually do anything but he looked quite menacing and the lady used to be an exotic dancer, so it was quite racy for Camelford. To me it was pure show business and I hung around in my grey shorts getting in their way. They called me Posh Boy and got me stacking seats. At the end of the week I breathlessly asked for their autographs.

Before I give the wrong impression, I would like to say that most small circuses in this period were run by highly-respectable talented families. However, the next year we stayed in Woolacombe, North Devon, and I came across a boy pasting a telegraph pole with a poster advertising Bronco Bill's Wild West Circus. (Cowboy themes were the rage in the mid 50s). It was run by a real rogue called Major Russell. He had been uncovered by the *News of the World* that year running a bogus Madras State Circus round the North of England and he'd jumped all the way down to the West Country to try and escape. There was absolutely nothing in his show. He started it late so that people didn't realise it was so short. He did about forty minutes ending with, 'Thank you very much, it's a very hot day. I'm sure you want to be on the beach.' It was an absolute con and he was locked up two or three times for different scams later on, but I was inspired and spent most of my time practising walking backwards on an old oil drum. (The rest of the time was spent rolling around with a farmer's daughter. My first real girlfriend. One morning I came down to breakfast covered in grass. Dad looked up from his newspaper and said, 'Son, next time take a groundsheet.')

Despite being so small and seedy these two circuses only increased my enthusiasm. I liked the idea of living in a bus, going to a different place every week, the rough living, the colourful characters. It was everything my life in suburbia wasn't. Looking back it seems pretty appalling, but then it looked glamorous and romantic; and they had shown me one important thing. You didn't need to be Bertram Mills or Billy Smart to have a circus. In fact all you needed to have was a single-decker bus and a lot of cheek. Both of which I reckoned could be picked up pretty cheap. Suddenly my dream of owning a circus seemed possible. I decided to start training seriously.

There are some basic skills which form the base of most acts in the ring, and every child born into a circus family will be taught practically from the womb – how to juggle, how to do basic acrobatics and how to walk a tightrope. Now, I knew which knife and fork to use and how to pronounce my vowels, but I had some serious catching up to do when it came to performing. It was difficult. Nowadays you can buy proper props with instructions in every decent-sized town. In those days circus folk kept the secrets of their trade very close to their chest. So I started to spend hours locked in my bedroom juggling oranges and cut-up lemonade bottles – the ceiling was permanently scarred. Poor Mum trying to do her baking in the kitchen was constantly saying, 'Don't bruise the fruit. Put the eggs down, Gerald, I've only got two left.' I practised juggling for hours on the rola rola (a plank of wood balanced on a twelve-inch-long cylinder) in the back garden. But the bit that must really have amused the neighbours was walking round the house on stilts holding on to the guttering. When I was thirteen, I was good enough to make my first public appearance. Dad was a grand master in the Masons, and when it was his turn to host ladies night I was hired as the entertainment. I appeared at the Connaught Hotel juggling, with my sister Jane acting as my assistant. I was very nervous, but it didn't stop me becoming something of a local celebrity. I opened local fêtes as a juggling clown, wearing a lady's wig and terrible orange bobbly hat with make-up running down my face. I made the local newspaper and appeared on *The Carroll Levis Discovery Show* on ITV as Britain's youngest schoolboy juggler. I was so bad I can hardly bear to think about it.

That might have been the highlight of my circus career if I hadn't found the perfect opportunity just round the corner. Chessington Zoo was five miles down the road and boasted a permanent circus run by a colourful old family called the Paulos. Like many circus families this was not their real name. They were actually the Thompsons, but if you could spice up your image by adding the odd 'o' or 'z' or 'illi', then so much the better. Hence famous circus families like the Rosaires were the Rosses and the Hoffmans the Macks. The Paulos were run by their womenfolk. Large formidable ladies with big blonde or auburn hair, they reminisced every Sunday evening about the old days and who was the best at this or that act. They often ended up having huge slanging matches, with plenty of colourful language and some of that lovely hair ending up being yanked. Imagine, Aunt Emily Paulo was the same age as my mum, but every night she dressed up in top hat and tails and fishnet tights, and pretty good she looked too. To a young lad of thirteen this made a deep impression.

One day I hopped on my bike and cycled over to Chessington. I went straight to the boss, Bill Thompson.

'Sir. It is my ambition to one day own my own circus, but as I do not come from a circus family I need some help. I would be willing to do any job for no money, if, in return, you let me spend time here at your circus and have the odd juggling lesson when someone has a moment.'

Now, usually circus people are wary of outsiders, but I reckon Bill could see I was serious.

'OK, Gerry, how are you at mucking out horses?'

From then on home became a mere hotel. Every moment I wasn't in school or in bed, I was up at Chessington, mucking out the horses, clearing up the litter, tidying the seats. Eventually I was given a uniform and allowed to sell candyfloss. I worked extremely hard for hardly any money but Bill's son, Billy Boy, and his uncle Frank did give me those juggling lessons and introduced me to the extended close-knit family that make up the circus community, including the Roberts brothers.

I began to bunk school pretty regularly to work at the circus. Mum had made sure that I scraped into the posh grammar school which had recently converted from a public school. I hated it. It was the sort of place where if you misbehaved you were stood against a brick wall and a prefect swotted you every time you moved your head. I never liked wearing ties so I was always being swotted. Schools in those days weren't interested in you, what you wanted to do, why you weren't good at something. The physics teacher just used to read the lesson straight from a book. Blenkinsop could have come straight from the pages of a *Boy's Own Annual*. He had a black gown like Batman and was never seen without his mortarboard on his head. I just had no interest in school.

Well, from now on my school career went from worse to non-existent. When the circus season started after Whitsun I stopped going to school altogether. A chap called John used to write letters for me and I used to write letters for him. School was so impersonal they never even phoned my parents or wrote letters home. I still can't quite believe I got away with it. But by the winter of my fifteenth year, I was in a right pickle. My exams were approaching. I begged my parents to let me leave school early, as you could do in those days, but they weren't having any of it. So, as you know, I ran away to join the circus.

I officially joined the Roberts Brothers Circus a week before Easter as an apprentice artiste on £5 a week. I arrived at their headquarters in Oundle with a change of clothes, my juggling props and a cake baked by one of my auntie Joans.

It was here I had my first brush with a ghost. I woke up one night with a terrible cold shiver running down my spine. I looked up from my bunk bed and saw a shadow of a person slowly walking the length of the room. I have never felt so cold in my life. I was quite literally petrified. The next morning I mentioned it to the Roberts:

'Oh yes. That's the ghost of the young Dutch lion trainer who thought he knew better than us. He used to sleep in your room.'

Apparently ten years before they'd had a young trainer who had difficulty getting his lions under control. Refusing the friendly suggestions of the Roberts family, he had gone off on his own to practise with the pride one lunchtime. The lions pulled him to pieces. I decided, whatever I did in the circus, caged animals were not for me.

There was a real pecking order to circus in those days. Roberts Brothers was a middle-ranking circus, with Sir Robert Fossett and Lord George Sanger as their main competition (it had been fashionable at the turn of the century for the big circus families to give themselves titles). Below these were at least thirty smaller shows and above them were the three leading circuses of the time – Bertram Mills', Billy Smart's and Chipperfield's, known as 'The Big Three'.

Roberts Brothers Circus centred around the two brothers, Bobby and Tommy, their hard-working wives Kitty and Marie, and their children. Bobby had a son called Bobby and Tommy had a son called John, who was my age and with whom I was friendly. Originally a German family called Otto, the Roberts were probably the only circus in the country to change their name to sound more English. They were a big outfit with lions, bears, camels, llamas, a zebra, horses and ponies, dogs, six elephants and a boxing kangaroo.

As my juggling was not good enough to be let loose on the public, I was supposed to be trained on the horses. But I had two mornings trying to vault on a horse and they never taught me again. I suspect they were not going to put me in a position where I could become competition to the family. I was eventually allowed to play the behind of a pantomime horse, not altogether successfully. The starring role in the front was reserved for a boy of my own age, Gordon Howes, the son of the lion trainer 'Captain' Sydney Howes. My diary records how in the last show on Whitby, 'We fell in the box and couldn't get out.' At Inverness I fell over the ring fence coming in, lost a nail and slashed my arm. Dangerous business being a pantomime horse. That was the sum total of my performances in the ring.

Instead I was stuck doing whatever menial task was left – to begin with I was just moving the props and picking up rubbish. Later, I graduated to rolling in the huge elephant tubs and getting a flick from the Roberts' whip when I crashed them. Because I was the youngest I also had to shovel up their mess. Shovelling up elephant shit is definitely the worse job in the circus. You have to do it in front of the audience, it's embarrassing, and there's nothing worse than an elephant doing a handstand and peeing at the same time. Mind you, it always gets a laugh. When the show wasn't on there were always plenty of other tasks to keep me busy – collecting sawdust for the ring, painting and repairing the wagons, running errands for the Roberts' wives. One of my least favourite tasks was tossing the sods. The circus would move from site to site in dribs and drabs. Before a journey every driver was given directions how to get to the next ground, but in 1961, when there was much less traffic and the shows moved at daybreak, the time-honoured method was for a driver who knew the route to lead the way and for his mate, usually me, to mark the way at road junctions by dropping sods of earth out of the cab window. Occasionally there was the opportunity to have some fun. When Sir Robert Fossett was playing in Manchester at the same time as us, our routes kept crossing. One day, under orders from Mr Bobby, I moved the Fossetts' sod markers. I had a great feeling of satisfaction when a couple of hours later, as were putting up our tent, the Fossetts' lost lorries came trundling past. We bombarded them with much jeering and name calling.

The Roberts family were tough. They had very high standards and this meant the show was really hard work. The fencing had to be painted every month, if they bought a new lorry it had to be painted straight away. No one had much fun. Imagine us doing two and three day stands (mainly two), for eight whole months, which meant the show had to be packed up and moved three times a week. They would get you up at the crack of dawn, and when you are up in Scotland in the summer that is literally four o'clock in the morning. The first job was to load the horses and the elephants into the lorries. Then you had to take down the stables and the elephant tent and then drive to the next town arriving about seven or eight o'clock in the morning, and then put up the Big Top, tents and seats straight away before you were even allowed to have breakfast. When I look back in photographs I look very tired and grubby with long hair everywhere. Because of the old Sunday performance laws we did at least have one day without a show, but then we still had to parade the animals through the town. You had absolutely no time for yourself and were permanently knackered. Here's a typical diary entry describing the move from Grantham to Long Eaton on 6 April 1961:

Call at ten to five. Most lorries got off well, then started to rain. All got off ground about 8.30. Went wrong way in Nottingham. Had to bumpstart Mrs Marie's Vulcan twice. Started build up about 10.30. Rain all the time.

What Will the Neighbours Think?

Built up on car park. Didn't finish until 4.30. Wire snapped on lorry. Not all seating in but enough. Did comedy horse with John in front, two shows. Better. A new man joined us. When it came to pull-down, after carrying some seat boards he collapsed [fainted]. When he got up, he left.

Bobby Roberts had ginger hair and the temper to go with it. On the 12 April I wrote, 'Paddy had to go to hospital. He has a broken jaw (Big Bob hit him. I think he deserved it).'

Roberts Brothers started off with twelve tent men (the men who not only put up the tent but did all the manual labour on the circus) at the beginning of the season and by the end it was just old Jock with his elephants and me.

The brothers weren't the only thing that made our lives tough. The real enemy was the elements. The mud used to get so bad we had to use the elephants to heave the wagons off the ground. At Whitehaven we were accosted by an old local prophesying doom, 'You shouldn't be here at this time of year, it always floods.' We took no notice because we seemed to be miles away from the river. But later in the day there was a high tide and water came pouring on to the site. Before we knew it waves were lapping up the steps through the doors of the caravans. There was a mad rush to get the animals and the caravans to higher ground, and we mostly did, but there were a few casualties like the bandleader's tin bath, which floated off down the river. Young Bobby Roberts couldn't resist the temptation to use it for target practice with his air rifle. But the wind could be absolutely terrifying. At Hebden Bridge we had the tent laid out ready to put up, but the wind just got stronger and stronger and we had to miss two shows, a very very rare event in the circus.

But the trouble really starts when the Big Top is already up and the wind picks up. This happened during our stay at Elgin. We were all hauled out of bed at two in the morning to take down the seating. This time the tent survived, but later on that season, three weeks after we had collected a beautiful, brand-new tent from Newcastle, we had one of the worst disasters that can befall a circus. It was mid September and we were staying in a valley at Galashiels on the Scottish borders when a ferocious wind suddenly whipped up. In that situation you can either close all the openings, pull out and tighten the canvas, and park trucks and trailers close to protect it, or pull the tent down damn quick. Mr Tommy gave the call to get the tent down. We all rushed to help. Someone called, 'Cut the ropes!' The tent started flapping about in mid-air like a balloon and ripped, and all the poles bent.

The work was hard and the living conditions weren't much better. It was OK if you were top of the pile. The top shows like Bertram Mills' had the most beautiful custom-made railway coaches from America, as they still travelled by train. Circus bosses like the Roberts would have their own big caravans, not quite as beautiful but they were always wired up to the mains and had running water. I lived in a bus. In the front was the Roberts granny, an eccentric old lady who could have had her own caravan but didn't want one. Her job was to sit all wrapped up in front of the big animal cages taking money from children eager to get a peep. Everyone knew Mother was keeping a large chunk of money for herself, but no one had the courage to confront her. She wanted to live in the bus to be next to Frank, the circus cook. He was a gay old stick, a circus fan who always used to get the butcher's boy to have a coffee with him. I don't know whether he ever scored but he was a bit of a character. He wore a gypsy scarf. If he was in a good mood you got a decent meal; if he was in a bad mood you got a maggot in your sandwich. At the back of the bus was John Roberts. Again he should have had his own caravan but there had been some falling out in the family. And then sharing a bunk bed was myself and Gerald Buttery the Midget. He wasn't the cleanest of guys and was known as Butter Bean because of his prolific rear. To be fair, keeping clean was an art in itself. The day after I arrived my diary records I 'had a good wash in a bowl that I found'. On the 8 April I 'walked two miles to have a bath'. My mum was quite shrewd in her way and said that once a week I must send home my laundry. So I always had clean clothes and my parents always knew where I was.

It sounds like I was having a terrible time, but don't get the wrong impression. I wasn't. I was loving it. I couldn't believe my luck. Just a year ago it had seemed beyond my wildest dreams that I could ever travel with the circus. I was drinking it in, even the bad bits. I loved all the characters. Old Jock the elephant keeper who drank a lot and slept with the elephants in their hay. Old Pop Glitter and his wife Ethel who balanced on a plank on his head. The poor man eventually went bald. Willie Cottrelli and his wife Joanna with their hand balancing act. I was constantly pestering them to tell me stories about their lives and teach me how a circus worked.

It was the best apprenticeship I could get. It's always good to spend time at the very bottom of your chosen occupation. By the end of the season, still just sixteen years of age, I had survived a year at the sharp end of circus life. Not only had I learnt about tents and their seating and endless bits of practical knowledge about bell-rings, tow bars, stringers and generators, but I had also been taking notes about the business, recording in my diary the size of the population of the places we visited and how well or badly we did there. I also got in the habit of hard physical graft and came to accept constant physical exhaustion as a necessary part of the business.

However big a circus may become the fundamentals stay the same: the rain is just as wet, the wind just as cold and the mud still slows everyone down. Behind the sequins and feathers this is the harsh reality of circus life. It was during my first year on the road that I really came to appreciate that fact. If the physical graft tends to become hidden by layers of sawdust and spangles, the wind and the rain, the mud and the snow or even the desert heat and tropical storms are never far away.

It was now late October, and it was time to leave. My relations with Roberts Brothers had gone downhill. I was never going to be more than a simple workman in the Roberts' circus. They saw me as an outsider, a 'flattie' or 'josser' as circus folk call them. I was accepted as long as I was happy to carry seatboards and heave canvas, but they would not tolerate me in the ring. I later learned that this attitude was typical among circus folk and only the most determined josser could break through. I'd had my juggling props with me and practised when I could but by 20 June I'd been lamenting, 'Practised for a bit but seem to be getting worse.' I would have loved to be a clown and I remember buying a large pair of clown boots which I saw in a shop in Consett. The Roberts Brothers' sons were unbelievably cruel saying, 'You'll never be a clown, you're only a tent man.'

The tent master was a top-class clown called Jacko Fossett. He took me aside one day:

'Listen, Gerry. You're worth more than just shovelling elephant shit. Don't hang around here. Go to a small circus. They won't be so particular about who they let star in their ring. You'll get the chance to try your hand at anything you want. You don't need to be amazing, just cheap and keen.'

I liked the sound of this advice, so when the circus ended, I went to see Joe Gandey.

The Gandey's was a real family circus, the like of which has pretty much died out these days. At the centre was Old Joe Gandey. He had been on the circus all his life and still spoke the circus language. In the 1920s his dad, Bob Gandey, had been a famous theatre impresario who, seeing the way the old music halls were going, thought there might be more longevity in the circus and invested his money in a small tent. Joe inherited the tent and had just about managed to keep the family business going. When I joined the circus it was twelve people, including Joe's hard-working wife Mary and his son Michael, who was my age, and baby Phillip. The main acts were Bob Del Rio, who had been a real star of the music hall and played the London Palladium, but was now reduced to touring with a cowboy act, which was in turn on its last legs because of his asthma attacks when he got overenthusiastic with the lasso; Ivan Karl, the world's smallest strongman; and Billy Gunga, the Indian chair balancer. Joe's publicity was done by the man who hit the gong at the beginning of Rank films, Carl Dane, although all he seemed to do was sit in the pub all day. The tent was one pole, some patched canvas and a domestic light bulb. And Joe practised a 'no play, no pay' rule. If business was bad, as it invariably was when the hot weather came in June and July, Joe would simply cancel the show and you went without your wages. Of course, we would try to second-guess this and sometimes Joe would blow the whistle to begin at the last moment, just to see you running around in a flat spin trying to get ready in time. Then sometimes he would see you hanging around in your make-up and decide not to go ahead. Although he was having a laugh, I sometimes got to the point where I couldn't see where my next meal was coming from.

But I really enjoyed myself and stayed for three years. I was at the centre of the show and Joe let me try anything I liked in the ring. I was never one for aerial acts or animals, so I started out juggling but I could only do three or four balls at a time. I soon realised that I had to devise some exotic props to try and hide the fact I wasn't really very good. I did learn fire eating but gave up after six months because I couldn't bear the funny taste of paraffin in my mouth, so I began to concentrate on clowning. I started off as JoJo the clown (all clowns seemed to be called JoJo at one time or another) until Joe gave me the name Scats after being stuck behind a Southern Counties Agricultural Trading Society lorry on the A303 outside Andover.

It soon became clear that while I enjoyed being in the ring (it was a great opportunity to show off to the girls), I did not have the talent to make it to the top of the Big Top. If I was going to be big in the circus world the only way was to be the boss, and I'm not talking ringmaster. This is where Old Joe Gandey was really good to me. He taught me the basics of how to manage a circus. He took me everywhere with him and treated me like his son. I learnt to start by putting posters in the high street, and to concentrate on the better shops. I learnt that when you went to ask for a ground, let the farmer name his price first because it was often a lot less than you were going to offer. I learnt not to raise expectations, no flash posters with pictures of animals you couldn't deliver. Joe was laid-back and used to sell the tickets over the door of his wagon. I used to say, 'Joe, why don't you get a smarter ticket office?'

Joe said, 'Stop going on about this bloody ticket office. They come up and see a little circus and this old clown selling tickets over the door of the caravan, so they're not expecting much, but by the time they've seen Tommy the Talking Pony, you juggling and Ivan Karl it's been much better than they expected. They go home happy and tell their friends about it.'

Most of all I learned the patter. Joe used to get the audience on side at the beginning of every show with, 'We're only a small circus but I'm sure you will enjoy it.' If you put a new trick in your act and it didn't work, then Joe would explain it – when I dropped my balls, as I did quite frequently, he would pipe up: 'Ladies and gentleman, please excuse Gerald here. His wife's just had a baby and he's been up all night feeding it,' or 'Gerry's hurrying because he can hear his new baby crying and he needs to get back to feed it,' or 'He's just got married and isn't concentrating,' (thereby also squashing any chances I might have with any good-looking girls in the audience).

Joe was an instinctive showman. In his own way he had a kind of genius. It was Joe who turned plain Tony Carroll, the lorry driver, into Ivan Karl the world's smallest strongman – giving him the launchpad to tour with Smart's and eventually end up at the top of his profession, travelling all round Europe with the big Hagenbeck German Circus.

Joe kind of adopted me and I think it was probably quite hard on his older son, Michael, who was the same age as me. But Michael was terribly scatty and didn't really want to be in the circus. He was in charge of the electrics for the show and was constantly blowing the generator, so we often had to go and beg electricity from the nearest house. Joe had rented an electric baby from a music hall act, Professor Sparks. He would put this metal baby on the laps of the audience and offer a fiver to anyone who could manage to wash the baby. They'd start merrily enough and then the current would come on and your hand couldn't get near to it. But Michael kept forgetting to charge the car battery which powered it, so the baby ended up polished till it shone. Joe was absolutely livid, £5 was probably worth about £50 today, and we never heard the end of it. Michael and I never really got on – we often ended up rolling round the floor fighting, although I think that was more because I was better at getting the girls than him.

You see it wasn't all work. Somehow I found the time and energy to do quite a bit of playing. When the circus rolls into town it always has, and always will, attract a lot of attention, sexual attention that is. There is something intrinsically exciting about dark strong strangers who can do wonderful tricks. For a lot of young ladies in the days before travel, before television, we were a breath of fresh air and were relatively sophisticated compared to the local lads. My first season with Joe we spent touring around the mining villages in the North. We played in little tiny places and pitched ourselves in the car parks of working men's clubs or on the black slag heaps which were hard but at least you didn't get stuck in the mud. In these godforsaken spots we were little stars. Girls used to hang about after the show wanting a bit of your circus magic. I would start off with a bit of patter, 'Did you enjoy the show? Do you want some free tickets?' and before I knew it I would end up having one, sometimes two, girls a night.

I'd fairly leapt for joy when Joe announced that he'd rented Gordon Howes' baby elephant for the season. Gordon and I were perfect partners in crime. He was tall, good-looking and slightly older than me, so when it came to chatting up women, I watched and learned from a master. We got on famously. One day, just half an hour before the show was due to start, we were approached by two of the local girls, 'We'll do it with you if you give us free tickets,' they said. Well, being seventeen this seemed like too good an offer to refuse. I dashed round breathlessly to Joe's caravan to ask. I was a bit nervous, he was quite unpredictable: sometimes he'd go along with the joke, sometimes he'd tell you where to go.

'Joe, see those girls over there. I need some tickets for them . . . Please?'

'What's wrong with them paying like everyone else?' he said with a twinkle in his eye. He knew where this conversation was going and was determined to get the maximum out of it.

'Well. How can I put this?' I paused. 'Look. Joe. Look at them. They've said they'll sleep with us before the show if we can get them tickets. What do you reckon?'

'I reckon I must need my head testing. Here you go.'

I didn't wait for him to change his mind.

Confessions of a Showman

I was all right but when poor Gordon made his move he was told quite firmly, 'United is playing at home.' It's the first and only time I've heard it referred to as that.

My amorous pursuits were complicated by the fact that although the whole back of the converted ambulance I lived in was a huge double bed, I shared the van with Billy Gunga the Indian chair balancer. But where there's a will there's a way. We started off taking it in turns to bring our girlfriends back to the ambulance and then sometimes we would just pull the blankets over our heads and pretend we were on our own. But these girls did tend to look a bit rough when you caught sight of them in daylight, off to work with rollers in their hair so they could hide the fags they were nicking from the tobacco factory. I remember one time I was talking to my date from the night before when her husband and father rounded the corner on the look-out for her (she'd obviously pulled this trick before). Without pausing for breath she said, 'Pretend you're asking me for directions.' I never walked off so quick in all my life. Joe used to enjoy all this naughtiness.

Sometimes he would help you along: 'Gerry, there's a nice-looking girl in the hairdressers, why don't you go in and offer her some free tickets?' Other times he'd set you up. Tell you he'd managed to chat up the good-looking girl in the sweet shop and I should go and try my luck. You'd be sent away with a flea in your ear and, 'I already told that old man I'm married.'

At the end of the season I had the dilemma that all circus artists face: what on earth to do for the three months in the winter when the circus can't tour? Luckily Joe offered me a job working with him in a Santa's Grotto in the BB Evans department store on Kilburn High Road. We put on a half-hour little circus show with Tommy the Talking Pony and three little dogs, and I did some juggling and clowning. As soon as enough children had gathered we would have to start. We were paid a fixed salary no matter how many shows we put on. One Saturday we ended up having to put on sixteen shows. Joe absolutely loathed it and spent most of his time trying to scare the children away by taking out his teeth and pulling his hair over his face when their mums weren't looking.

What Will the Neighbours Think?

However Joe did like the opportunities the job gave to sample London's nightlife and he decided it was time for me to be introduced to the delights of Soho. In those days it was a very edgy place. The bars were run by Maltese or Cypriot gangsters. It was much darker. It always seemed to be foggy or misty – I guess it was the last days of smog. Policemen would be walking the streets in capes and the girls would actually stand on the street corners under lamps wearing skirts with slits up them, fur coats and carrying large handbags. Joe teased them shouting, 'The Rozzers are coming!', and laughed as they scarpered. That is until one night he got hit over the head with a very large handbag when one of the ladies recognised him as the joker from the night before.

The West End was much more theatrical in those days. There were a lot of variety artists down on their luck who worked as barmen or doormen. We used to end up in the Bear and Staff, round the corner from Leicester Square. It was full of theatrical agents, variety artists, showmen and girls of all sorts, and Joe knew all of them. Although I never liked drinking alcohol (most of my life I have been tee-total) I loved hanging out with Joe. I sat open-mouthed, just lapping up the atmosphere, while Joe worked the room catching up with all his friends and contacts, swapping theatrical tales of derring-do and debauchery. One night I had an uninvited initiation into Soho life. An infamous old transvestite known to all as Mrs Shufflewick squeezed next to me:

'What is your name, young man? I don't believe I have seen your face around here before. I would have remembered it.'

I started to feel very nervous.

'Do you know London? Perhaps I could show you the sights? Would you like to have dinner?'

Everybody started to listen and enjoy the show. Joe looked at me and said with a completely straight face: 'Come on, Gerry. Mrs Shufflewick's a nice lady. Let her take you around, show you London. It would be an experience you'd never forget.'

I was completely lost for words and deeply embarrassed. I had been brought up not to be rude to strangers, but I also knew enough to know that this was the kind of sightseeing I never wanted to experience. You have to understand those days were very different to today. Homosexuality was still illegal. Coming from Cheam I had never met anyone gay before, or at least to my limited knowledge. I just didn't know how to handle it. I got up and made for the nearest loo thinking that if I waited in there for long enough he would get the message and be gone by the time I got out. But the rogue followed me in there and standing next to me in the urinal made, let's just say, a very definite physical pass at me.

'Get your hands off me or I swear I'll knock your block off!' I yelped and rushed out of the gents and out of the pub all a fluster. Joe came running after me delighted. We caught a bus back to Kilburn. I can still remember the journey. The smog was so bad the conductor walked in front with a flag. Joe spent the whole of that interminable journey teasing me. I'm glad I managed to give him so much amusement, but it was a long time before my pride had recovered enough to venture into the Bear and Staff again.

I had more luck in Joe's favourite haunt, the Hippo Club. Soho was full of drinking dens in those days. The Hippo, so-called because it was behind the Hippodrome, was mainly frequented by theatrical types (I saw Jeffrey Bernard in there once). It was run by a Spanish lady called Harriet, and she had three rooms upstairs which girls worked from. There were various girls of various types – something to suit everyone if you were that way inclined, although the ladies were all rather older than they looked at first glance. Joe only came there to drink and talk his way through the night with his mates, but he was very keen for me to sample the extra services the club offered. I was very nervous but after several nights he persuaded me to be introduced to this lady, let's call her Susan. She was not your average working girl. In fact she was a wealthy woman, a doctor's wife. The couple had this arrangement where a couple of nights a week she was allowed to come up to London. I don't know definitely that her husband knew what she was up to, but I think he did. Sex outside marriage was seen differently in those days. It was not unusual for a wife to accept and turn a blind eye to a husband's sexual infidelities, but this way round was much more unusual. Anyway, Susan was in her late thirties. Very sophisticated and classy. She wore very trim expensive suits and black stockings. I was totally in awe of her and she taught me a thing or two. I don't know why she did it, it certainly wasn't for the money, but I thought she was great and saw her many times. I liked older women for a long time afterwards. (Now I don't – but then I am sixty.)

This meeting was to have other long-term consequences. I developed a taste for that whole scene – the over-the-top characters, the sexually-charged atmosphere and the feeling of doing the forbidden – like a duck to water. Maybe it was the rogue Cottle gene. The male Cottle has often had a weakness for women. Uncle Sid I have already mentioned, but my grandfather was also reputed to be a dreadful womaniser. My grandmother may have committed suicide over his passion for a barmaid called Maud. My great uncle Sid allegedly poisoned his wife. Whatever it was that drew me to dangerous ladies, it was a fatal attraction that was to get me into no end of trouble later on.

Ten things you didn't know about
British Circus Families

1. Philip Astley was the father of all modern circus. Yes, circus was invented in Britain in 1768, when the former cavalry officer started to give public riding displays in Lambeth. He built a timber amphitheatre and added acrobatic, balancing and tumbling acts.

2. The most famous British circus showman was Lord George Sanger. His parade was over two miles long with 200 horses.

3. The first Sir Robert Fossett was a champion circus jockey, winner of countless cups and medals in the 1930s and 40s.

4. In 1854 William and George Pinder started the first Pinders' Circus in Scotland. Arthur, one of their sons, established a circus in France which is still touring there today.

5. The Rosaires were all good-looking and very talented, especially with animals – from elephants to Pekinese dogs.

6. The Chipperfields go back the furthest of all the British circus families. They first performed before Charles I with a bear and found their fortune at frost fairs on the frozen Thames.

7. Billy Smart was a large funfair operator who kept going through the blackouts by putting his rides under circus tents. The big show stopped in 1971 when they opened Windsor Safari Park.

8. Bertram Mills was a coachbuilder who after seeing a very poor circus at Olympia in 1919 bet one of his friends £100 he could do better.

9. The old circus families still running today: Phillip Gandey and his Spirit of the Horse show; Tony Hopkins leases the name of 'Billy Smart's'; Zippos is a good traditional, very nostalgic show; Santus Circus travels round the south-east; Hoffmans' Circus is now trading as Uncle Sam's American Circus; the Roberts Brothers Circus – I still love going to see the matriarch Auntie Kitty Roberts. The biggest operators in the UK are the EEC run by my old partner, Brian Austen, and Peter Featherstone. They still bring the Moscow State Circus and Chinese State Circus to Britain every year.

10. Giffords Circus was set up 5 years ago by Nell Gifford. She has no circus background but has created a magical small circus which travels to Cotswold villages too small for most circuses.

Chapter Two

How to Marry into the Circus
1966-70

I first spied my wife Betty when I was seventeen. The problem was she was only twelve.

Gandey's circus had joined up with a small family circus called James Brothers to play a rather curious regular gig for the Birmingham city transport authority. Every summer they hired a circus to give a free performance to their employees and families – a genuine busman's holiday played out on their municipal playing fields over the course of a week.

I was having a brief but intense fling with Betty's cousin Pauline who was a juggling rope spinner with James Brothers. She was a warm lovely circus girl who absolutely refused to go to bed with me. One night after the show I was desperately whispering sweet nothings in her ears when I spied the most exquisite dark-haired beauty, scowling at me from the corner of the tent.

'Who's the beauty in the corner?' I asked without thinking.

Pauline drew back and narrowed her eyes at me.

'Why do you want to know?'

I thought it best to change the subject, but I was completely distracted. Maybe it was what they call love at first sight. Certainly I was all weak at the knees and butterflies in the stomach. You see, this young girl was the embodiment of all my adolescent fantasies about circus girls. She was tiny yet curvy with very dark beautiful long hair, stunning in her sequins and feathers. It was as if Gina Lollobrigida had walked off of the set of the film *Trapeze* into the small circus ground at Aston. (She also looked a bit like my mother, very pretty and dark haired – make of that what you will . . .)

Having lost all concentration, I made my excuses to poor Pauline and crept off to make some enquiries. The results were very exciting. The 'beauty' was none other than Betty Fossett, a princess of Britain's oldest circus family.

The Fossetts are this country's greatest circus family. They have been riding horses bareback for nearly 200 years. One half of the family are dark (they're the good-looking ones), the other half are ginger (enough said). The men are all called Robert or Tom or Harry except for Betty's branch, which tend to go for John or James. It was quite possible to have an old Harry Fossett and a young Harry Fossett and a middle Harry Fossett all working on the same circus. This prolific family always made a habit of having lots and lots of children, many of whom in turn went off to run their own circuses and many of whom either married each other (with 'jossers' instinctively distrusted, marrying second cousins was not uncommon) or they married into the other big circus families – the Chipperfields, Smarts, Sangers etc. The Roberts brothers had a Fossett mum, hence the red hair. Not only did the Fossetts infiltrate the whole of British circus but there is a Fossett diaspora across the globe. There is a huge clan of Irish Fossetts running the biggest circus on the Emerald Isle. There are thousands of them in the States. Sarasota, Florida, is the place where all American showpeople base themselves – half the population of Sarasota are related to the Fossetts. They went over in the 1950s with their riding acts. In the UK, one branch of the family is very rich – Uncle Bailey Fossett had hung up his riding boots and owned half of Northamptonshire – and the other half is not so rich. That is Betty's lot. But they are good-looking. They never sleep, work like maniacs and have quick tempers. Even among circus folk who, let's face it, are more colour-ful than most, they are known as 'The Mad Fossetts'.

There were lots of romantic reasons why I wanted to marry a cir-cus girl (next time you're in on a rainy afternoon take a look at Claudia Cardinale in *The Magnificent Showman*). But there was one far more important practical reason. I was a 'josser', not of circus blood. If I had any real intention of becoming Britain's biggest circus owner I was going to need the contacts and cooperation of the circus community. I was only going to get this by becoming one of them. Marrying Betty should get me a VIP invitation to join the club. I saw the whole progress of my life laid out in front of me.

There was one small problem. She didn't really like me very much. It was rather unfortunate that the first time she saw me I was manhandling her cousin and the next time she saw me I was in the middle of a blazing row with Ivan Karl. He had a gift for winding you up, but when Betty walked round the corner it just looked like I was being aggressive. I tried to introduce myself.

'One day I'm going to own the biggest circus in Britain,' I said.

She looked at me as if I was a piece of elephant shit on the heel of her glorious silver stilettos. 'If I had a pound for every josser who said that,' she spat as she strode off, tossing her gorgeous black hair.

I thought she was magnificent and had no doubt that she was the woman for me. I decided to play a long game. She was still only twelve years old after all.

After two more seasons with Joe Gandey, I was ready to move on to new pastures. I really wanted to gain more circus experience, but I was lured away by the promise of some very lucrative work manning the ropes of Kirby's Flying Ballet, keeping the actors floating in the air in Peter Pan. It was working with them in the Theatre Royal in York, I saw my second ghost. One night up in the dark spooky grid, manning the ropes, a terrible chill went through my bones, my hairs stood on end and a shadow passed over me. I felt a terrible tragic presence brush past me. At the end of the performance I asked the theatre staff if they had any supernatural inhabitants. They told me the story of the poor nun who got pregnant and was apparently bricked up in the theatre to die a terrible death. I was relieved when we moved out of York and spent a season touring Europe.

It was a great experience. I travelled across the Eastern Bloc and ended up in Israel on a kibbutz. (Remember, these were the days before interrailing and package holidays. It was quite heady stuff for a boy from Cheam.) It was through this experience that I got a job working on Holiday on Ice, again travelling across Europe. I wasn't doing anything particularly glamorous (ice skating is not really me), but helping with the equipment was surprisingly profitable. I certainly was earning more than I would have done on the circus. I put everything away into my little circus fund, in full expectation that one day I would have enough money to buy my very own circus.

But I was feeling homesick and I knew I needed more time on a real circus. And I couldn't get Betty Fossett out of my mind. As it happened, Betty's father, Jim Fossett, was the owner of the James Brothers Circus, who Joe Gandey joined with for the bus workers' show. It was a small traditional circus built around an extended family. There was Betty and her two elder sisters Juliana and Babette, otherwise known as Julie and Baba, and her brother Jimmy. It was a good little show for what it was. Always immaculate, it was called the 'mini Bertram Mills'. But it was in need of shaking up. There was no publicity to speak of. Every year it went to the same old small towns and fields, hardly venturing out of Warwickshire. It struggled to make enough money in the season to keep everyone fed during the winter. Their farm had no running water.

I went round to see Jim Fossett. With my heart in my cowboy boots I knocked on the door. I had no plan B. I offered my services as a juggler and more importantly to take over their bookings and publicity. Jim Fossett saw I meant business and I was hired. I pulled on at the family farm in Lowsonford in Warwickshire with my converted ambulance in the summer of 1966 and immediately started my campaign to win over Betty. Now at fifteen she was even more beautiful than I remembered. I watched her every night in the ring, in her tight black trousers presenting her clever ponies, commanding her performing dogs and throwing her lasso around. Betty was tiny but so strong, I'd never seen rope spinning like it. Her skill with her hands was wonderful to see. I adored her, but she still showed absolutely no interest in me.

I began a war of attrition, my tactics – to wear her down through sheer persistence. I had absolute confidence I would have my way in the end. I used every opportunity to get close to her, whether it was squeezing in the van beside her or chatting her up behind the curtain or taking her hand in the cinema. This was the first time I had had to chase any girl that hard, but then I had never fancied any girl that much. Maybe that is what kept me enthralled. But circumstances were going my way. Her two sisters were already paired off. Betty needed a partner to go to the pub or the dance in the local town. In reality I was the only available young man in the world of James Brothers. In the end she gave in. I'm not sure when or how, but soon we were an item. By the time Betty was sixteen I had scraped together every last penny and bought a caravan for £200 – a lot of money in those days. I think it was the best caravan I ever had. It was a gorgeous 'Rollalong' with thick oak panelling and a coal fire and a curved roof. It was the heaviest thing on the show but exquisite. I used it as bait to get Betty to move in with me. Caravans are very very important to circus folk. It worked, she couldn't resist. She moved in the week it arrived although it was hardly the done thing in those days. My mother was horrified – yet another thing she couldn't tell the neighbours. Betty's parents turned a blind eye. I think I was proving too great an asset to the circus, they couldn't afford for me to leave. But her brother Jimmy made no secret of his fury.

'How the hell are we going to move such a bloody big wagon?' he seethed.

'The same way we move every other bloody wagon.' I snapped back. Although Jim did have a point. In the end I had to exchange the Rollalong for something more practical. Sometimes you have to learn the hard way.

James Brothers was great fun. It was a very young circus, with the three sisters and their boyfriends all on the show and then Jimmy and the cousins too. The Fossett sisters were (and still are) a force to be reckoned with. They are very very close. When they were children, they all slept in the same bed like puppies. They were all beautiful with their long black hair and gypsy eyes. Baba and Julie caused a stir wherever they went. They would wear hot pants to the local disco and masses of make-up. Betty is a bit more reserved, but they all like to drink. One night we had to take Julie home from the pub strapped to the car's roofrack because she was so plastered and making so much noise. I liked Baba and Julie, but they were slow to accept outsiders and they didn't make my life easy. They teased me constantly. It hurt at the time, I desperately wanted to be accepted. I got on better with their boyfriends. Mike Denning lived with Baba. He was incredibly nice, laid-back and full of bonhomie. Everyone loved him and he's one of these people who makes friends instantly wherever he goes. Billy Wild was a bit different but we were still great friends. He was ambitious and organised. He had long hair and looked like Buffalo Bill and was desperately in love with Julie, but she wasn't in love with him. She broke his heart in the end. It has to be said, she was very very sexy. Betty's brother Jimmy was a different story. Circus families are very traditional. The eldest son is the heir apparent and expects to be treated with respect. Well, Billy and I were never going to accept this and there was a clash from day one. It was a classic fight to be the alpha male. I guess the caravan incident says it all. I'd only been on the circus five minutes and somehow I managed to find the money and the cheek to buy a caravan that outshone them all. Jimmy resented me and showed it.

Even though everybody was working very hard in the ring, they also worked very hard to have a comfortable home life. The Fossetts' caravans were always warm and cosy and spotlessly clean. The whole extended family gathered in Betty's parents' caravan every night to eat. Julie would dash back from the ring, put a pinny over her leotard and cook my favourite stuffed apples. I loved it. Talk round the table was always about the show, what we had done, what we hadn't done. Billy, Mike and I were always coming up with ideas to make the circus better, which Betty's father and brother invariably shot down.

There was lots of laughter and teasing. Betty's father could be very dry. They were all part of one big extended family that worked, ate and laughed together, and sometimes had the mother of all rows. It felt incredibly warm and lively and real. So different from my repressed middle-class home life. I wanted to be part of a family like this – but with myself at the head of it.

We were in our caravan one night after the show. Betty was doing some sewing – she loved making things for the wagon – red velvet cushions, matching curtains, sofa covers with gold tassels on. 'I'm going to ask your father if we can get married,' I said.

Betty looked absolutely shocked. There was silence. 'Oh, all right then,' she muttered, sewing rather furiously, avoiding my eyes.

I don't think she really wanted to get married. I was very definitely in love with Betty. I'm not sure she was in love with me. What I do know is that she was under pressure from both the mothers. My mum kept asking, 'When are you going to get married?' Her mum kept saying, 'Isn't it about time you got married?' That's what it was like in those days. London may have been about to swing but the rest of the country was still stuck in a world of Green Shield Stamps and Izal loo paper. Betty was very young, I was so much older I think she just went along with what I wanted, but looking back she wasn't very enthusiastic.

I strode straight out of the caravan and made the short walk across the ground to Jim's caravan and once more banged on the door with my heart in my boots. He ushered me in.

'I've come to ask if I can marry Betty,' I announced.

Jim looked surprised and didn't react for a few seconds. He was a man of few words but the ones he used were important. 'You're not in love with her, you know,' he said.

I said nothing, although I think he was completely wrong. I was very definitely in love with Betty. There was a pregnant silence.

'But I know that whatever happens you will take care of her,' he added.

Our interview was over. I took that to be a blessing of sorts and thought no more of these wise words until years later. Instead we rushed headlong into wedding preparations so that we could get married as soon as the tenting season was over. I picked 7 December because seven is my lucky number. I was born on 7 April 1945. As soon as we announced the date, Jimmy true to form announced he was getting married two weeks earlier.

On a bitterly cold but sunny December morning Betty and I were married in the little church of Rowington in Warwickshire, the Fossett family seat (as much as any travelling family can have a family seat). It was quite a do. The guest list was bizarre – a mix of my parents' gin-swilling Surrey stock-broking friends and the circus elite. Like any royal family wedding, representatives of all the major dynasties turned up – a full complement of the Roberts, not to mention the head of the Fossett clan himself, Uncle Bailey Fossett, complete with his Rolls-Royce. In fact one of my abiding memories is the procession of huge cars that glided up to the church. In those days any showman worth his salt owned a big Mercedes – they were the only big diesel cars you could get in those days – so it was quite an impressive show. Considering Betty and I didn't have two ha'pennies to rub together and I was a virtual unknown in the circus world, it was a very good turnout. I guess as usual I had somehow managed to punch above my weight.

Betty's sister Julie has always been a dab hand with a needle – whizzing up the most fantastic sequined circus creations. She made Betty a turquoise velvet wedding dress trimmed with rose pink velvet. She looked amazing. She was flanked by the Fossett sisters in rose pink velvet. Betty's favourite uncle, Sonny Fossett, was supposed to be my best man. Unfortunately he got drunk in the pub beforehand, so my dad had to do the honours. We all retreated to a local pub afterwards. Betty and I left in my terrible Hillman Minx estate car with my dog Barney. It was so rusty rainwater leaked through the floorboards. Betty desperately tried to mop it up with copious amounts of newspaper. We ended up in a very posh stale hotel in Stratford-upon-Avon, Betty very much the worse for wear. Then it was straight off the next day to start in pantomime in Leicester. It was not a good honeymoon and not a great start to our marriage.

How to Marry into the Circus

One good thing to come out of our Big Day was a real change in my mother's attitude to my life in the circus. Dad had always been more laidback and cheerful, but seeing her beloved Gerald as a rough tent boy living in back of an ambulance had been a difficult pill for Mum to swallow. Once I went into the ring at Gandey's they used to come up in the holidays to watch me perform. My parents arriving was always a bit of an event. They were seen as very posh and everyone treated them with great respect. Joe always invited them for a meal in his caravan. And although there's no denying I had rebelled in a quite spectacular fashion, I always played the dutiful son ringing home once a week and sending the odd postcard. While everyone was very British and polite about it, I still felt my mother's extreme disappointment. But my wedding was a turning point. At last I was doing something 'normal' – something the neighbours' children did, something she could talk about – and I think the wedding and the quality of the guests surpassed all her expectations. Maybe the circus wasn't so bad after all.

So I had my wife and I was a fully paid-up member of the circus community. Now I had to get my circus. But I needed some help if I was ever going to own Britain's biggest circus. Luckily I had struck up a rather unlikely friendship that was to change my life.

One of the great things about circus is all the weird and wonderful things you do to keep yourselves from starving in the winter when the circus is off the road. It can also be one of the biggest nightmares. I met Brian Austen working as an extra on the set of the film *The Evil of Frankenstein* in 1964. I was dressed as a stilt walker. He was dressed as a lady snake charmer in a long dark wig, gold-encrusted bra and see-through trousers on account of the fact that the lady performer who was supposed to be doing it had run off with a young man the day before. Luckily there were no close-ups, so he got away with it.

Brian and I got talking and immediately hit it off. We were an unlikely couple. We had both run away to join the circus when we were fifteen but there the similarities ended. Brian had a hard start to life. The eldest of three brothers and three sisters, his father was in and out of jobs and his mother never stopped working just to make ends meet. From the age of eight he worked at the local stables and went door-to-door selling horse manure to boost the family finances. He walked out of school before he could take any exams and got a job on a circus mucking out horses. Unlike me he didn't fall in love with the circus itself, for him it just offered an escape from home. But the way of life suited him. Brian discovered an unparalleled talent for the mechanics of circus. Even today there are few people who can get close to Brian's expertise and talent for moving a circus. More galling for me, the man who had little interest in what went on inside the Big Top effortlessly turned his hand to animal training, tightrope walking, knife throwing, whatever. But Brian certainly hid his talents under a bushel. He lacked my confidence. Brian was, and despite becoming a rich man is still, very shy. He had much less interest in the management of the circus – publicity, posters, booking sites. My strengths were his weaknesses and vice versa. In that way we complemented each other perfectly.

Now at this time Brian had got work on *The Evil of Frankenstein* because he was hanging around with the eccentric Count Lazard, who I had first met many moons ago on my childhood holiday in Cornwall. The camp count had never really left my life. I liked him because his was the only circus run by a josser. He looked the part of the circus impresario – he was never seen without his long pointy beard, Stetson and gold chains. He was great friends with Joe Gandey and when the circuses toured in the same part of the country, they would, as was customary, pay each other a visit, watch the show, drink a few polite beers and then sink a whole lot more while exchanging the latest gossip.

The flamboyant count, self-declared son of a Bulgarian nobleman, actual former miner, former hair-gel salesman from Nottingham (a mixture of glycerine and turpentine) liked to keep a small circle of young men around him. Somehow Brian had managed to get himself adopted. But hanging out with the count was not a fast track to fame and fortune. After they finished the filming, the count and his crew had nowhere to go. All their lorries and wagons were stuck on the green outside Shepperton studios.

In the end the council got fed up and sent in a load of bulldozers to tow them away. The count's stepbrother, William, got out a cine camera and started filming 'to use as evidence against the violence of the council'. Instead he found himself being arrested by the police. The drama queen count wailed, 'What are you doing to my beloved brother? Take your filthy hands off him!' and was promptly arrested too.

In those days a lot of showmen, including the count, couldn't read or write. I was seen as well-educated. I got hold of Bill Bailey, a well-respected friend to all showmen, who ran his own very successful insurance business. Bill sorted it out and got the count released. Meanwhile, the whole charabanc had been towed out of the field and left sprawled along the roadside right on a busy roundabout. A Mini promptly went flying into the back of the tent pole trailer and caused a nasty accident. The police accosted the count once again.

'Is this your circus, Sir?'

'My circus? No this isn't my circus. I wouldn't leave my circus lying around like this. My circus is over there,' he said pointing to the field. 'Oh no. Where's it gone? Someone's stolen my circus!'

The count screamed hysterically at which point the police were so irritated they nearly took him in again.

Something had to be done. By chance I came across an advertisement in a circus trade paper: 'Circus wanted for South Africa'. It looked perfect for the count. For a small fixing fee the count could take the whole circus on tour in the sunshine. I wrote a letter on the count's behalf and they left a couple of months later. Unfortunately the fixer turned out to be a conman. When they arrived, there was neither sight nor sound of him – the tour didn't exist. The count was all washed up with nowhere to go and no money to leave. Well, all credit to his lordship, he pulled himself together and eventually managed to get a circus up and running and touring not only South Africa but Swaziland and Rhodesia as well.

Brian prospered. He learned how to train animals and fix the circus machinery. He also learned a few other useful tricks and ended up running off with the count's stepbrother's wife, May – formerly the renegade snake charmer from *The Evil of Frankenstein*, now the snake charmer on the Lazard Spectacular. The count was livid. Brian was out of a job. Penniless he fled back to Britain. He found himself at the tender age of seventeen unemployed with a twenty-nine-year-old wife and two children to support. Now in the scuffle with the council at Shepperton Brian had managed to leave his one and only pair of shoes in the back of my car. Back in Britain, in desperation, he wrote to me saying he was coming to collect his only pair of shoes, no matter that nearly three years had passed. Strangely enough I had actually hung on to them. I wrote back telling him to come straight over to James Brothers and he could have his shoes and I might even be able to get him a job. Brian fitted in straight away, Jim Fossett gave him a caravan and I had the last piece of the jigsaw I needed to get my own show.

I was very happy on the James Brothers Circus. But my ambition to own the biggest circus in Britain was keeping me awake at night. I felt I was getting too comfortable and being sucked into the family circus. I wanted to be head of my own family circus and I felt ready. My frustration grew, especially as many of my ideas to improve James Brothers fell on deaf ears. I had already made a difference booking bigger towns, changing the design of the posters and doing some publicity with the local press. It seemed obvious to me that James Brothers could so easily move into a different league and take on the likes of the Roberts, if only they would take a few risks, but Betty's father Jim just wanted a quiet life. He didn't like it when the circus was full, he worried that a fight would break out. He was always grumbling, 'Gerry, don't work so hard, I don't like these big towns,' 'The circus isn't good enough for this town,' 'The seats might collapse.'

But worse was Betty's brother, Jimmy. He found it difficult to accept an ambitious young man suddenly beside him at the family table. A classic example is the time I managed to get Betty's father to allow me to sell sweets. We were paid basic wages, but the family were also given concessions – Julie did the orange juice, Baba did the programmes and Jimmy had the concession for the candyfloss. All the profits could go into your own pocket. Of course as soon as I married Betty and qualified as a member of the family, I lobbied hard to get my own concession. In the end Jim reluctantly gave in and said I could sell sweets. Well, you can imagine what happened. He thought I would be dealing with a few Sherbet Dib Dabs. Instead, I scoured the country and found a fantastically reasonable confectionery wholesaler in mid Wales. I borrowed the biggest truck I could find, drove a hundred miles and filled it to the brim with everything from pear drops to Mars bars. There was absolute uproar. Everyone accused me of trying to steal their business; Jimmy called me all the names under the sun. After just a week Jim took me to one side.

'Gerry son, I think the only decent thing you can do is give up the sweets. It's bad for everybody's business and bad for the family. How about toffee apples?'

Well, there was no way I was going to let Jimmy Junior get the better of me. I went down to Kent and bought hundreds of apples at an ultra-low price. I got Betty making toffee through the night and when the show opened the next day the caravan was decorated with a thousand toffee apples. There were trays and trays of them from every window, the door and even the roof of our caravan. It really was time for me to move on.

I had been working on my escape for a long time. I had my little pile of savings from my season travelling with Kirby's and work with Holiday on Ice. It was time to use it. First, I had come across a circus-loving director of Tesco's, Jack Maclaren, when he had hired me to do some stilt walking for a 'Money takes bigger strides at Tesco's' promotion. He agreed to put up some money for me to run my own circus. Then I found a man who called himself Captain Lewis. (My father had always warned me not to trust anyone who used 'Captain' or similar in front of their name.) Captain Lewis was one of those characters that you find hanging around the periphery of show land. He was a marquee hirer. He offered to give me a tent and all the equipment I needed in return for a share in the circus. With Brian back on the scene I had found someone who could not only perform lots of acts in the ring but most importantly take care of all the mechanics of the circus, the building and the moving of it. Not many people can do that. I had everything in place to leave, but I had one more hurdle to jump – breaking the news to the Fossett family. I knew it was not going to be easy. Staying long term had never been an option but you can imagine my trepidation as I took that short walk across the ground to Jim's caravan. He ushered me in cheerily, thinking probably that I wanted to talk about the latest poster design. Instead I dropped my bombshell.

'I've come to tell you Betty and I will not be travelling with James Brothers next year.'

Jim's face said it all. Total shock. I ploughed on.

'I think you know it has always been my ambition to manage my own circus. I have been working very hard and I am now in a position to launch the Embassy Circus next season with myself as the manager and co-owner.'

I thought I could detect just the hint of a raised eyebrow and twitch at the corner of the lips. He was making me nervous.

'Brian and May will also be coming with me.' I was starting to stammer. Jim was not going to say anything.

He got up and held open the door for me to leave. As I was halfway through the caravan door he spoke for the first time, 'Obviously you won't be spending the winter with us then. You'll be looking for somewhere else to build this Embassy Circus of yours.'

I was shocked. This was a serious blow. I had just assumed, naïvely, it was going to be OK for us to use the Fossett farm as a base to build the circus and get on our feet. I was going to have to find somewhere else to go, and fast.

Then just as I reached the door of my caravan Jim seemed to relent a little. He shouted across the field, 'I know I will never have to worry about Betty while she's with you. You're never going to let the grass grow under your feet.'

★

How to Marry into the Circus

It was the nearest thing to a blessing I could have hoped for. Despite everything I had said right from the very beginning, everybody presumed that now I had married into the family, I had also married the James Brothers Circus as well. Now I was splitting the Fossett family up. I was taking away their beloved youngest daughter, who moreover by this time was pregnant with their first grandchild.

Betty was distraught. Our caravan rocked with weeping.

Her mother shouted at me, 'It's not right taking Betty away at this time. About to have her first baby. How could you?'

Her brother tried to punch me. I ducked and he put a hole in the wardrobe instead. For years we had to hang a picture over it. The last few weeks were miserable but I wasn't going to give up. I had a very strong feeling that if I didn't make my move now, I never would. I certainly would never own the biggest circus in Britain. I stuck to my guns despite intense pressure from all around.

The day dawned for us to go. Until then the family didn't really believe we were going to leave, but when they saw our caravan all packed up ready to go an almighty row broke out. I can't remember the details except the sound of weeping, which still rings in my ears. I know that Betty's mother shouted at me and I know I ended up arguing with Jimmy. Worse still was the fact that Betty's father, who I really liked and respected, stayed locked in his caravan. He never even came out to say goodbye. We pulled off the ground in disgrace. As we went through the gate, Julie and Baba were leading the horses and dogs back up the lane after their morning exercise. They came running up.

'Where are you going?'

'Betty, why are you going?'

'Why are you going now?'

'Don't leave, Betty.'

'Gerry, you can't take her.'

They were distraught. It was awful. Betty had nightmares about it for weeks afterwards. The Fossetts were an incredibly close-knit family, but I think it was Jim who suffered most. The girls were all devoted to their daddy and he to them. He had an especially soft spot for Betty as the baby of the family. She had been quite spoilt, but with Betty that was easy to do. She was very pretty and charming, the sort of little girl who melted old ladies' hearts in supermarkets. Jim ran the circus, not just because he loved circus, but because it kept the family living and working together. I think Betty leaving broke Jim's heart. The girls said that he was never the same afterwards. He felt betrayed, although he did tell the sisters, 'I know whatever happens, Gerry will always look after Betty.' My entrance and then exit from James Brothers was to have huge consequences for the whole family.

Banned from the Fossett family's winter quarters, my sister Jane managed to persuade an old school friend to let us camp on his pig farm outside Reigate while we built the new circus – or, to be more specific, while Brian built the new circus. Drowning in mud and pig excrement, Brian sewed the tent and made the seats out of old scaffold planks. Brian's younger brother Michael also joined us. He was a wiry bundle of energy. A fantastic worker, he couldn't keep still, and nothing was impossible. He was full of fun and practical jokes, just what we needed at this stage. The Austen brothers had great fun teaching themselves basic circus tricks, learning to walk with stilts and on the tightrope. They made a comedy bike out of an old iron bedstead. The pregnant Betty went to stay with my parents in Cheam. I went off in search of a job in the pantomime to earn the money to keep us all.

Aladdin starred Tommy Trinder. He was a real household name in his day and a real pain for us young budding performers to work with. He was very precious and superior. I was playing the part of a Chinese policeman with blue comedian Chubby Oates. There was a real tradition of playing practical jokes on the 'serious' talent. Well, we did our utmost to make Tommy's life a misery. We kept him talking so he missed his entrance, and shouted, 'Oh Tommy, you're on,' so he'd go rushing on stage at completely the wrong place and look a right prat. The final straw came when we changed the words on his song sheet to something very rude. He was apoplectic.

'I know it was you two bastards. You're the clever circus boy who can tie knots and you're the budding comedian who thinks he's funnier than me.'

He tried to get us sacked. The stage manager was in a tizzy, 'Whatever you do just deny it. He's determined to see you out of here.'

Well, we kept our heads down and managed to keep our jobs. But Tommy was determined to get his revenge. The next night at the part where us policemen had to stand frozen on stage while he cracked a joke, Tommy decided to do the longest stand-up set in history. He went on and on, the jokes just kept on coming. We got cramp and felt faint. It's funny how often comedians can't take a joke.

By February it was clear that the money from the pantomime was not going to be enough to get the Embassy Circus on the road. I managed to get Brian a job in a zoo in Cambridge. While I went round putting posters up all over town, twice a day he walked the tightrope over a cage of hungry roaring lions. It was an instant hit. I racked my brains to think of other ways we could use Brian's extraordinary talent. I saw a poster for local stock car racing. The track's managers were more than happy to advertise a man walking the tightrope as cars raced underneath him. Brian was less happy.

'You must be joking.'

'Get lost, Gerry. I am not doing it. I AM NOT DOING IT.'

'If it's such a good idea, you bloody do it.'

'Look, you can shove your circus right up your . . .'

Somehow, I'm really not sure how, I managed to persuade Brian to do it. He started off cheating it – waiting until the cars had started before walking which meant they'd already gone under by the time he was over the track. The manager complained, 'You're not getting your money unless he walks with the cars actually underneath him.'

Poor Brian had to do it again It was absolutely petrifying. I'm pretty robust, but my heart stopped beating. Suffice to say he only did it the once.

★

By March we were ready to go on the road with the Embassy Circus. Looking back now I don't know how we faced the audience. Although we were a big outfit – about twice the size of James Brothers, it was all very tatty – the tent poles were pine trees with the bark still on. The tent and the trucks the captain had loaned us were horrid. The artists had mainly come from an advert in *World's Fair*. We had a pair of brother clowns who spent the whole time arguing. Never the best way to assemble a circus.

From day one it was a disaster. We opened at Petersfield in Hampshire in the pouring rain. No one turned up. We didn't even take £100 and we were working like dogs. I was working all hours booking the sites, doing the publicity, managing the circus, then appearing as the ringmaster, juggling and presenting the ponies. Brian was doing five acts in every show, twice a day and then had to organise the pull-down of the tent, move the whole circus and then put it up again. Most of the equipment that the captain had given us was totally rubbish – it took a day and a night just to do one move. I was making no money at all. Brian was just getting paid a pittance.

Despite all this the dreadful captain had the nerve to keep coming down and hassling us for money. 'Ooooh well, when am I going to start seeing a return on my investment?' was the constant refrain. He was completely paranoid about being ripped off. He couldn't understand why vast profits weren't rolling his way – although I challenge anyone to show me a new circus that has managed to make any real return in its first six weeks. When the circus got to Beaconsfield, the captain called a meeting via a very pompous letter asking that all petty cash vouchers, receipts and the wage book be available for inspection, as well as the staff contracts and the receipt and registration for a car Brian had bought.

Now on his way into this meeting the captain spotted some fire extinguishers in the back of Brian's old car which he was using to transport equipment between towns. In front of everyone the ridiculous captain opened the meeting by accusing Brian of stealing the fire extinguishers. All hell broke lose.

How to Marry into the Circus

'You can shove them up your arse. In fact you can shove the whole circus up your arse. I'm not working that hard for anybody,' Brian shouted and stormed out.

I rounded on the captain, 'You idiot. Without Brian there is no bloody circus.'

A fight started. Somewhere along the way I managed to push the captain through a wardrobe. That night I penned my letter of resignation.

Holtspur Playing Fields,
Beaconsfield.
10th June 1970

Dear Sirs,

Due to the recent accusations and mis-trust, I feel strongly that as from last night, I am compelled to resign from the company. Loath as I am to do this, it having caused me a lot of unpleasantness, I feel the onus has fallen on me. May I take this opportunity to wish you every success if you continue with the Embassy Circus.

Yours faithfully,
G W Cottle.

So ended my first ever circus. We packed our belongings in a solemn mood. We had lost all our savings. Betty was seven months pregnant. We had nowhere to go. The next morning our little tribe of myself, Betty, Brian, May, their children and Brian's brother Michael, set off along the A40 with no plan. We stopped in a lay-by to do some hard talking in the back of the van.

Betty wanted to go back to James Brothers. 'What's wrong with you, Gerry, why won't you? You know they'll have us back straight away. With the baby coming it's not the time to start anything new. We haven't got any money anyway. What choice have we got, you stubborn pig?'

In my mind was a picture of Jimmy Fossett laughing. Hell would have to freeze over. I would have to be diplomatic with Betty, though.

'Look, Betty. I know in the short term things would be a lot easier for all of us, particularly for you. But that's not the answer and you know it's not. We've done the difficult bit. We've actually left. To go running home to your mum and dad would be a huge step back. We've got to keep going forwards if we're ever going to get that circus I said we'd have.'

Betty shook her head, bit her lip and looked as if she was going to cry. The windows were beginning to steam up in the rain.

Brian as ever had remained pretty silent up to this point, but I knew he had the same picture of Young Jimmy in his head that I did. He rubbed the van window with the sleeve of his jumper and seemed to be staring into the distance, I thought pondering our limited options. Instead he piped up, 'Gerry, have you noticed what's on the poster on the pole over there?'

I strained my eyes. I thought I was seeing things. Through the driving rain I saw a picture of a roaring lion and a Big Top – Chipperfield's was in town.

'Wait here,' I shouted as I ran and leapt into the van. Just up the road I found Dicky Chipperfield and his enormous circus.

Chipperfield's had just got back from a few years in South Africa and was suffering from an attack of disorganisation. They were particularly struggling to move the huge tent and equipment. Although Dicky and I didn't really hit it off he was in a bit of a spot and didn't need much persuading to take us on. We were hired as casual labour at the rate of only £25 a week, but grateful for anything we pulled on to the ground.

Within a few weeks Brian and I had taken over the moving of the circus. It was operating like they had never seen it before. I was getting them a couple of new sites a week. Brian was saving them a day and a half on moving the circus. We asked for more money and Dicky refused. We had a huge stand-up row and before we knew it we were once again packing up and heading off into the unknown.

How to Marry into the Circus

Once more we camped on a lay-by, this time on the A30, with nowhere to go and no money to live on. Betty was now eight months pregnant. We decided that the only way forwards was to start our own Cottle and Austen's Circus straight away. But with no money, no equipment and a baby about to arrive, we weren't quite sure how we were going to do it.

Ten things you didn't know about
The Ring

1. The ring is traditionally 42 feet in diameter. This was probably established over 200 years ago as the ideal size for the horses to canter around. You never see a circus ring or stage larger than 42 feet.

2. Ring boards are the large pieces of wood put into the ring for trick cyclists and magic acts. The ring carpet is for acrobatics. The ring fence is the box surround that establishes the ring area.

3. The sawdust which coats the floor must be soft white wood to give the proper effect, reflecting the light and looking clean. Often nowadays white wood chippings are used instead of sawdust.

4. In the US and South America the tradition is for a three ring circus, sometimes with two stages in between, all surrounded by what is called a hippodrome track for parades.

5. The audience sees the ringmaster introduce the acts and direct the show. Behind the curtains he also performs a costume inspection. No holes in the tights allowed and ladies are sent to change if their costumes are too revealing.

6. Under the ringmaster is the ring foreman. He organises all the staff, called ring boys. Except they are very rarely boys. In fact they are usually ancient, being ex-artists who are too old to perform.

7. In Britain the ringmaster is traditionally dressed in top hat, red tails and white gloves. George Lockhart started the tradition of the ringmaster wearing a red tailcoat during Bertram Mills' Olympia Christmas circus in 1922.

8. The most famous ringmaster in Britain is Norman Barrett, now in his 70s and still working with Zippos. As a boy Norman always wanted to be a lion trainer but his father told him to be a ringmaster because they live longer – it certainly worked for him.

9. In the last few years ring mistresses have been very fashionable in either hot pants or cut-away leotards. Yasmine Smart, granddaughter of Billy Smart, has been one of Britain's finest.

10. Without all the animal acts ringmasters are no longer necessary. Shows tend to follow a storyline so need less announcements. You have more of a stage manager now, who rarely appears front stage.

Chapter Three

The Smallest Circus on Earth
1970-72

I screeched into the car park of the Royal Epsom hospital in a converted bread van with a picture of Brian walking the tightrope on the side. I was in a hurry. The baby was finally on its way. Mum had rung first thing that morning, 'Gerry, you had better get here quick as you can. Betty's in hospital, the baby's coming.' God, I was in a flat spin. I was a hundred miles away in darkest Dorset and had to pick up a hundred old school chairs from an old circus man in Twyford before I could get to the hospital.

Well, as it happens I could have walked and still got there in time. The baby took forever. I sat in the delivery room reading *Circus Lady* with my gown on back to front, eventually falling asleep with my feet in the air, snoring. Betty says I was a waste of space. Over twenty-four hours later Sarah came into the world. She was beautiful. I was impressed with her long black hair. Visions of a troupe of beautiful dark Cottle trapeze artists flashed before my eyes. Anyway I held her and then had to say goodbye. There was important work to be done. The brand-new Cottle and Austen's Circus was waiting to get on the road. It would be a good few weeks before I could see Betty and Sarah again.

...

How do you start a new circus from scratch?

1. Find somewhere to build it

As we sat in that lay-by on the A30 pondering our future, I peered out of the window. In the days before the M4 had been built, the A30 was the main route down to the West Country. I watched the cars fly past and read the signpost on the other side of the road. It said 'Berwick St John'. The name rang a bell. Chipperfield's old publicity man had told me about a friendly farmer in Berwick St John called John Pocock. 'Gerry, if you ever get in a spot around there, he's the man to go to. He'll never refuse a circus in need.'

I leapt in the van and drove straight there. It was seven o'clock on a Sunday evening when I walked into his farmyard and knocked on his door. A patrician man in tweeds opened it.

'Mr Pocock? I'm sorry it's so late, Sir, but I'm in a bit of a spot and I've been told you're a good friend to the circus,' I said.

'Well, you had better come in and tell me all about it then,' he said.

John Pocock was a real gentleman. Without another word, he ushered me straight into his study. It was rather chaotic, with a big old roll-top desk overflowing with bits of paper. I explained our dire situation but also my enthusiasm and determination to start a circus of my own. Something I said managed to capture his imagination.

'That's very exciting, Mr Cottle. As it happens I do have a field you can use. It's small but you can pull on to it straight away and stay however long it takes to get your new circus up and running. Just let me know if I can be any help to you. Don't worry about the rent, we'll sort it out later.'

Well, this true friend never did ask for any rent and, although he never gave us any money, he did a deal with the village. We were only charged half price for whatever we needed for the circus and he made up the rest later out of his own pocket. We never knew anything about it. For years we came back to the blacksmith in Berwick St John because he was so damn cheap. It was only at Mr Pocock's funeral many years later that I found out about his incredible generosity without which we would never have got Cottle and Austen's Circus on the road.

2. Buy a Big Top

I had another piece of good fortune. Driving along one day I noticed a marquee set up by the side of the road. I stopped the car and asked whether I could buy it. The owner happened to be the father of an old school friend of mine and he took a shine to me. We couldn't have the marquee but he did have an old flower tent we could have for £60 and, moreover, he offered to take just £20 up front and let me pay a pound a week for the rest – which was good because there was no way I could have laid my hands on £60 at that moment in time. He also threw in the poles and ropes and tipped me off where I could get the stakes from a scrap heap. My dad lent me the £20.

As for the rest of the equipment, we were so poor, Brian made the ring door curtains out of his brother's stripy bed sheets, the seats were the old school chairs I'd picked up the day Betty went into labour, so rotten that every time you folded them they disintegrated, and the ring fence was made with old deck chair canvas. The tent had so many holes we often had to stick it back together with Copy-dex glue.

3. Paint your circus

On our travels we had made friends with a bus driver called Barry Walls. He used to do a great turn lying on a bed of nails in fairgrounds but was now working on the Green Line buses. Barry used to turn up in his London Transport uniform and paint all our vehicles a nasty blue colour with pictures of our acts on the side. Not long after this Barry joined us full-time and stayed with us for many years as one of our most successful acts – every year he had a different incarnation: Tutankhamen, El Hakim, Chief Sitting Bull, whatever, he was very popular!

4. Find some artistes

I reckoned that between the Cottle and Austen families, we could just about pull it off. Brian could do tightrope walking, knife throwing and a bit of clowning. May could eat glass and lie on a bed of nails. Michael could dance on the stilts. Of course I would do my turn as Scats the clown and a bit of juggling. Betty would have to go straight back in the ring as the ringmistress and we could take it in turns to change the music on the record player when we were back stage. The one thing we were missing was the animals. In those days you weren't considered a real circus unless you had animals, but we just didn't have the money to buy them or the means to transport them. I would have to put into practice all the spin doctor tricks I had learnt from Joe Gandey to turn this vacancy to our advantage, and I promised myself that just as soon as we made any money at all we would invest in something four-legged and furry. It probably wouldn't be an elephant but even a performing pussy would be an improvement.

5. Book some sites

With the circus coming together, I started to look for some places to go. In the age before mobile phones, the village phone box was my office. It was the bane of my life. I had to make arrangements with pockets weighed down with change and Les Dawson type ladies banging on the windows as they queued up to ring their daughters. You'd be told the farmer would be there to take your call at seven o'clock in the evening, but the chances of the phone being free at seven were very slim. If you had more than two phone calls to make, forget it. You were likely to be lynched by the mob waiting outside. If the farmer was engaged I felt like committing hari-kiri. When we got on the road I'd be dashing off between acts, wrestling with my clown costume, the coins, a pencil and paper and the telephone receiver. I hated it.

6. Let the audience know you are coming

In these early days we're really talking about posters. Joe Gandey had taught me that even the smallest circus should take the trouble to print their poster properly and, instead of writing on the location and date, have slips printed that could be stuck on the posters so it looked like the circus coming to your town was a proper event. Also keep pictures to a minimum, don't draw elephants and lions if all you have is a three-legged goat. Just your name will do and then people don't know what to expect.

The Smallest Circus on Earth

It was a horrible job putting up posters. You'd go into a garage and ask if you could put one up and they'd say, 'How many clowns do you have? Do you want some more? We've got plenty of clowns here.' Well, it's funny the first time you hear it, but after the fourth or fifth time the joke starts to wear a bit thin. Or people would say, 'Have you got any elephants?' and when you said you didn't they'd go, 'Oh well, it's not a very big circus then, is it?' Some posh shops would be very rude and tell you where to go, although strangely enough the more difficult it was to get people to put your posters up, the better the business. There is a hell of a difference between places. Somerset and Northamptonshire were always terrible for circus — maybe it's something about places that make shoes . . .

By the beginning of July everything was finally in place. Sarah was born on 2 July 1970 and we pulled out of Pocock's on the sixth, heading for our first stop, Sturminster Newton. We were the smallest circus on earth but I felt totally optimistic and excited — probably because we had absolutely nothing to lose but the shirts on our backs and a dodgy bread van.

Which was good because we got off to a really rocky start. The audiences were hopeless. Again, we only made £100 in the first week. After we'd paid rent, petrol and the posters there was barely enough to feed ourselves. Things were pretty tough.

It was such damned hard work for a start. Our day ran as follows. Get up at the crack of dawn (we're talking 4.30–5.00 am) and start the trucks. They were so old they had to be run for an hour to get the pressure up. As the field filled with clouds of smoke, the wives fed the men and children then packed all the furniture — all the ornaments (and circus ladies tend to collect china for some perverse reason) had to be wrapped up in newspaper and stored in boxes in the caravan. Brian got the vehicles ready, which was no mean feat because in those days they were always breaking down. The circus travelled in convoy in case anyone broke down. Devon roads were not built for a thirty-foot lorry towing a thirty-foot caravan. We caused some terrible traffic jams when we got stuck. Poor little Moretonhampstead was a village with just one street. Our lorry got totally stuck trying to turn into a gate and blocked the high street for two hours, with all the holiday traffic building up behind. Murder was nearly committed.

When we reached the new site, we would mark out the pitch. There's quite an art to working out the best place for the tent. It needed to be seen from the road but also protected from the wind. All our lorries would be parked out front so the circus looked as big as possible. Brian and Michael would then put the tent up, with Betty and May pulling on the ropes. Then there were the props, generator, lights, cabling, ring and seats to be put out. Dressed in my one blazer and old school tie I would be off booking more sites, and talking to councils. I worked at least one week ahead which meant I travelled miles in the car every day. I would put up posters going from shop to shop, giving out free tickets all over the place. Michael would get on his stilts, go into town and hang round the local school giving vouchers for cheap seats. Then we would dash back for the show. Betty would sell the tickets from the caravan door. May would stand at the entrance to the tent, take the tickets and sell programmes. When it was time for the show to start Betty would put on her top hat and tails and as mistress of the ring blow the whistle for the artists to assemble. The programme ran as follows:

Me as Scats the clown warming up the audience
Brian and Michael juggling
Me doing some magic
May as Yacarna, Britain's only female yogi – in silk pantaloons, washing hands and face in broken glass, and dancing on it

Interval – May would sell candyfloss, 6p raffle tickets for a teddy bear prize and circus balloons

El Briarno walks the tightrope
Scats the clown would become the ballerina of the wire, walking the tightrope very badly (no problem for me!)
Michael stilt walking

The Smallest Circus on Earth

Brian as a clown getting children out of the audience to perform
Juggling Melvilles – Betty and I doing our regular juggling act
Pawnee Joe – Lots of whips and fire eating as Brian threw knives at May

As the audience left one of us would make a last desperate attempt to sell some circus balloons as the rest pulled down the tent around them. Lights had to be dismantled, chairs stacked and lorries loaded before we could go to bed. We usually finished at midnight ready to be up at five the next morning to move. There really wasn't much time left for anything else.

Occasionally if we had found a very good pitch we would stay for three days, but we usually moved every day. By the end of the season we had been to forty-one places in just thirteen weeks.

It was particularly difficult for Betty. Especially as she didn't really want to be there in the first place.

After the baby was born, Betty went up to the Midlands to stay with her family on the James Brothers Circus. It was her first time back since our fraught exit the year before, and once she got there she really didn't want to leave. Her family were over the moon to see her and made a huge fuss of the baby. Jim Fossett loved baby Sarah, she reminded him so much of Betty as a baby. He walked around the ground, town, supermarket, anywhere, holding her so gently, and proudly showing her to anyone who would look. Betty was able to go shopping with her sisters who showered her and baby Sarah with presents. She even made it to the disco once or twice. It was the best time Betty had had since we left. She was still only twenty after all. Every few days we'd speak on the pay phone and she'd make another excuse why she couldn't join me. Eventually I lost my temper.

'You're my wife and you belong here with me,' I shouted.

Betty realised that she could delay no longer. It really had become a choice between me and her family. I found out later that she nearly didn't come back to me. It would have been very easy to stay and bring up Sarah on her own at James Brothers – the whole family would have rallied round and there were none of the usual stigmas on the circus about being a single mother that there were in suburbia.

But in the end she broke her father's heart all over again and left, this time with his beloved first grandchild. Billy Wild drove her all the way down from Warwickshire to Charmouth in Dorset where we were pitched. It was a long journey, especially with a new baby, and Billy had to literally drop Betty and Sarah in a field and zoom straight back to the show. Poor Betty. I was out as usual and no one came out to welcome her. She was horrified by the sight that greeted her – a field knee-deep in mud, a two-pole flower tent full of holes, an old lorry and two tiny caravans. Not a soul in sight. Betty struggled into the caravan, baby in one arm, suitcase in the other and promptly spent the rest of the evening in tears asking, 'My God, what have I done? Is this going to be my life from now on?' Unfortunately the answer was 'Yes'. There were no luxury caravans like there are these days. No flushing toilets, no showers, no central heating, not even any running water. Water had to be collected in stainless steel cans from wherever we could find a tap. Sometimes you would have to walk a mile. Sarah's bottles had to be sterilised with jugs of water, her towelling nappies had to be left soaking in Nappysan in tin buckets in the caravan. Betty used to have to rinse them out in buckets in the middle of a field. I was never there and she was very lonely.

Looking back now I'm not proud of my behaviour. Faced with harsh domestic reality I had started to wander (something that I would continue to do throughout my life). With the wives busy with the children, Brian, Michael and I went looking for fun. It wasn't difficult to find, although we did get in terrible trouble in Puddletown where there was a certain girl who liked the men. Her father found out what she'd been up to and being distinctly unamused banged on my caravan door. Betty answered.

'Mrs Cottle? I want to speak to your husband. Some of his men have been messing around with my daughter.'

Betty, suspecting nothing, replied, 'Oh dear, you'd better come with me.' She brought him round to the back of the caravan where I was fixing the generator.

'Mr Cottle?'

I sensed trouble. 'Can I help you?' I asked, dreading the answer.

'Some of your men have been messing around with my daughter.'

'Oh that's terrible,' I did my best to look shocked. 'Look, I'm really sorry but we've got a show starting in five minutes. Could you come back in the morning and maybe we could sort it out then when we've got plenty of time?'

He stomped off mollified for the moment. The next morning we packed up and left in record time, before the old devil could catch us.

At the time I was just glad to get away with it and promised myself to be more careful in future. Now I feel bad, particularly for Betty. You do see things very differently as you get older.

So we were working very hard but still losing money. I decided to take a risk.

So far we had only been to places that hosted circuses every year – Shaftesbury, Gillingham, Sturminster Newton. But Joe Gandey had taught me that it could be very lucrative to go to places which hadn't seen a circus for a while. I drove around the pretty lanes of the West Country and stopped where I saw a nice-looking field. With a bit of investigation and persuasion I managed to book tiny places with sweet names like Crewkerne, Chard, Ottery St Mary, all virgin territory for the circus. Our first new spot was the Isle of Portland – no circus had ever been to the Isle of Portland. It turns out they had missed out big time. On the first night we took £40, the second £50, the third £74. By the end of the week we had taken £295. It was such a great feeling to perform to a tent at least half full and have some loose change jangling in our pockets.

Flushed with success I made a few discreet (or so I thought) enquiries about men who might want to join us from other circuses. But word travels fast in our game. As we left the isle we were stopped by a policeman who demanded to look at our tax discs. Brian and I were all in the clear, but poor Michael was caught out – he simply had not had enough money to buy one. I was furious. I was sure there had been some foul play. Portland hadn't seen a circus before – why had we been stopped?

'You've been tipped off by someone,' I said.

'I'm not allowed to say,' the country plod said.

'I tell you what. I'll guess the town you got the phone call from and you just say yes or no.'

'OK.'

'Manchester.'

'Yes.'

Count Lazard was on tour there. I suspected he felt we were getting a bit above ourselves and was a bit cheesed off that I was trying to nick one of his staff. All this is perfectly normal in the world of circus and I thought I would have plenty of opportunities to get my own back on his lordship later. Anyway I was no saint. I saw Chipperfield's was billing for Weymouth and decided to have a bit of fun. We managed to squeeze into a site just down the road in the town and opened two days before them. I was desperate to show Dicky Chipperfield that we might have only just started, we might only be small, he might have sacked us only a couple of months ago, but we were already capable of spoiling his business. It worked. I was already well on the road to making myself deeply unpopular with the old circus families.

The gamble to play in new towns was really starting to pay off. By the beginning of August we had enough money to start investing in some animals. Our first purchases were very much token efforts – there to amuse the children rather than show any great prowess in the ring. For £60 we bought a pair of ponies. Donald and Smokey were so old they were going grey and were completely hopeless in the ring. Brian presented them but they basically did what they liked. One of them would always walk round the ring one more time than he was supposed to. They would lie down and Brian would pick a cute child from the audience to give them a lump of sugar to get them to stand up, except that one of them would always stand up just as the child got in the ring anyway. Hopeless.

A farmer gave us two goats but they just ate the costumes. One day I part-exchanged them for a generator, but I couldn't bring myself to tell Betty. She is very close to her animals. Brian and I tried to load them into the van without her noticing, but we forgot to close the door at the front. The rascals were in one door and out the other and before we knew it we had two goats running amok around the circus. Betty caught us chasing after them.

'What are you doing with those goats?'

'I've part-exchanged them for a generator.'

'You *what*?' She stopped in her tracks. 'How the hell can you part exchange two goats for a generator? Only you, Gerry Cottle, could part exchange two goats for a generator. You are unbelievable,' she screamed, totally exasperated.

She still has not forgiven me.

We also got our first member of staff. Local orphan Neil Warley used to help out at John Pocock's farm but reckoned he could reincarnate himself as JoJo the clown. He was a bit of a wild card, but JoJo had his uses. It struck me that JoJo the clown could do with being christened. So we invited the public and of course the local press to witness the first ever christening in a Big Top. The circus had a sort of unofficial circus vicar, the Rev Dr Donald Omand. He was always turning up to shows with a different young lady 'driver' and had a heightened attraction to the dark side – seances and the supernatural and the like. Mind you a lot of people in the West Country are like that. Well, he was only too happy to perform the ceremony and we had baby Sarah and Brian's children, Mark and Suzy, christened at the same time.

One of the most interesting Big Top religious services ever to be held will take place in the car park at Seatown next Wednesday. The service will be conducted in the Cottle and Austen's Circus and is due to begin at 3.15 pm.

The unusualness of the event lies in the fact that three separate religious ceremonies of the circus – the blessing of the circus tent, the baptising of children and the blessing of animals (in this instance Shetland ponies) will be included in one service. In his long association with the circus Dr Omand has never known this to happen before. Another unusual feature of the service is that it will be open to the general public. This was decided upon by Messrs Cottle and Austen so that a collection might be taken in aid of St Giles Church, Chideok nr Bridport, of which Dr Omand is vicar.

The service on Wednesday will embody the traditions and pageantry of the circus. The artists will appear in full circus attire – to signify that they bring all their talents and skills to lay before God. Animals will be present throughout the service. By insisting on this, circus people believe they are keeping alive possibly the oldest tradition in Christian worship, for the adoration of the shepherds in the stable at Bethlehem took place with animals present.

Bridport News, August 1970

Our first publicity stunt was a total success. Six local newspapers previewed the event and afterwards we made all the front pages, most of them printing a lovely big photo of us looking very solemn in clown's make-up and spangly leotards with our heads bent very low over our prayer sheets. Even the vicar had a straight face.

JoJo himself was not such a hit. One night after far too many drinks he took the bread van and managed to drive it into a ditch. Petrified, he just abandoned it and ran off across the fields. He carried on running for several days, avoiding all roads and travelling cross-country because he thought we were scouring the countryside desperate to give him a good hiding. He arrived back at John Pocock's farm a few days later, exhausted and starving with his clothes in rags. JoJo was obviously not the full pint. I wrote in my diary that evening, 'JoJo crashed the van and did a runner. Scratch on van cost £5, owe JoJo wages £15 – net profit £10. A good day!'

Right from the start I reckoned if I could just get an extra pound from every person who came to see the show, I would succeed. (It's been my mantra throughout my career, whatever I have done, and still is.) The money I saved by JoJo doing a runner helped us to invest in a candyfloss machine. Only made abroad, these nifty devices are surprisingly expensive. I think we picked ours up for £200 second-hand. However, the profit you can make on a bit of fluffy pink sugar is just as astonishing. It can quite literally make or break a circus. I remember the Moscow State Circus taking £10,000 in one week from popcorn alone. The candyfloss machine raised our takings by a much more modest £100 a week but when you're only making around £300 a week, enough said. (I loved the days when Tesco's would use sugar as a loss leader and offer two packets for the price of one – we'd go in there and remove the whole shelf, to the manager's extreme annoyance.)

But probably our biggest piece of luck came from a member of the audience. By mid August we were pitched under the picturesque ramparts of Corfe Castle in Dorset, again another spot that was a stranger to circus, and we were doing pretty well with most seats full. Betty was selling tickets through the caravan window, when a well-spoken man in a trilby got to the front of the queue with his teenage daughter. He tried to buy a half-price ticket for her. Well, Betty was having none of it.

'No sir, only under thirteens can go half price.'

'She is thirteen.'

'Well that means she's not under thirteen then, doesn't it?'

'Look, can't you just make an exception.'

'No I can't, Sir. Now there are customers waiting. Do you want to come to this show or not?'

Well, the gentleman paid up. After the show he approached me.

'Are you Gerry Cottle?'

'What can I do for you?'

'My name is Trevor Philpott. I'm a reporter for the BBC. I'm currently making an hour-long documentary called 'The Entertainers'. At the moment it features a concert pianist and a wrestler and I am looking for another performance to make up the last twenty minutes of the programme. I've just seen your show. I think you would be perfect. Can I have permission to film you?'

Always game for a bit of publicity, I agreed. We had great fun. It was only our second month on the road and there we were with a BBC camera crew following us. They were all charming and we really enjoyed ourselves, but we thought it was just a bit of fun, no more than that.

By the time our short season ended we had made £2,676. All our profit had gone into buying more animals and machinery and employing more people, so that in just thirteen weeks we had become a much bigger circus. In October 1970 I sat down and wrote my formula for circus success:

1. The right locations
2. The right posters
3. Giving away lots of discount tickets
4. A few well-placed publicity stunts
5. Being cheeky
6. Working bloody hard and being a good team
7. Oh yes. Most important – putting on a pleasing show, which people will recommend to their friends.

Now I had to take this formula and use it to make a bigger and better circus next season. I was not going to be happy until I was the owner of the biggest circus this country had ever seen.

> In this day and age, when one hears of the larger travelling circuses folding their tents for the last time, we feel to survive we must now consolidate. Not to be as large as the pre-war circuses, but to have a compact mobile unit with a traditional yet modern programme with the accent on quality entertainment. Not too sophisticated, so it can be enjoyed by all ages (are we not all children at heart?). Yet we must never relax in the challenge to produce an ever better performance.

So ran the rather pretentious letter I sent to the councils in the Christmas of 1970. What was the point in wasting time? I decided to try and get the biggest and best grounds straight away. After all, you can but ask.

This is where my middle-class background made a difference. Normally a circus owner would just turn up on the council's doorstep in their muddy wellies. I presented us as a proper business. My letters were written on headed paper titled 'Cottle and Austen's Circus Spectacular' with a drawing of a lion roaring and my parents respectable Surrey address at the top. There were photos of Brian and I all scrubbed up in our dinner jackets, arms around Donald the pony, with our best (and only) painted lorry behind. I attached facts regarding the general running of the circus, a list of towns visited in 1970 and a copy of the programme. I also put in a couple of articles I had managed to get placed in the national newspapers:

The Smallest Circus on Earth

Gerry ran away to join the Big Top

Running away to join the circus has a fairytale ring about it, but it does sometimes happen. One day when he was fifteen, Gerry Cottle left his comfortable suburban home in Cheam, Surrey and his parents (his father is a member of the Stock Exchange), his grammar school and his O level swotting – and turned up in Newcastle where he landed a job with Roberts Brothers Circus.

The start of the career he had chosen for himself was unglamorous; 'I wanted to learn trick riding,' remembered Gerry wryly, 'but I only learnt how to carry seat boards.'

. . .

The audiences came and the show grew so that this season their big top can accommodate 800 spectators. They provide a fine bill, strong on humour and excitement.

Gerry's parents are now his staunchest supporters. His father told me, 'We admire his initiative; I wouldn't normally cross the road to see a circus, but I enjoy going to see him perform. And I love being in the pay box!

Observer magazine, December 1970

How the jobber's son ran away to start a circus

What is so surprising is that anyone should contemplate starting a circus when you keep hearing about others folding up their tent for the last time. Certainly their numbers have dwindled and there are now only about a dozen in the UK. But then as Cottle says starting a circus is largely an act of faith:

'If we had worked it all out on paper beforehand we would never have started.'

Neither Gerry nor Brian come from circus families. They started in true storybook fashion by running away to join the circus when they were lads.

The Sunday Times, December 1970

Then I got on the phones. I bothered the councils relentlessly. People got so sick of me they started to give me dates. First we got Southport, then Crewe, then Wakefield. I was dead excited but also in a bit of a spot – we didn't have anything like a big enough circus to put on these grounds – a two-pole flower tent and two ancient ponies simply would not do.

Luckily I had time to work on it. In the absence of winter head-quarters, Cottle and Austen's Circus had pitched on a car park behind a large pub in Barnsley. It wasn't as grim as it sounds. In fact I look back with great affection – it was all concrete so there was no wading through mud, we had access to flushing toilets and the landlord let us plug into the mains. Believe me, these things matter when you've got to spend the winter in a caravan.

At night we were appearing in *Little Red Riding Hood*. Brian and I were the villains and utterly hopeless. 'For God's sake, try to look menacing,' the director, Duggie Chapman, hollered at us.

Really I think we were too busy playing tricks on the principal and larking about with the chorus girls, if you know what I mean. The good thing was, the job left us with the whole day to get on with building the circus. Most of the time, Brian was making and mending in the car park and I was doing deals.

My first task was the tent.

Fire ravages Eisteddfod
Welsh national festival cancelled as tent goes up in flames.

So ran the headline in the newspaper. I sniffed a bargain. I made a few enquiries and found out that the damage done to the tent was bad, bad enough for the owners to want to sell it cheap. But perhaps not so bad that our man of genius, Brian, might not be able to make a Big Top out of the remnants.

I needed money, but I had run out of options. Dad had lent me the money for our last tent, I just couldn't face asking him again. I went to see Mum. Bless her, she had no money of her own. She really was not keen on the circus, she always said, 'But what about the poor animals, Gerald?' She clung to the hope that I would see sense and join a bank. In the meantime, knowing how much it meant to me, she took me upstairs to her bedroom.

'Don't tell your father, Gerald. He really would not be happy.'

She opened her jewellery box, a very rare event. I had never seen inside. She took out her mother's ring.

'You can do with it whatever you want, sell it, pawn it, use it as security. It's yours, I never want to see it again.'

I took her at her word.

I went to see my old friend Joe Gandey. With the ring as security he lent me the money.

It was midnight by the time I got back from Chester with the tent. We rolled it out on the concrete and gazed at it by the light of the winter moon.

'Jesus, Gerry, what the hell are we supposed to do with that?' said May.

'How much did you pay for it?' said Michael.

'It's not a tent, it's a string vest,' said Betty.

To be fair, it did look a lot worse now that I had actually bought the thing. I tended to agree with them, not that I would admit it in a thousand years. But it was Brian's verdict that mattered. He walked round and round it in silence, stopping every so often to flash his torch over the worse holes. It was an uncomfortable few freezing moments. Finally he said, 'You know, I don't think it's so bad. Give me a week.'

The next night *Little Red Riding Hood* was stopped in its tracks by a terrible clunking noise. The audience all peered up expecting the ceiling to come down on their heads at any moment. The wolf missed his cue. Upstairs Brian had discovered an ancient sewing machine. Luckily no one discovered Brian. Every night for a week when he wasn't on stage he was patching up the tent. No one managed to connect the noise with Brian's absence. Instead the cast talked of ghosts and curses. The management talked about the boiler and sent for a man in overalls. He spent an afternoon tapping a few pipes and twiddling a few knobs and said the problem was fixed. By this time Brian had fixed the tent. We had a new Big Top.

Next I needed some animals worthy of a proper circus. In those days Britain was full of small zoos ready to raise a bit of extra cash by selling you the odd chimpanzee or boa constrictor. In my dreams I wanted a pack of hungry wolves. I had this image of Brian walking across the tightrope with a wild hairy pack, baring fangs and baying for blood beneath him. Unusual and effective I thought. Brian was less impressed. Anyway I scoured the country and eventually tracked down a pack to a small zoo in Yorkshire. I was dying to try out this little trick and the very day they arrived we rigged up a little practice pen in the car park and Brian strung up a tightrope between two poles. He started cautiously sliding along the wire over their heads. The wolves were lying on top of each other asleep. As Brian came directly above them I thought I saw an ear twitch. Puzzled, particularly as they hadn't had their breakfast, I stamped my feet and roared. I clapped my hands and waved them in the air. A wolf yawned, rolled over and went back to sleep. With a rising feeling of panic I ran into the caravan and looked out my well-thumbed copy of an animal almanac:

Canis Lupus: The wolf is the primeval wild dog. Hunting in packs, they are primarily scavengers and can go for a long time without eating.

Damn lazy, in other words. Oh well, maybe the excitement of the ring, a little reduction in rations, they might perk up.

I had the opposite problem with the baby bears. We'd only had them for a couple of weeks when one night as Brian and I waited in the wings, a breathless stagehand ran up. 'Brian, Gerry, the bears have escaped and are running wild in the pub.'

There wasn't much we could do about it right at that moment – we were within seconds of mugging Little Red Riding Hood. Brian's dad, Henry, who had joined us after Brian's mum died, was supposed to be in charge. Henry was very laid-back. He fancied himself as an animal trainer and the bears and wolves were his first charges. Well, he didn't get off to a great start. The bears were in a cage in the back of the lorry. As Henry went in to feed them, they dashed past him straight through the open door and proceeded to skip and dance around the pub car park. Luckily Henry managed to keep them contained with a broom handle until we ran back, still in costume. The landlord came out to see two comedy criminals in stripy T-shirts and black masks with bags marked 'SWAG' chasing two bears round his car park. He wasn't too impressed and we had to part with a couple of pantomime tickets to stay in our car park.

Meanwhile our departure had unwittingly caused the complete breakdown of James Brothers Circus. It's something that can be seen over and over in circus families. When they work together they prosper, but when they start to bicker (and that tends to be when the younger generation take over) they very quickly unravel. The Fossetts were well aware of this and the sisters swore they would never let this happen to them. They were so close and content they never dreamed they could fall out so badly.

Unfortunately it proved only too easy.

Betty made her usual weekly phone call home to find that her sisters Julie and Baba had had a row with their dad and left. No one knew where they had gone.

It was a sad tale. After Betty and I left, things had never been the same. Jim fell into a depression. He seemed almost to be looking for his other girls to 'betray' him as he believed Betty had done. And of course it became a self-fulfilling prophecy. To replace me doing the circus publicity, he had hired Dicky Sandow. He was well known on the circus circuit and not popular. I felt his self-interest came above the interests of the circus. He teamed up with young Jimmy and the two of them started ganging up on the girls, whispering in corners, telling tales to their dad. The most damaging rumour being that the girls were passing information to me and plotting to join Cottle and Austen at the first opportunity. Nothing could have been further from the truth. Julie and Baba were devoted to their dad and what they saw as their circus and couldn't understand what was going on. (Maybe Jimmy wanted the girls to leave so he could have the circus all to himself.) Well, his wish came true.

Usually the family agreed any changes collectively, but when Dicky arrived he put paid to that. All sorts of humiliating changes were introduced without the girls being consulted and Jim, a defeated man, just let it happen. The final straw was when Dicky and his wife set up a staff canteen and told the girls they would have to pay for their tea in the interval. Julie and Baba marched into town and bought some cheap paper cups from Woolworth's so Dicky Sandow had no excuse to charge them. When the girls produced them in the interval and refused to pay for their tea an almighty fight broke out. Julie marched round to see her dad. He was in his old brown overalls and beret putting out the rubbish.

'Daddy,' she started.

Old Jim stopped her, 'Whatever it is you've got to say, I don't want to know.'

Poor Julie was stunned. She felt if her father didn't want to know, who could she turn to? Baba and Julie and Billy and Mike held a crisis conference in a caravan. They decided they were never going to get on in the circus as it was and they may as well leave. As the girls packed up the next day, Jim came to see them.

'Here's a hundred pounds each for you and Baba to help you on your way,' and he turned and left.

Julie and Baba were devastated; they really didn't want to go. All Jim had to say was, 'I don't want you to go,' and they would have stayed. As it was they pulled off later that day. With nowhere else to go and no jobs (most circuses had just finished employing for the season) they went back to the family farm at Lowsonford. I contacted them there and offered them jobs with us and confirmed all Jim's worse fears.

Jim was never the same. Even though he was reconciled with his daughters briefly, he died broken-hearted a year later. A few years ago James Brothers Circus stopped travelling for good.

By the middle of this second season Cottle and Austen's Circus had become a real family enterprise. We had most of Betty's family with us, Baba and Julie on the trapeze, Billy Wild as Buffalo Bill and Mike Denning clowning. As well as Brian's father Henry, his little brother Patrick also joined us. Patrick was definitely one of the lads. Big and bulky, he enjoyed going out with the men, but underneath it he was the gentlest of men and again a good worker. He never cut corners. Then his brother Michael fell in love with a church organist on the

Isle of Portland. Deborah joined us and became our band, playing the keyboard. Against the odds, the change in lifestyle suited her and, three daughters and forty years later, they are still together.

Other new recruits included a rather uneducated mining lad who'd never been out of Yorkshire. Then we had a camp couple, John the ringmaster and his much younger boyfriend Roger, who walked on stilts. Peter Norris, a very round jolly cinema manager, joined us to help with the office. Ray Maxine and his wife Lynne came with their magic act. Lynn was very pretty. Brian and I tried it on with her and got absolutely nowhere, and then we hired a very good-looking juggler called John James. Like me he was a middle-class lad from an ordinary family in Northamptonshire who had run away to join the circus. He had taught himself to juggle and was a really decent bloke, that is until he ran off with my wife, but more of that later.

Perhaps the most important person to join us was John Levine. He was a huge ex-bingo-hall manager who ate too many chips. But he knew his publicity. He had done a couple of seasons working for Billy Smart's Circus and taught me how to do publicity for a much bigger show. He bought an old mobile library off the council and made a box office. His wife travelled a few days ahead of us in it and for the first time we were able to sell tickets in advance. He taught me how to work a big town – as many posters as possible, publicity stunts, doing parades. He would do deals with newspapers where you offered readers cut-price tickets in return for free advertising.

As you can see, in just a year we had grown into a medium-sized circus – the like of which could compete with the Roberts and Fossetts of this world and certainly knocked my old friends Count Lazard and James Brothers into a hat.

Our second season was very different from the first.

'Do you think the youth of today are getting more badly behaved?'

'I'm afraid to say I definitely do. The language they use, well it's unrepeatable. They no longer respect authority. If you tell them to stop throwing stones at the clowns or rocking the caravans, they laugh in your face.'

I was being interviewed by Radio Merseyside in March 1971.

'And this is a new phenomenon?'

'Oh, most definitely. Of course there have always been certain areas where the circus knows there will be a rough element looking for trouble. But we're used to that and in the past we have been able to sort out these kind of problems ourselves with a few strong tent men . . . looking menacing . . . if you know what I mean. Put it this way – I've never had to call the police before.'

'Does this mean you will think twice about coming to Liverpool again?'

'Oh, most definitely. We wouldn't come back to the Kirkby site. Maybe if I could find one in a better area I might consider it, but this may well be the last time Cottle and Austen's Circus comes to Liverpool.'

Absolute rot of course. We were plagued by horrible rough little boys. (It's easy to forget what things were like then, but we could have done with some Asbos even in those days. Joe Gandey used to say 'they eat their young in Kirkby,' and I know exactly what he meant.) We even had to cancel the show because of a massive fight and leave a site early because they overturned a caravan with Barry Walls in it. However, I milked it for all it was worth – made sure it was the top story in all the local rags, I made guest star appearances on local radio etc – and boy, compared to what we could make in the little villages of the West Country, did we make money. Those northern industrial towns at that time were grim, dirty and depressing, but in our first week alone we made £774. My gamble to go for the big council sites had come off and again all our profits went into expanding the Cottle and Austen empire. More trucks, more props, more people and a new car for myself and Brian.

God was on my side in 1971.

There was decimalisation for a start. On 1 April 1971, when we went from shillings to pounds and pence, we were able to more than double our prices overnight (tickets went from seven shillings and six-pence to seventy-five pence, the equivalent of fifteen shillings) and the audience were none the wiser.

Then we hit another stratosphere when Trevor Philpott's BBC documentary hit the screens. Unbeknown to us, the pianist and the wrestler were left on the cutting room floor and we became the stars of a whole hour-long documentary entitled '*What do you expect, elephants?*' Suddenly a photographer turned up wanting to take our photo for the cover of the *Radio Times*. The documentary went out on a Saturday night in May 1971. We closed the circus for the night, crowded around the TV set. The effect was amazing. For the first time in my life people started to contact me – and I said yes to everything. Before we knew it we were appearing at Oxford May Balls, book festivals and children's television programmes. We were the first circus to be invited to the Channel Islands for fifteen years. At the end of the season we had pulled on to forty-four grounds in twenty-seven weeks and made £20,000, equivalent to £200,000 today, and every penny went back into the business. Things were looking really good. But I knew I needed another piece of good fortune to really become a contender for Britain's biggest circus.

Ten things you didn't know about
Elephants

---

1. It's usually the smaller Indian elephant that performs in a circus, and it's almost always a female. They can reach a height of 10 feet and they usually die at 60 to 70 years of age.

2. If you ever go into an elephant tent on a circus there will always be one elephant standing up. It's on guard while the others are asleep. On smaller circuses with only one elephant, it usually pals up with a small pony or donkey. They need the company.

3. Elephants are strictly herbivores and eat at least a bale or two of hay a day and nearly every type of fruit or vegetable. They drink 30 to 50 gallons of water a day.

4. The first elephant to appear in British circus was at Covent Garden in about 1810. By 1920 there were performing elephants with most circuses.

5. The most famous elephant in the world was Jumbo, an African elephant who had grown to a size of nearly 12 feet and weighed over 6 tons. P T Barnum offered the London Zoological Society $10,000 to take him to the US.

6. Despite a campaign that included Queen Victoria and Parliament, Jumbo was sold. Barnum claimed it cost him $30,000 to transport Jumbo, but he soon got a return on his money, taking $3,000 a day showing Jumbo for years.

7. Circus elephants, apart from always leading the parade, have been known to perform many tricks – from driving their own especially-made jeep to wire walking, with two wires I hasten to add.

8. In the old days the Americans exhibited a white elephant. It worked as long as it didn't rain . . .

9. Elephants are often considered a lucky omen. Ornamental elephants should always have their trunks up and face the door. My elephant Rani used to attend at least 10 Indian weddings a year.

10. In 1990 there were 30 performing elephants in the UK. Now there is only one and she is only used for souvenir photos in the interval. But I would estimate there are still over 500 performing elephants worldwide, with 100 in Germany alone.

Chapter Four

One Elephant or Two, Sir?
1972-74

'How many elephants would you like?' Brian Williams asked me anxiously.

'Well, I was only really looking for the one, but if you've got more ...'

'Twenty.'

'Ah. I see ... well, I really can only afford the one but if I can help you get out of a spot ...'

'Look, Gerry. I've got twenty elephants stuck in containers at Stansted airport, what do you think?'

'Well, perhaps if you were prepared to be flexible about payment.'

'Done.'

This is how I went out to buy one elephant and came back with three (we called them Sarah, Jane and Suzy after mine and Brian's children). Sarah was paid for in cash, the others on credit. Brian wasn't impressed (for a start our animal trainer, Marcel Peters, had to make the hundred-mile round trip three times with the trailer to pick them up), but I believe you have to seize these opportunities when they come up. An animal dealer called Brian Williams had been employed by three of the big circuses to bring in the elephants, but no one had bargained on the introduction of VAT on 1 April 1973. Suddenly the circus owners who had agreed to pay £1,500 each for the elephants were presented with an eight per cent VAT bill on top. Well, there was no way these old-fashioned circus folk were going to pay the VAT. Instead they insisted that Williams drop the price. He refused to be bullied and there was a stand-off with the elephants stranded in a container going nuts. Which was great news for me because I was under pressure to find some big animals.

So how did I get to the point of such success that I was scouring the country for big game?

I blame my insurer Bill Bailey. He surprised me over a polite cup of tea at the end of the 1972 season.

'Gerry, why don't you take your lovely circus to the London parks?' Bill said.

I was taken by surprise. 'Well, for all the reasons you know, Bill. No one has been on them for years. The councils won't let them out.'

Bill was a great circus fan. Let's face it, there aren't many people who would insure a circus. One of the things he loved was the gossip and I loved going to see him in the quiet days of the winter break. I always learnt something useful.

'But what about the festivals of London? All the councils are running around desperately looking for things to fill their programmes. If a circus could just get in there, it would clean up. If you don't do it, someone else will. Don't you think the Roberts and the Fossetts of this world aren't right at this moment plotting how they can get in?' Bill argued.

'I hear what you're saying, Bill, it's just that I have a real problem with London. It seems so huge. How would you ever organise the publicity?'

'Gerry. You're looking at this all wrong. You've got to treat London as a series of little villages, each with its own centre and high street. Publicise them individually, tailor your publicity to the nature of the village. Never play next-door villages consecutive weeks. All the normal rules of the route apply to the London villages.'

One Elephant or Two, Sir?

It was a road-to-Damascus moment. I suddenly saw a way to make London work and I walked out of Bill's office itching to start writing those letters to the councils.

It didn't take me long to work out that circuses weren't getting sites in London because they were always asking for grants, so I did the opposite – I offered to pay rent.

It worked. Letters started arriving thick and fast from councils offering us sites. Parks were opening up to us that hadn't seen a circus for decades, if at all. Wembley, Merton Park, Islington, Hackney and Dartford, to name just a few. I managed to get from February to May booked up with sites within the M25 area. I took care to 'zigzag' our bookings across London – so for example if we were in Islington in North London one week, the next week would be in Clapham, South London. We would leave at least a month before going to Camden (next to Islington), to make sure we weren't dominating the area and still seemed fresh. On 8 March 1973 we took Cottle and Austen's Circus into London for the first time. Driving in was so exciting – it seemed so busy after the country. We had a devil of a trouble getting the lorries into our first stop, Clissold Park, in Stoke Newington. The gateway was too small and the traffic ended up backed up right down Green Lanes. A huge crowd gathered to watch us pull on. I had butterflies in my stomach. Then, as the time drew near for the show to open, I just had to stop what I was doing and watch the crowds. It was mesmerising. There were hundreds of people waiting to buy tickets. The queue went right across the ground, out of the gate and down the street. I had never seen anything like it.

At that moment I knew we were about to make it really big. I could see my ambition to become Britain's biggest circus owner within my grasp. And the rest of the season carried on just like that. These were the days before political correctness and before the animal question reared its ugly head. Londoners had been deprived of the circus for a long time and were loving it. Of course some places in London were better than others, often places right next door to each other can get a completely different turnout – Deptford was bad but Woolwich was all right – but overall takings far exceeded anything we could get in the rest of the country. The councils were pleased as well. So the next year we were allowed to do the whole thing again. From 1973 our seasons basically followed the same pattern – February to May in London, then down to the coast for the summer holidays, and when the kids went back to school in September we went back to London until the end of the season in October. One year we did thirty-two places within the M25. We became known as London's Circus and London is where the money is. We prospered.

But you can't be the London Circus without some serious beasts.

I was lucky to find our three wonderful elephants. I also managed to get camels and lions. In the end we were travelling with five elephants, six lions, ten horses, ten monkeys and baboons, three camels and five llamas, all with men specially dedicated to look after them. Having what is essentially a travelling zoo made running our circus a completely different operation. How do you look after such a great menagerie in the centre of London? Answer – with great difficulty.

Just getting rid of the elephant mess was a job in itself. Where do you put it? There's vast amounts of it and the smell . . . well, I'll leave that to your imagination. The first season in London with the elephants we got away with selling it for manure to the park keepers. But next year we were told where to go – they'd found the only thing that would grow in elephant pooh is sunflowers. Their gallons of pee rotted the wooden floorboards of the tent, so we had to constantly replace them. Their tent had to be specially constructed with the poles placed so they couldn't reach them with their trunks, otherwise the cheeky things would spend the whole time pulling it down on their heads.

Then all these animals had to be fed. You'd arrive in a town and have to find a butcher who could supply you with four ox heads a day for the lions. For years our lion trainer kept his own little black book with the name of a friendly butcher in every borough. We employed a boy known as 'the beast boy' specially to prepare the animals' food. We had the same one with us for years nicknamed Robert 'Gunther' Raven, after the famous American animal trainer Gunther Williams. He fancied himself a bit. He used a big chopping board and an axe to chop the ox head to pieces and the dogs would hang around and catch the scraps.

Moving all these animals was a feat in itself. Every time we moved the lions, their cages and props had to be packed up. Even the horses needed two men dedicated to taking down the stable tent, loading them on to the lorries and clearing up the straw. We had to have a double-decker bus travelling with us just to carry all the straw we needed. Occasionally the animals would escape. I was woken up by a telephone call from the police in the early hours one morning when one of our lorries had had a minor accident and the llamas were running amok on the M6. They were soon caught with no harm done, I hasten to add.

Then we had to find somewhere to put all these animals in the winter when we weren't travelling. We couldn't just park up behind a pub anymore. The animals still needed to be fed and exercised and men kept on to look after them. So we invested in a farm in Cricklade, Wiltshire. Our first headquarters.

Looking back I can't quite believe we travelled with so many huge animals. Residents often complained about the lions roaring at night. But that was nothing compared with the old days. Betty's granny remembered the Fossett family circus travelling with over a hundred horses running free alongside the procession, with the elephants pulling the wagons. All the villagers used to line the side of the road to watch the spectacle. You see this was a way of life. No one questioned it because this was the way it had always been. The people who worked on the circus didn't live in any better conditions than their animals, and sometimes worse. At least the animals were always well looked after, fed and groomed. Of course there are rogues in every business, but I picked trainers from the old school who took pride in their animals. My trainer looked after his lions so well they had special supplements in their food and a day off meat every week, just milk. Their coats shone. At the time I loved my big circus, but would I want to do it now? Elephants in the centre of London? Not really.

With the purchase of our big beasts, especially those three elephants earmarked for our bigger older rivals, we attracted a lot of attention from our circus colleagues, and not the sort of attention you particularly want.

In theory the circus families were supposed to cooperate with each other. In practice they were deeply competitive. A circus party wasn't considered a proper get together unless there was a good fight. Even the biannual meetings of the Circus Proprietors' Association, which were supposed to be friendly social gatherings – let's face it, we were all related to each other in one way or another – were always fraught with petty jealousies and history (think of those Christmases you dread). Unforgotten slights and insults created currents running under the polite talk. It was terrifying to a newcomer like myself, half the time I didn't have a clue what was going on. I remember the great matriarch Mary Fossett kicked off the meeting one year by leaning across the table and saying menacingly to Peter Featherstone, 'I knew we'd upset you Peter, when we didn't get a Christmas card this year,' and it just went downhill from there. The main purpose of these meetings was to put our cards on the table and tell everyone our routes. But there was the most ridiculous amount of bluffing and double bluffing going on. Everyone was desperate to nick someone else's plum site or 'jump them' (go in the week before and spoil the business) and, hands in the air, I could be the worse culprit. I guess I felt a need to prove to the other rascals that I was snapping at their heels. And although we were under oath never to reveal anything outside those four walls, they were as leaky as a sieve.

Spoiling each other's posters was a bit of a game. As long as I was the winner, I loved it. We wasted masses of time running round taking down our rivals' posters or, even worse, papering ours over the top. I got a special kick out of doing it even in my very early days – Roberts Brothers stormed Joe Gandey's Circus threatening to kill me after I Evo-sticked a Gandey's poster on to a Roberts' lorry. Evo being the glue they use to mend tents, it was absolutely impossible to get off. See, I'm chuckling as I write this. Now I had my own circus I made sure my posters were plastered absolutely everywhere, especially in

One Elephant or Two, Sir?

London. The other circuses got totally fed up. We mostly fell out with the Roberts and Fossetts – old Uncle Bailey Fossett said to me one year, 'God Almighty, Gerry, your posters are everywhere on the North Circular. You're advertising three different circuses at once.' His nephew, Robert Fossett (Betty's cousin, a red-headed Fossett with a temper to match), ended up knocking me unconscious when he caught me papering over one of his posters for 'Sir Robert Fossett's Circus at Blackheath' with one saying 'The Big Circus is now at Peckham Rye'. As soon as I had regained consciousness I went over to the Fossetts and after an hour of shouting we agreed a truce. None of us ever really wanted all-out war.

The next year the Roberts, cheesed off because we had yet again managed to bag Wembley during September, turned all our direction arrows round the wrong way so the public were going round and round the North Circular completely lost and fuming. I was down to their site like a shot. Well, they gave me a cup of tea and pretended to be sorry for a nanosecond before their real animosity burst forth and we ended up having another huge shouting match. But circus folks' bark is worse than their bite and most quarrels are resolved in the end. Although it has to be said everybody ignored me at the Circus Proprietors' meetings from about this time on.

Rivalry between the circus and funfair folk is something completely different and much more nasty. Sometimes circuses and funfairs get on well together, but sometimes – particularly among the tent men and workers – things get horribly tense. People tend to join the circus for the glamour and the animals. Fairground men tend to be younger jack the lads who have joined for the girls. Whereas circuses will go all over the country, fairgrounds tend to move in a very small area. This makes them much more territorial and they don't much like a circus appearing on their patch. Fairs have a totally different rhythm to circuses. They take a whole week to build and then will be open for just two days for very long hours. The workers can be treated much more harshly. Both sets of men like to think they are stronger and tougher and have a harder life, and enjoy provoking fights to prove it. The male ego, eh?

One September we got into a terrible fight. We were pitched next to a funfair at Wembley. My heart sank when we arrived on site – I knew it meant trouble. One of our workers called Ricky (glasses so thick they looked like magnifying glasses) chatted up one of the fairground worker's wives. Big mistake. This massive bald bloke walks on to our ground looking for a fight. Before anyone could stop them, they were throwing punches, the fairground worker fell straight down, staggered to his feet and in his confusion hit Brian. An almighty fight then broke out. Brian picked up a wooden torch. I could see this was really getting out of hand so I ran across the road to where there was a police station. Unfortunately the police ran over and the first person they saw was Brian. He was nicked before he could draw breath. The fight broke up as quickly as it started. I looked for Brian but couldn't find him anywhere. I tentatively knocked on all the caravan doors thinking he might be up to a bit of mischief, but no sign of him. I never thought he'd been arrested – that wasn't the plan at all. Eventually I found him in the police station. He had to spend the night in jail but we managed to bail him in the morning. My solicitor persuaded him to plead guilty in order to avoid a custodial sentence. Brian did, but it meant he got a criminal record which is a shame because he's not a violent man.

All this was nothing compared with my relationship with my wife. Betty and I had not been getting along at all well. From the moment she arrived on Cottle and Austen's Circus she was lonely and miserable and I have to admit that was largely my fault. I was never there, always off booking sites, putting up posters and being naughty. I don't think she knew that I was playing around that first season. But she did catch me wrapped in the stage curtain with one of the chorus girls in the Barnsley pantomime. It was a long time before she spoke to me again. Things trundled along – Betty was preoccupied with the new baby and I was totally obsessed with work, but we weren't happy. My sister remembers one occasion early on in our marriage when I turned up on my parents' doorstep first thing on a Saturday morning. I was in a bit of a state.

'Dad, I can't stand it any more. I've left Betty.'

Dad was very calm and dealt with it in his own wise way. 'Come in, son. Before you say anything go upstairs and have a bath. Mum will cook you breakfast. Then we'll talk.'

Well, after I had been washed and fed, Dad very calmly and deliberately started to ask questions:

'Where are Betty and the baby?'

'How far away is the circus?'

'Mother, go and ring the station and find the times of the trains.'

'Now listen to me, son. I'm going to give you a lift to the station. You are going to get on the train and go straight back to your wife. You don't walk out on your wife and family. They are your responsibility. Your place is with them, not here.'

He said it kindly but firmly. There was to be no argument. I returned. Nobody had even noticed I'd gone.

We reached an all-time low in 1973 when Betty had our second baby, April. Right from the very start things didn't go smoothly. Betty went into labour in the middle of the pull-down in Reading. We decided to drive to our next pitch in Stockwell, London, and find a hospital there. All the way Betty was in terrible pain. In the end I just had to abandon the caravan and race around looking for a hospital. From the car window we saw the Clapham Hospital for Women – it seemed auspicious, overlooking one of circus' great grounds on the common. Well, it wasn't lucky for us. It was terrible. It was dirty, babies screamed all night and the midwife was horrible. It closed a few years later. Betty had a long painful birth that went through the night, and when I finally emerged the next morning my car had a puncture. Even worse, in the confusion Betty's beloved Jack Russell, Clyde, went missing. After putting up posters all round South London, we got him back the day Betty came home.

That was just the start. April was the most terrible baby. A fiend. We were totally unprepared because Sarah had been so easy. But April never stopped crying. My sister Jane remembers her first visit. We had a big caravan with a veranda in front of it. As she approached she saw me hanging on to the railings, knuckles white with anger. Without even saying hello I said, 'I can't go in. If I do, I'll kill her.' For a second Jane thought I meant Betty, then she realised the awful wailing noise was not one of the animals, but the new baby screaming. April never stopped to draw breath, we could do nothing with her. She drove poor Betty into postnatal depression and me into the arms of my girlfriends. Betty wanted to go straight back in the ring like she had after Sarah, but with April it just wasn't possible – she wouldn't stop screaming for long enough. She never slept. So Betty was stuck on her own in the caravan with this devil and I stayed away as much as possible. I think Betty was very very lonely.

So Betty did something very unlike her.

At the end of 1973 the circus was in Croydon, but I'd been away for a few days supposedly seeing London councils. In reality I was having a good time with an old girlfriend. Joy and I had instantly fallen in lust with each other when we both appeared in *Peter Pan* years before. I was only sixteen at the time and very keen and impressionable. Joy was playing the maid and Nana the dog. She was tiny and blonde, bubbly and flirty. As you can imagine, we hit it off instantly. I was a frantic adolescent bee drawn to this heavily-scented honey pot. She was going out with someone else, but that didn't stop us. In fact for the next twelve years it didn't stop us. Meeting up was always a bit of a game. I could never ring her at home. I would always get a message from her best friend to ring a certain phone box at a certain time. So we didn't manage to get together very often – maybe two or three times a year – but it was always a pleasure. This time we had managed to grab nearly a whole week (I think her husband must have been away on business).

After this week of illicit fun, I walked back in the caravan door bracing myself for a barrage of abuse. Instead I found suitcases everywhere and Betty packing.

'What's going on? Why have you got the suitcases out?'

Betty looked like a rabbit caught in headlights. But she soon regained her composure.

'Oh, I'm glad you've graced us with your presence. You're back just in time for me to tell you I'm leaving you.'

'What do you mean? Don't be stupid Betty. You've got nowhere to go.'

'Oh that's where you're wrong. I'm leaving with John.'

'John? John James? The juggler?' I was dumbfounded.

'Yes, Gerry. You have no idea about my life, what I do just to get through the day. Well, it's time you realised the world doesn't stop turning round just because you've walked out the door. I'm sick of being lonely. I'm sick of waiting for you to come home. I'm not going to do it any more.'

'Just hang on a minute. You know why I can't be here. I'm working bloody hard getting this circus up and running. Making it the biggest and the best. And who do you think I'm doing it for? For you, for the family. You've got everything you want. The biggest caravan, the best car . . .' I stopped. She looked like she was going to hit me.

'Shut up, Gerry. The one thing I want above all is a proper husband. I am so lonely. You are never here. I never have a clue where you are. You're not a husband – you're a lodger and a bloody ungrateful one at that. And don't even try to pull that biggest and best line on me. This circus is for you, Gerry Cottle, and no one else.'

She had a point there.

'And John is the answer?'

'He is certainly a lot more like a husband than you are.'

She had a point there too. John James was a gentle man, dark curly hair, calm, totally different from me. The kind of boy she likes. In fact I don't know why she did end up with me.

'We're leaving tonight. John is taking me and the girls to stay with his parents in Northamptonshire.'

I was so shocked. I stood rooted to the spot. For once in my life I had run out of words. In the absence of knowing what else to do I walked out the door. I didn't see them go. Instead I walked the streets of Croydon for a long time. It got dark. I didn't care what was happening to the show. It was very late when I went back to the caravan. It was cold and dark and very very quiet.

I think it was no surprise to everyone on the circus. They all knew John and Betty had been having an affair for months, but I guess no one told me because they thought I deserved it. I was totally devastated. It might seem strange because of course I couldn't behave myself. All I can say is no one likes to be rejected and I guess Betty was my home, my rock. I didn't blame Betty and I certainly didn't hold it against John. I knew it was my fault. She was still my beautiful circus girl and I loved her.

I didn't cope very well, I couldn't stop crying for a start, and I was hopeless at looking after myself. I wandered around the circus ground looking a mess and hungry, until McGinty, our gay Irish poster man, took pity on me, and became my butler. It was actually a job he'd been born to do. When we went putting up posters in a town, we would split it in half and meet up at the end of the day in the local Wimpy. He'd stagger in and plonk down plastic bags full of second-hand tea towels and tablecloths he'd picked up in the charity shops. He'd use them to make pretty curtains for the tent men's wagons – no circus was as dainty as mine. So he naturally enjoyed putting on a pinny and walking round all day twirling a feather duster in my big caravan.

So my domestic needs were looked after, but mentally I was still in a real state – as I said, I couldn't stop crying. In the end, Joy, worried about me, came up to give me solace. We were holed up in the caravan one afternoon, keeping each other warm as it were, when out of the blue Betty's car with the children inside pulled up on the ground. Brian, totally aware what was going on, shot out of his caravan and offered to help Betty with her luggage. Like a scene from a bad sitcom, he grabbed a suitcase and ran across the ground with it. He banged on the door and yelled loud enough to wake the dead, 'Gerry, are you there? Betty's come back.'

Brian managed to keep Betty at bay out front while I pushed Joy out of the back. Luckily Joy had a sense of humour.

I welcomed Betty back with open arms, but within weeks couldn't resist going walkabout again. Betty was not amused and once again packed the children into the car and headed off for Northampton.

This time she was away for a lot longer. By this time we were working very hard in Cornwall, doing two shows a day. I was at the end of my tether. One day I was driving down the A30 and passed a café called Betty Cottle's. I had to stop. I tried to open the door to the caff, but I couldn't go in, I wasn't fit to face the public. Instead, propelled by an unknown force, I walked behind Betty Cottle's to a field full of ripe corn. I started to wade right through the middle of it. It was a beautiful summer's evening. I pushed my way through the acres of ripe corn with tears streaming down my cheeks. Then I suddenly saw what I must look like – a complete nutter. It was there and then that I pulled myself together and vowed never to cry over a woman again. A resolution I kept . . . well, for many years anyway.

Betty meanwhile was living in Northampton with John James and his parents. They must have had a hell of a shock when Betty arrived on their doorstep. I think it was bad enough for this respectable middle-class couple when their son ran off to join the circus, but when he came back with someone else's wife, a circus girl at that, and her two children, it must have been the last straw. Things were different in those days, it was the early 70s after all – The Nolans were pop stars and *Ask the Family* was prime-time viewing. People wouldn't bat an eyelid these days. It was as much a shock for Betty. This was the first time she had lived in a house for any length of time. She didn't take to it at all. She was used to a new town every week and looking gorgeous every night in the ring. Betty was deeply in love with John but she could see no future for them. She believed that I would block anything John tried to do in the circus and she couldn't see herself ever being able to settle down and become an ordinary suburban housewife. She also wanted the girls to grow up on the circus with their real dad. After six months away she made a snap decision to return.

They arrived back together one morning out of the blue. I was delighted. Well, I needed them both. John was an excellent juggler and Betty looked great in the ring. It might seem strange that we could just settle down after all that and live and work together, but you can do that sort of thing on a circus. John left us eventually, his heart broken, apparently, but Betty never left me again. Betty found it difficult for a long time afterwards, but once she has made a decision she sticks to it. Our marriage fell into an uneasy truce.

My life with Brian was about to take a turn for the worse too. Again it was my ambition that got the better of me.

The main headache for every circus is what to do in the winter. If you could take money twelve months a year, the world would be a very different place. We'd tried extending the season by visiting the Channel Islands for a few weeks, but we could hardly sustain a three-week run, never mind three months. We'd also had moderate success putting on a small circus inside Britain's first shopping mall – the Tricorn Centre in Portsmouth. But the amount of money we made barely made it worthwhile. We were probably not helped by the fact that our Santa was rather uneducated. He was the ex coal miner who we had picked up in Barnsley, working as doorman at the theatre. He'd never been out of Barnsley so nobody in Portsmouth could understand a word he said and he couldn't tell the girls and boys' presents apart. In the end we just had to give him Smarties to hand out. I washed my hands of the whole project when one of the clothing stores caught fire, the brand-new shopping centre was nearly razed to the ground and the animals had to be turned loose. There were camels, llamas and horses running wild all over Portsmouth.

Instead I looked to the continent for an answer. In Europe, especially in Italy and Paris, it was traditional to have a circus on ice at Christmas. I'd had that bit of experience with Holiday on Ice and I really fancied the idea. In the winter of 1973 I persuaded Brian to put on a Circus on Ice at Cardiff's Sophia Gardens.

The first thing I had to do was find the performers. We put together a rather eclectic mix of circus performers who quickly retrained themselves as ice skaters and Home Counties young ladies who had done ice skating as a hobby and wanted to make a career out of it. In general the ice skaters were a bit of a liability. While they looked amazing and were good on the ice, they had a job adapting to circus life. Living in a caravan without running water and electricity is a big task for nice girls from detached houses in Surrey. Also Bob Moore, our manager, was very professional and demanded a lot. There were a lot of tears and a lot of them left pretty quickly. The male ice skaters were all gay and very promiscuous and caused a bit of a stir with the residents. By contrast some of the circus performers became real stars. We had a mother and son juggling act who within three weeks had taught themselves to do their act on the ice. David Lorenz, a circus boy born and bred, went on to become a star with Holiday on Ice, travelling the world and earning hundreds of thousands of dollars as an acrobat and juggler on the ice. We had a Highland scene, a Spanish scene and a lady presenting pigeons on ice. The stars of the show were the Cimarro Brothers from Germany, who did their sensational high wire act over the ice. Thomas stood on Matthias' shoulders while he walked the high wire blindfolded to the music of *Jesus Christ Superstar* (they stayed with me for many years after this). We even had a man dressed as a huge pink elephant skating doing tricks. We had an enormous cardboard and plywood pink elephant made for publicity and Bob decided to attach it to the top of his van. On his way down to Cardiff, he went over Clifton Suspension Bridge in the wind and never saw it again.) The Cardiff show was very glamorous and did very well. Before our three-week run was over I tackled Brian.

'I love this show. Don't you think it's been good?'

'Not bad. Better than I thought. Yes, Gerry. What's your point?' He knew me too well.

'You know we've got the spare tent.'

'No, Gerry. Don't even think about it.'

'You haven't even heard what I'm going to say.'

'I don't need to. It's a rubbish idea.'

'What's the point in having a spare tent hanging around doing nothing when we've got a ready-made show we can put in it?'

'Yes and who's going to manage it?'

'Me. That's the beauty of there being two of us. You can manage Cottle and Austen's and I'll take the Circus on Ice. We can go to opposite ends of the country so we're not in competition with each other. We've put in so much effort getting this show together, it would be daft just to dismantle it after three weeks. Especially as it's making so much money.'

'Aren't you forgetting something?'

'What?'

'The ice. Where are you going to get the ice from to fill a tent every night?' He was right – this was the Achilles heel of my plan. But I was prepared.

'There's a turkey refrigeration plant in Cricklade up for sale.'

I'd won the argument but Brian was not happy. I think the bottom line was he just wasn't as ambitious as me and was perfectly happy running one successful circus. It doesn't matter what I have, I always want more.

If I'm really honest, Brian does tend to make steadier business decisions than me. Right from the start, the reviews of the new touring Ice Show were not encouraging. I think the British public weren't ready for a big ice show in a Big Top. Torvill and Dean hadn't hit our TV screens yet. 'How can you have an ice rink in a circus tent?' reviewers asked. A very good question.

By far the biggest problem was the ice. The turkey refrigerator plant turned out to be a damp squib. We spent a whole day dismantling it. Old pipes were disintegrating in our hands. Fibreglass was everywhere and we were itching for the rest of the day. It was useless. Then one of the skaters tipped me off about a new kind of transportable ice manufactured in the States. I sent off for the brochure and it looked amazing. I went to visit the States for the first time. (It blew my mind. Times Square at night in the days before it had been cleaned up – it was full of dodgy people, but it had a sort of dynamic edge. I thought I had died and gone to heaven.) I met the managers of the ice company. They were a couple of real shady gangsters. I was wined and dined but they never seemed to get to the point. Eventually I got to see their headquarters. It was a Portakabin on an industrial estate in the hinterland of New Jersey. I just didn't trust them. Actually, I didn't have the money anyway. I went home empty-handed. In the end I got a local refrigeration firm to make an ice rink. The base folded into three pieces. When we wanted to move, the men would chip away at the ice at the hinges with pick axes, splitting the ice into chunks which would be stored in dustbins. When we arrived we would put the ice together again, spray some water over it and refreeze it. In theory it worked. In practice it was a nightmare. Our poor technical manager, Marnie Dock, almost became an old man overnight. The wind on they road was the biggest problem – it melted the ice. Brian had to make a special cover for it, but still to keep the ice cool we had to have big generators running all day. They rattled so much the pipes were always breaking and clouds of CF gas would go pouring over the circus ground. Every move would take all night. It was hard going and the public, who obviously couldn't grasp what a circus on ice, in a tent, was all about, were staying away in their droves.

It was also incredibly difficult to communicate with Brian. We were travelling up north; he was down south with Cottle and Austen's. We had to make appointments to speak to each other on the public telephone. If there was an urgent problem we would have to send a telegram, 'Call me at such and such a number at such and such a time,' or sometimes I'd pretend to the local police that we had a serious problem or someone had died and ask them to pass on a message for Brian to ring. We were losing money at a frightening rate. I had told Brian we were £12,000 in debt. He found out it was actually £40,000.

'That's enough. We're scrapping it,' Brian said

'But we're just about to go into Scotland. We're bound to take money.'

'At this rate we'll be bust before we get there. It's just not working.'

It was time to split. On 15 June 1974, Brian's birthday, we met half way at our printers in Bradford. They gave us a room to ourselves. I had read a story about what Lord George and Lord John Sanger had done when they split their great circus at the turn of the century. Apparently they had both written their own list of what they wanted from the circus in order of preference and the value they put on each item. They then tossed a coin. Whoever won got the item from the top of their list and had to pay the other person the value they had written beside it. The other person got the next item and so on until there was nothing left. Brian and I went into separate rooms to write our lists. Funnily enough we both valued our equipment almost exactly the same, we were never more than a couple of hundred quid out on anything. It was uncanny. I tossed a coin. Brian called 'heads' and heads it was.

'I want Cricklade,' he pointed to our winter headquarters at the top of his list.

I breathed a sigh of relief. Brian could keep the farm, I had never liked it that much anyway. 'I will take the big tent then if you don't mind.' It was the brand-new tent we were using for the Circus on Ice.

Brian nodded his head. He didn't look too gutted. The rest of the list went just as smoothly. It was an amicable separation. Brian would carry on down south with the traditional circus renamed Austen Brothers. I was left on my own with only a loss-making, broken Circus on Ice for my future. Ever the gambler, I thought if I could get the show to Scotland and the peak summer business my luck might just turn.

Ten things you didn't know about
Circus Lingo and Superstitions

----

1 The circus has a language all of its own. In the past it was very common, especially with the smaller family shows. It's a mixture of cockney rhyming slang, Romany and many other things besides.

2 Words special to the circus: *josser*: someone not born into a circus family (like me); *flattie*: an outsider, not a circus person, with the idea that 'they're all dull'; *jags*: the person over there; *her jillpots*: the woman over there; *nanti*: no, not at all.

3 You can also trace the lingo to Italian and in fact much is Army slang: *carsey* (karsi): the toilet (used in the army), probably derives from the Italian *casa*; *polone*: a girl, a woman; *ohmy*: a man; *chavy*: a child.

4 Animals all have their own descriptions: *buffer* is a dog, *slanging buffer* means performing dogs; *prad* is a horse; *pigs* are the elephants (not used very much); *cats* are the lions and tigers (used all the time).

5 The *Big Top* is the circus tent, the main poles are the *king poles*. Before plastic tents, there was another row of poles called *quarter poles*. The tent is *pulled out*. Putting the tent up is called *build up* and then you have the *pull-down*, and the journey from town to town *the move*.

6 'Circus' is probably the most universally used word to describe our form of live entertainment. In Italy, Spain and South America, the circus is called *circo*; in France it's *cirque*; in South Africa, *sirkus*.

7 Circus people are very superstitious. Just a few: you must never wear real flowers in an act; green should not be worn in the ring; a bird flying round inside the tent is very bad luck, the programme cannot continue till the bird is chased outside.

8 We could fill a book with ghost stories, in fact two branches of the Fossett family still live in their caravans in their winter quarters because they think their farm homes are haunted.

9 A very grave superstition is that you must not go back to your caravan or dressing room if you have forgotten anything. Send someone else instead.

10 Wherever possible the old circus families would try and put the circus next to a graveyard, citing it as 'the dead centre of town' and good for business. Funnily enough, in my experience it always was.

Chapter Five

My Wagon's Bigger than Yours
1974-76

Four weeks after the split with Brian, I nearly died.

'Do you know what's wrong with him?'

'Haven't a clue.'

'No. I haven't either. At first I thought it was a thrombosis, now I'm not so sure.'

'Much more likely to be the Big C.'

'Yes, that's what I think. But I've really never seen anything like it. What would you do?'

'Don't know. I suppose you could have a go at opening him up. See what's in there.'

'I suppose there's no other option really.'

'No not really.'

I had an enormous, excruciatingly painful, lump in my leg. My whole body had swollen up, I was throwing up and fainting and the doctors had no idea what was going on. I could hear them talking about me on the other side of the curtain around my bed, oblivious to the fact that I could hear every word they were saying. Scary.

My Wagon's Bigger than Yours

The lump first made its appearance on the long drive up the west coast of Scotland. I was driving a huge old Scammell showman's tractor pulling two trailers. It had a very stiff clutch. By the time I had been at the wheel for six hours, I had a strange protuberance straining at my trousers' seams. Not a good sensation for a man. When we pulled on to the ground I fell out of my lorry, tried to stand up and promptly fainted with the pain.

I spent the next two weeks in hospital while the doctors scratched their heads. My timing couldn't have been worse. It was our final week as the Circus on Ice. Business hadn't picked up and I had booked three weeks in Aberdeen for an ordinary circus, in a last ditch attempt to stop myself going bust. The thing about circuses is if the public come in you can make money very fast, but on the other hand a few bad weeks and you can lose money just as quickly – circuses are very expensive to run and there's very little you can cut back when times are hard, so owning a circus is a good way to go bust. The people who succeed are those who know when it isn't working and react quickly. Much as I loved it, I could see this Circus on Ice was in danger of losing me everything.

I lay in my hospital bed and got down to business. I had one week to transform the circus. My first visit was from my friend and artist, sign painter and poster designer, Tony Shuker.

'What name do you want me to paint on the side of the wagons?'

'I don't know. Something foreign and exotic. I'm quite taken with Scarletti's. You know the circus in Enid Blyton's book?'

'Naff. What's wrong with just calling it Gerry Cottle's?'

'Cottle's not a circus name. It's boring.'

'It's a good name. It's an unusual name and circuses always work when they are identified with a strong boss, look at Billy Smart's.'

He had a point.

Luckily most of the ice skaters were circus artists anyway. So the Salvadors transformed from the Skating Salvadors into globe walkers. Peggy Lorenz and her son David put their juggling act back in the sawdust ring and Peggy got back on the trapeze. The Cimarro brothers walked the tightrope over the lions' cage rather than the ice. Meanwhile I was trying to earn some extra money by hiring out Vicky, our baby elephant (named after my first Devon girlfriend), to perform with the Sri Lankan mass band in the Edinburgh Tattoo. The negotiations were protracted. Everyone got sick of me. The nurses were forever shouting, 'Cottle, you're wanted on the phone. It's the wretched elephant again.'

Matron would have given Hattie Jacques a run for her money. She was old-fashioned and terrifying, 'Cottle, you're putting my patients' health at risk with these incessant telephone calls.'

She moved me into my own room with a telephone. 'You're making everyone ill, just listening to you,' she complained.

After two weeks I couldn't stand it any longer. My leg wasn't getting any better and my beloved circus was going on without me. I discharged myself and headed up to Aberdeen. That night I had the most excruciating headache and collapsed. Betty called an ambulance and before I knew it I was back in my hospital bed. That's when I heard the doctors. The next day they took me into theatre and took something out, although no one was any the wiser what it was. Afterwards I felt much better, I just couldn't walk – my leg wouldn't bend. I was sent on an intensive course of physiotherapy, but Matron had her own ideas.

'Start walking up and down those stairs, Cottle.'

I hobbled over to the first step and tried to hoist my leg up on to it. It must have been a pitiful sight.

'Come here, Cottle.'

She beckoned me over. I approached cautiously.

'I'm not going to hurt you.'

Her voice softened as if speaking to a small fluffy kitten. As I got within reach she lunged at my leg, grabbed it and with all her might bent my knee. My scream would have woken the dead. I lay poleaxed on the floor, my leg finally bent. I was fine after that and heading for my circus by the end of the day.

Our new circus was doing fantastic business despite my hospital stay. Scotland is always good for a traditional circus: the people are relatively old-fashioned in their tastes, the weather is only good enough to have a circus for three months in the year and only good substantial circuses travel that far north. Well for whatever reason, people were queuing down the street to get in. I managed to book Inverness after Aberdeen and cleaned up there as well. Just a few weeks before I had been staring into the abyss. Now I had enough money to look for some new acts.

I started going away every weekend, visiting different circuses to get ideas. My guide was the most extraordinary circus agent, Billy Arata. Small and dishevelled, talking nineteen to the dozen, he lived in a council house in Birmingham but travelled the world. He had the most amazing gift for foreign languages. Billy spoke everything – every European language, Chinese, Russian, you name it. Even if he wasn't fluent in a particular tongue, he always knew the essentials for cutting a deal – namely the numbers. He had started off as a circus performer and had made friends and kept in touch with everyone he met in the business. He had a real nose for an outstanding or unusual act and was invaluable in introducing me to the best acts in Europe. Europe has a great tradition of circuses. Nowhere else in the world are they so popular or such big business. German circuses are probably the best, closely followed by the Swiss. But every country has its strengths. The Germans are great animal trainers and high wire walkers, the Italians are very stylish, good-looking and are great acrobats, the French have done more for alternative circus than any other European nation, the Hungarians are masters of the large springboard troupe. If you see a good juggler chances are they're either Dutch or Swedish. We do the best clowns. But it was in Ireland that I found probably the best act I ever had.

I went to see Duffy's Circus. When Khalil the Strongman walked into the ring, I knew he had to be mine. He was an enormous Persian man with a great big bushy dark beard, tanned face and flashing eyes. He dressed in a simple loincloth and used old-fashioned Eastern weights with a ball on each end. His muscles were unfeasibly large. You can have so much fun with a strongman. If you put a man in a cannon, once he'd been fired into the net, that's it, act over. They're a one-trick pony. There are no limits to the number of tricks a strongman can do. A strongman could walk into the ring and ask the audience to try and lift his weights, which of course they wouldn't be able to do. Then he'd struggle but eventually succeed in lifting them himself. Then he'd lift double the weights and then lift double again, all accompanied with plenty of moans and sweat and the audience would be amazed. It's one of those acts where you could really get the audience involved. Khalil used to have ten of them sat on a board balanced on his feet and push them up and down using his legs. And he could lift a baby elephant. We also decided to run a car over him. We used to get twenty people from the audience to sit in a four-wheel drive and drive over Khalil very very slowly. He'd be groaning and howling and as soon as it passed over him leap up with an enormous roar, shake his fists in the air triumphantly and do a little dance. That's the sort of thing that sticks in the mind.

The other act that people remembered was Barry Walls, my old sign painter and former bus driver. He turned out to be a whizz on a bed of nails and climbing up a ladder of swords, in fact he was a good old-fashioned fakir.* It wasn't so much what he did, but the way he did it. He used to test out the sharpness of his swords by grabbing a member of the audience and slicing off a lock of their hair with a great flourish. Although sometimes he forgot to sharpen his swords so it got a bit clumsy. Personal hygiene wasn't high on his list of priorities either – Betty refused to be his assistant any more because of the state of his toenails. He was a bit vague as well. One night moving from Ealing Common to Richmond, he hooked up his caravan with his wife and children inside to a lorry and drove off. It wasn't until he got halfway down the Kew Road a couple of miles later that he looked in his wing mirror and realised the caravan was no longer there. He found it lying on its side in the middle of Chiswick roundabout with his family still inside . . .

Other acts in the new Gerry Cottle's Circus included Klemendore, The India Rubber Man (he was from Sri Lanka). He had the ability to cross his arms in front of his body, pass them round his back and clasp his hands at the front again. Granted he was thin

---

* Traditionally in the circus a fakir goes into a trance and performs feats of endurance. It's a great act that plays on the supernatural.

and used lots of grease, but it was still an amazing thing to see. Klemendore was a bit of a prima donna. He came up to me one day and said, 'Gerry, it is always raining in this country. I must have someone to carry my umbrella above my head when I walk from my caravan to the ring.'

As politely as possible I said, ' Klemendore, if you want someone to carry your brolly that's fine. But it's your problem. I am trying to run a circus here. If you can find someone and are willing to pay them, then you just go ahead and do it.'

Well, we had a nymphomaniac box office lady at the time, let's call her Frenchie because she's now a respectable married lady, and she was willing to carry Klemendore's brolly and put his grease on for him for very little money indeed . . .

I didn't have to travel very far to find my animal trainer and boy did it cause ructions in the circus world. Captain Sydney Howes was getting on. He'd been with Roberts Brothers for over thirty years and of course I'd got to know him when I'd worked there. (His son Gordon was my great partner in crime from the days of Joe Gandey.) I had bought six lions that could not be trained. I knew Syd would be able to do it. The Roberts were playing in the North. I paid a polite social call, watched the show and made sure I bumped into Syd afterwards.

'You know Syd, you would be welcome to join us at any time. I would love you to train my new set of lions.'

That's all I said. That's all I needed to say. Syd was unhappy. The Roberts' sons had taken over the running of the circus and, as was quite common, Syd was finding it difficult to adjust to the new younger generation of bosses. One day he just packed up and drove the length of the country to join us. The Roberts were not happy bunnies. Circus people don't take kindly to their staff leaving mid season. One family, who shall remain nameless, accused a mechanic of stealing all their tools after he did a moonlit flit. The first thing the poor mechanic knew about it was when the police pulled him up.

Syd set about training the lions. I watched fascinated as he worked. Training animals is all about repetition and gaining the animals' respect. Syd would take the lions into the ring one at a time. Using a stick he would push a piece of meat near the pedestal and as the lion wandered over to pick it up, he would move it up on to the pedestal. Gently he would manoeuvre the meat so that only when the lion had sat down on the pedestal would he be rewarded with the meat. All the time he would be quietly talking to the lion, it was almost a purr. He was praising it in German (the traditional language animal trainers used). It was hypnotic for me, never mind the beasts. Once all six lions were sat obedient on the pedestals he would make them stay still and watch him for long periods of time. 'Sit Rajah. Watch me Rajah,' he would say, using their names over and over again. He clicked his fingers to get them into line. At the end of six weeks, Syd had them practically eating out of his hands.

By June 1975 we were like Lazarus back from the dead. From the jaws of disaster a fabulous circus had been born. Our acts were good and audiences healthy. After Scotland, we went down to London and repeated the success that we had had as Cottle and Austen's. The one thing we were lacking was a home. Brian had kept the farm at Cricklade so we no longer had anywhere to go when the season ended. I was starting to feel a bit desperate. It's difficult to find the right site. A circus headquarters needs easy access for all the big vehicles, a yard (the more concrete the better), plenty of ground for the animals to roam and not too close to a residential area in case one of them escapes. On a visit to some old showmen friends, I mentioned my predicament.

'You ought to go over to Addlestone Moor. There's a rich gypsy family with a derelict farm who are desperate to sell. Go and see them,' one said.

I left the showmen and drove straight up to Addlestone. I was greeted by the sight of an abandoned pig farm under some electricity pylons. It was perfect. It was close to London, our main business and my main playground. There was lots of space and a new motorway was being planned at the bottom of the garden. Moreover, it was derelict and the electricity pylons – well, they didn't bother me – we would be travelling most of the time, but I reckoned they did mean no one else would want it. It had to go for a good price.

I took Betty to see it. Unfortunately she didn't feel the same way.

'Gerry, it's horrible. How can you even think of us living here, making this our home? It's creepsville.'

'It's got great potential.'

'Look at the rats everywhere.' It was totally overrun with rats.

'It smells disgusting.' It was an old pig farm after all.

'They're building a main road outside its gate.'

'Well, I don't like it.'

Luckily Julie was with us and didn't see it the same way, 'I think it's perfect, Gerry. You'll have the best farm of any circus in the country.'

I was sure Julie was right. I was determined to make an offer.

Let me first explain a little about gypsies. Circus people are often confused with gypsies. We do both travel in caravans and in the old days circus folk sometimes bought their horses from gypsies, but there the connection ends. We are *not* related. However, that doesn't mean that we don't get on. The good old English gypsies are wealthy. Many have invested in property, and you never see a gypsy with the wrong motor. They are very shrewd.

Leslie and Reggie Hughes were definitely quality gypsies. They were wealthy – Addlestone was just one of several farms they owned. They had just been refused planning permission to build sixty homes there, so they were fed up and very happy to meet. I was greeted with the greatest courtesy and Mother Hughes made me a cup of tea in her finest bone china. There was a lot of polite conversation and sizing up before we got down to the real business of the day. I plucked up courage and popped the question, 'How much do you want for Addlestone?'

'£80,000.' (Remember this was 1975.)

My cup rattled in its china saucer.

'Oh. Really? If that's the case, I've been wasting your time.'

'How much could you give us then?'

'About half that amount.'

A look of disgust passed between Leslie and Reggie. Mother Hughes snatched the cup from my hands. Leslie and Reggie came over, took an arm each and escorted me firmly from the premises. Not another word was said. I put the whole episode down to experience.

A week later we were performing at Hersham Green in Surrey. The rain was pouring down and we were swimming in mud. I had to put a notice on the gate, 'No cars due to weather'. So when a huge Rolls-Royce shamelessly drove right across the middle of the ground, I shot out of my office hollering, 'Rolls-Royce or no Rolls-Royce, you can't park here.'

Leslie and Reggie Hughes got out, 'We've come to see you, son.'

I said no more about their parking and made them my best cup of tea. This time there was no polite chitchat.

'If you can pay us that money, you can have it,' Leslie said.

I was taken aback and in a bit of a spot. 'Well. When I said I could give you £40,000. I meant I could give you £40,000 in total . . . eventually.'

'What are you trying to say?'

'Look, I think that's the right price for the farm. The problem is I can't give you all that money at once. I just don't have it.'

I waited for them to walk out. They didn't.

'What can you give us now?'

'I can give you half that amount by the end of the month.'

'And the rest?'

'In ten instalments. £2,000 cash at the end of every month,' I said off the top of my head.

'Done. You've got yourself a farm.'

I was astonished. I felt like I'd won the pools.

'Well in that case, I'll get in touch with your solicitor tomorrow,' I said quickly before they had time to change their minds.

'No, no paper.'

'No paper?'

'Our word is good enough for you.'

I looked at them carefully. I wasn't a great fan of contracts myself. My instinct told me this was one deal worth taking a chance on. 'OK, I'll send round the first half by the end of the month,' I said.

My Wagon's Bigger than Yours

My solicitor thought I was mad, 'You're giving them thousands of pounds with nothing to show for it. They could just run off with the money and you'd be left empty-handed.' But our little arrangement worked perfectly. Each month I sent over someone different with £2,000 in cash. I reckoned that way if they reneged on the deal at least I'd have plenty of witnesses. By the time the season had ended we'd paid the brothers most of the money and they kindly let us move on to the farm. Unfortunately I couldn't pay the last instalment and they came over with some of their men, looking menacing. I had a lot of my circus boys on site who gathered round when they saw the gypsies getting out of their cars. It looked potentially very nasty. I walked straight over to the brothers and shook their hands.

'Reggie, Leslie. It's OK, I know why you're here. As you can see the circus is off the road. We haven't had any money coming in for a few months now. I have simply run out of cash. As soon as we're touring again you will have your money. Can you wait until Easter?' I said.

There was a long silence as the brothers stared intently at my face, then Reggie said, 'OK, son,' nodded his head, and his men retreated. As good as gold they got back into their cars and drove off. That was the last I heard from them. I sent round the last instalment at Easter, as promised, and we had our home.

I found out later that the brothers had let Addlestone go so easily because one of them had just received a huge tax demand and the other had just been told he might have a fatal illness. As it turns out, I think they're both still alive today. Lady Luck really was on my side that day because Addlestone turned out to be the best purchase I ever made. Rentokil got rid of the rats, the tent men made short work of the pig mess. When the M25 opened at the bottom of our garden we had instant access to all the major motorways in the country. The quarantine lady told me, 'I love coming to see you, Mr Cottle. This is the only circus headquarters in the country where I don't have to put my wellies on.'

I was making lots of money but Gerry Cottle's Circus wasn't famous yet. One man came into my life who was to change all that. Michael

Hurll was in charge of the BBC's Saturday night entertainment. The summer presented him with a bit of a problem. In the 70s, Saturday night BBC1 was dominated by big bold family variety shows. But in the summer all the artists went off to the coast to do their summer seasons on the end of a pier. Michael decided the solution was to take an outside broadcast unit to them – the 'Seaside Special' was born. Every week the show would come from one of Britain's great holiday resorts – the usual suspects, Great Yarmouth, Bournemouth, Weymouth, Blackpool. They were presented by the 'Smashey and Nicey' cheesy Radio One DJs of the day – Tony Blackburn, Noel Edmonds, David Hamilton – and featured all the big acts – Val Doonican, Rolf Harris, the two Ronnies, Sacha Distel, Little and Large, Ken Dodd, the Village People, Boney M, the Wombles etc. Just listing them now feels like a roll-call in 70s nostalgia. These acts were punctuated by a bit of singing, a bit of dancing and some acrobatics.

Originally Michael was going to use Pontin's Holiday Camps, but they didn't have a stage large enough, so he decided to use a circus tent. Researchers were sent round to all the big circus families to see if anyone was interested. Well, they didn't get much joy. The BBC needed a Big Top from Friday afternoon right through to Sunday evening – the time when the circus makes the most money – and the money they were offering didn't come close to matching what a circus would make from an ordinary weekend. Then Michael came to see me. I too wasn't impressed with the fee, but I could see the value of the publicity would be priceless. Every week millions of people would see the BBC's flagship entertainment programme coming from 'Gerry Cottle's Big Top'. Our posters could be emblazoned with 'As Seen on TV'. A few punters might be a bit disappointed not to see Ken Dodd and Cilla Black in the ring, but ticket sales would go up for sure. So I said yes. We made a second tent and got some more equipment and went down for the first show in Great Yarmouth.

Michael and I immediately hit it off. He said I was the biggest chancer he had ever met – the 'Arthur Daly of the circus world' – but

My Wagon's Bigger than Yours

I think he appreciated my can-do attitude and I liked the fact he was always game for a laugh. He got the DJs doing all sorts of circus tricks on the show, but insisted on doing them himself first just to prove they were safe. Barry Walls in his incarnation as Tutankhamen was supposed to take a cigarette out of Tony Blackburn's mouth with a flick of his whip. Michael gamely got in the ring only to have the skin of his nose taken off. Another week Michael went into the lions' cage with a humourless German lion tamer. 'Nothing in it. Lions seemed bloody scared of me,' he said. The next week the German was killed when one of his lions jumped on him – the lion caught its claws in the trainer's woolly jumper and broke his neck.

There were also a few complaints about Khalil the strongman. Michael had brought in some nice Portaloos for the TV crew. Khalil used to make the strongest Persian curries, but instead of retiring to his own caravan he would use the crew's loos. The smell was so rancid, no one could approach them for at least half an hour afterwards. He would persist in using them so in the end I had to give him a formal written warning, but I don't think it made any difference. He also annoyed Michael. I'd told him how Khalil could pick up the baby elephant and straight away Michael wanted to put it in the show, but each week Khalil came up with a different excuse ('Oh my hernia!'). So in the end Michael said to him, 'Khalil, this week no excuses, I've put it in the *Radio Times* for God's sake. You are lifting up that elephant.' We were in Poole at the time. Khalil trotted up to Sandbanks, a very posh Jewish area, and walked into a GP's waiting room in his loincloth, muscles rippling. I don't know how he did it but he came back with a letter which he thrust into Michael's hands:

Dear Mr Hurll,

I am writing to inform you that while Khalil the Strongman is fit enough to appear in the show, he is not well enough to lift the Baby Elephant.

Yours sincerely,
Dr Jacobs.

The fairground boys were a different matter. We got into terrible trouble in Southsea. A funfair was right next to the circus, a disaster waiting to happen. We'd only been there a few hours when the most almighty fight broke out – men were flying everywhere. Kelly my Irish tent man was a great worker and team leader, but he had psychopathic tendencies. If he caught any little boys peeping under the tent he'd chase them with a plank of wood. Imagine what he did to the fairground workers. A police superintendent came round to say Kelly had been locked up and charged with GBH. Well, I went down to the station, sorted it out and brokered a peace with the funfair owner. The circus men and fair men agreed to go out for a drink together to seal the peace. After the show had finished, Michael invited me out for a meal at the local Italian. We walked down Southsea High Street. It was a beautiful balmy summer's evening with no noise except for the odd seagull.

'What a wonderful evening. A beautiful spot. Just how a British holiday town should be. Quiet and tranquil,' Michael said.

'Yes indeed. This evening a Great Peace has broken out,' I replied.

With perfect comic timing, no sooner were the words out of my mouth when a funfair worker flew through the front window of a pub and landed at our feet. Once again the emergency services had to be called.

The shows were a huge success. They got 8 to 10 million viewers and the Cottle name became synonymous with family entertainment. Michael became a personal friend and through him I got some amazing work. We appeared on *The Two Ronnies*, *Morecambe and Wise* and *The Ken Dodd Show* many times.

By June 1976 Betty was very pregnant with our third child. She was desperate to have a boy and was convinced, as we all were, that this enormous energetic bump was Gerry Junior. Looking back now I was a bit daft, but I left her with our circus in Wimbledon to go and help put up the Seaside Special tent in Blackpool. Of course Betty went into labour in the early hours of the morning. My brother-in-law Billy Wild took her to St Theresa's in Wimbledon, a lovely little private hospital run by nuns.

My Wagon's Bigger than Yours

This time Betty had a much easier labour. By six o'clock in the morning she had given birth but I was still nowhere to be seen. When the lovely little Irish nun said, 'Mrs Cottle, you have a beautiful baby girl,' Betty burst into tears and wailed, 'That can't be right. He was supposed to be a boy.' At this point poor Betty just wanted to put the baby back, do it all over again and this time get the right result.

'But she looks just like you, Mrs Cottle. She's absolutely beautiful,' the poor nun tried.

It was no good. Betty kept crying and still I didn't come. Billy had rung the manager of the Blackpool circus, who I was supposed to be staying with. In fact I wasn't there. I was somewhere I wasn't supposed to be and missed the birth of my third child, something I will always regret. When I did finally get the message I leapt straight into the car. As I raced down the M6 in my Range Rover I happened to be listening to Radio One and I nearly crashed the car when Tony Blackburn announced, 'If Gerry Cottle is listening, his wife Betty has just had the baby. It's a girl.'

By lunchtime Betty was still crying in hospital and I still wasn't there. One of the nuns decided enough was enough, 'You know, Mrs. Cottle, you've got a beautiful baby girl and I know you wanted a boy. But you're safe and the baby's safe and you've really got to stop crying because you're going to make yourself ill.'

'But I wanted a boy,' Betty was inconsolable.

At three in the afternoon Betty finally heard the clip clop of my cowboy boots along the corridor outside her room. I came in and her first words were, 'I haven't given you the son you wanted.'

'And I wasn't here for you,' I said. It was a desperately sad moment. Then they brought the baby in and gave her to me. She was absolutely beautiful – the image of my beautiful circus girl, and there was no way I would have swapped her for any boy in the world.

'Little Juliette,' I said. Betty stopped crying. Juliette was the name of Betty's favourite cousin, very beautiful and very talented in the ring, a fitting name for such a perfect baby. Funnily enough, from that moment Juliette and Betty never looked back. Betty was and is a wonderful mother to all our children but she has been always been particularly close to Juliette and now they are more like sisters than mother and daughter. (The name itself didn't stick. As a toddler she talked so incessantly I said one day, 'She's a right Pretty Polly, isn't she?' From that moment everyone called Juliette, 'Polly,' and when she grew up she actually changed her name to Polly.)

When Betty left the hospital I arranged for an elephant, a llama and the most beautiful crib covered in pink to be waiting at the front door. The nuns crowded around tickled pink. Betty appreciated the gesture, although she was less happy about the press who had been invited along as well . . .

In 1975 my father was diagnosed with cancer and given a year to live. We were all totally shocked. He was just sixty years old. He had only retired the previous year, yet from the day he stopped work he had been feeling very tired and not himself. It was a double blow because Mum was the person we were supposed to be looking after and worrying about. She had been diagnosed with Parkinson's five years earlier, a terrible disease that results in you gradually losing control of your movements. It's generally associated with older people, but she was only forty-five when she was diagnosed.

The doctors were very precise about how Dad's cancer would develop. 'He'll have a course of treatment which will make him feel a lot worse to start with, but then he will suddenly feel a lot better. However you mustn't get your hopes up. This will only be temporary. He will then experience a gradual but irreversible deterioration which will result in death.'

They were stark words but very accurate. We tried to see him as much as possible that year, but it was very difficult – it was my second year without Brian and we were travelling all over the country, desperately trying to establish ourselves. For his last months Dad was moved to one of the country's first hospices in Sydenham. Almost a year to the day after he'd been diagnosed, I got the phone call I had been dreading, 'Come quickly, he hasn't got long.'

I had to drive from Weymouth. On the way I suddenly saw a motorway service station and on impulse quickly turned off. I got a coffee and a bacon sandwich and sat there for half an hour. Then I carried on with the journey. When I got to the hospice, Dad had died about twenty minutes earlier. I think I had known if I stopped I would miss him. I just wasn't ready to see a person die. I still haven't seen a person die, which is probably quite unusual in the circus business. I have so many regrets about Dad. He often accused me of taking him and my mum for granted, and I guess I did. Even so, Dad and I were quite close. Everyone says I've inherited his sense of humour and ability to get on with people. I know he was proud of where we had got to. I regret he died before he saw me make a real success of the circus. But I didn't grieve, I coped with losing him and my regrets about our relationship in my usual way – shutting it out and just working harder and playing harder.

I find it even more difficult to think about what happened to my mum after he died. It's a dreadful thing to say, but at least Dad's early death spared him from watching her terrible decline – I'm not sure he could have coped. At first she stayed living on her own in the house in Cheam. She was terribly lonely. The Joans had moved away by this stage and though she was a member of the Women's Institute and the Townswomen's Guild and things like that, you didn't make real friends there, or at least she didn't. She was a very proud, dignified, private person and it got very difficult for her to go out. She never knew when she was going to freeze in the middle of a conversation and not be able to finish, or even worse lose the use of her legs and fall over. She could no longer live on her own. Betty was very good with her, but there was no way my mum would ever come and live in a caravan on a circus. My sister did her best but she had four little girls of her own and a demanding marriage. So Mum went into the British Home and Hospital for Incurable Diseases in Streatham. It was full of people from all walks of life, with all sorts of horrible conditions, living on wards. Mum was quite aloof and she must have found it a kind of hell on earth. The nurses would chivvy her, 'Now come on, Joan. Let's have a smile.' It was well meant and they did a good job, but it was not the way my mum wanted to be treated. It was too sad. I hated visiting her. I used to take the children, but she really didn't recognise them. I had one decent conversation with her five years before she died. I had stayed later than usual to try and avoid the traffic and as we watched *Coronation Street*, she started to talk. She was completely normal. My mum was back. It was amazing, but it never happened again. That was the only conversation we'd had in a decade. Poor Mum was in the home for ten years before she finally died.

Luckily there was plenty going on in my business life to distract me.

The previous winter I'd had an unusually top-drawer clown called Peter Picton working for me. Aside from owning the original *Chitty Chitty Bang Bang* car, he had a lovely wealthy girlfriend with a mews house overlooking Hyde Park and great connections. He came to see me while we were in London with an unusual proposition.

'The Sultan of Oman wants to see a British Circus for his birthday.'

'Does he indeed? Well, that shouldn't be a problem. When does he want to come along?'

'It's more a case of when can you go to him?'

'What do you mean?'

'He wants a British circus in Oman in December.'

My jaw hit the floor. No British circus had travelled outside the United Kingdom since the turn of the century. Just moving fifty miles up the road was difficult enough.

'How much is he willing to pay?'

'£60,000.'

That is about half a million today. I began to feel excited. It suddenly all seemed a bit more possible. I flew to Oman to see the chief of police and the sultan's solicitors (who, curiously, were Jewish). It turned out the sultan had been educated at British public school, was very keen to see a circus and, as the Middle East had no circuses of its own, was willing to indulge our every wish to get us there. The Omanis would build a special stadium in the desert for us and the sultan's police would be at our service. In return we would perform for two weeks to his family, friends and workers, and have a special gala night for the sultan himself on his birthday. After the meeting I flew back to

My Wagon's Bigger than Yours

England on Concorde for the first and last time. The seats were a bit hard but, as I sipped the complimentary tomato juice, I decided to go.

It was very ambitious. No circus had ever flown before. We had to make special ramps just to get the elephants on the planes. Never one to miss a PR opportunity, I invited the nation's press to witness our embarkation. I held my breath as the elephants were led on to the tarmac, in a line chained at the ankles. They weren't sedated. All I could rely on was the skill of their trainer, Carlos MacManus. But he calmly took the harness of their leader, Rani, and they followed him up the ramps into the planes as if they were taking a stroll down the street. We made the front pages of all the newspapers with the headlines 'First Circus to Fly' and wonderful photos of our four elephants climbing aboard a Jumbo.

When we arrived in Oman we were driven for miles through the baking desert to the specially prepared spot. I got off the bus and had to pinch myself. It was like we had landed on the moon. We were in the middle of a perfectly flat plateau surrounded by mountains and not another human being to be seen. We worked hard all afternoon getting the tent ready. A royal box was installed, complete with leather sofas for the sheiks to lounge on. Another box was constructed with special net curtains for the ladies so they could see out but we couldn't see in. The showgirls' costumes were checked for propriety by the police officers. A job they relished and took full advantage of. There's a certain irony about being told to dress with due decorum and then forcibly pressed for sexual favours, but then it's a very different culture. By the time we had finished, the tent was up and glowing pink in the last rays of the setting sun. The peace of that spot was something I had never experienced. It was the most bizarre and beautiful backdrop my Big Top has ever had and I felt a real sense of achievement.

The next day the noise of whirring helicopter blades announced the imminent arrival of His Highness for his birthday performance. I stood in the receiving line of dignitaries in my newly-purchased safari suit, sweating profusely. Everywhere I looked the hills were alive with soldiers. Oman had its fair share of problems. The helicopter came down on target at the start of the red carpet. Everybody stood to attention. A white robed figure climbed out and was ushered over to greet us. As he approached, the line visibly relaxed and there was some laughter. I was confused until the police chief next to me explained that the Sultan's body-double had arrived. His Highness was arriving in another helicopter out the back as we spoke.

The performance was a huge success and for the next two weeks our Big Top was full. The sultan's friends and family came across the desert in a long line of limousines. They looked like a line of ants marching over the horizon. Lucky workers arrived in specially laid-on buses to see their first-ever circus. Everybody was incredibly helpful, especially the police, many of whom were ex British services or prison officers. Unfortunately a couple of naughty showgirls changed all that. They had enjoyed and reciprocated the attention of dusky men bearing gifts and driving sports cars. Word got around and by the end of our two weeks I think the local men felt all these girls were fair game. After the last performance the sultan's staff held a special party in our honour. A fleet of identical red jaguars came to pick us up and take us to the party on a recreation ground in the middle of the desert. The jag I was travelling in broke down with steam pouring out everywhere. They were hugely embarrassed that this British car, which had been purchased specially to honour us, had broken down so spectacularly. By the time I arrived the party was well underway. I had only been there a few minutes when blood-curdling screams started ringing out across the desert. Me and the men dashed round trying to find out where they were coming from. In the end we had to break down the door of a cupboard. One of our showgirls fell out half dressed with a flustered aggressive policeman behind. He'd got the wrong idea, bundled her into the cupboard, and locked the door. Nasty. The party ended very quickly and when we went to pack up the circus the next day, the police had locked up the forklift truck and none of the promised help materialised. We had to pack up the whole circus ourselves. It was a shame such a wonderful successful trip had to end on such a sour note.

The next day we flew to Bahrain. When I had accepted the Sultan of Oman's invitation I decided to look around and see if there was anywhere else we could go. After making a few enquiries I was paid a visit by Bahrain's minister of tourism. He was a very grand sheik who flew in specially to meet me and arrived in a stretch limousine in full Arabian gear. These were the days before the Arabs had started coming on their shopping trips to London, and he cut quite a dash in Fulham. We got on very well and he offered to pay me a generous deposit to go over. Our one disagreement was how long we should stay. He wanted us to go for four weeks, I really only wanted to go for one. I pointed out that there were just not enough people living in Bahrain to fill my Big Top four weeks in a row.

'But what if it should rain?' the sheikh asked.

'What if it should rain?' I replied.

'Mr Cottle, our cars do not have windscreen wipers. No one goes out if it rains. If it rains for the week you are with us, you will go home a poorer man and nobody will have seen the circus.'

I took his point and agreed to go for two weeks. Anyway I needn't have worried about filling the tent. We had the opposite problem. People went absolutely crazy. Fights broke out all over the place as men clambered over each other trying to get into the tent. Our metal barriers were warped and the ticket office had men scaling the walls and jumping off the roof. The police were swatting men like flies in a vain attempt to stop the whole situation turning into a riot. The overcrowding wasn't helped by the fact that some of the police were reselling used tickets. The bizarreness of the situation was compounded by the mountain of sandals that were left outside the tent. All the men took off their shoes before they came in as if they were going to a mosque, but when they came to go home the sandals were hopelessly muddled and they all left with odd feet. Again I managed to make a massive profit.

So when I got back to Britain I had money in my pocket, some new equipment and I had proved circuses could fly. I was having great adventures and these were great times. It felt as if the whole world was now Gerry Cottle's oyster. In just five years I had gone from a one-pole flower tent to really achieving my ambition of becoming Britain's biggest and best circus. I felt invincible and for the new British touring season, I felt it was time that Britain's biggest circus owner should have some accessories to match.

I decided to build the biggest caravan in the world. I do like to have the biggest. It's all part of showmanship and annoying the old circus families. The world's biggest caravan – it was in the *Guinness Book of Records* in 1976 and at least a few years after that. It was specially commissioned from a company in the Forest of Dean. I wanted everyone in the family to have their own bedroom and central heating and running water. In the end it was fifty-five feet long and had seven rooms. It was beautiful, all mahogany, and cost £20,000 – the equivalent of over £200,000 today. But we ran into trouble as soon as we picked it up. It's very nerve-wracking towing something like that for the first time. We hooked it up to an old Atkinson lorry and I just couldn't get it round a corner, so we had to go the wrong way up the one-way Chepstow High Street. It's a very steep hill and we were travelling on a busy Friday afternoon. Betty had to leap out and beat a path ahead of me. Luckily everyone was quite good-humoured about it, but it was a sign of things to come.

I only had one accident. When I backed into Torquay railway station I took the guttering down, but there was no one around and I got away with it. The real problem was the abuse we got trying to get it round the country. Cabbies in London were the worst. I got stuck at traffic lights in Fulham. A black cabbie was shouting the most filthy abuse. I marched over to his cab and lunged at him through the cab window. I managed to get hold of his tie. He shut the window, leaving his tie left hanging out, and called the police. When they arrived a couple were having a row in a telephone box across the street, so while they sorted that out I legged it. The next thing I knew I had a letter from the black cab association's solicitors demanding compensation for his loss of fares. Well, I wrote back and reminded them of all the black cab drivers' children who had free tickets to our circus every Christmas as part of a special evening for underprivileged children. We never heard anything more. But the world's largest caravan had to go. Its beautiful crystal chandeliers were a nightmare to pack up every time we moved. It bowed in the middle, the roof leaked and the chassis constantly needed straightening.

Now I was Britain's biggest circus owner it also seemed fitting that I play host to the Circus World Championships on Clapham Common which were broadcast across the world, and as an added bonus, I was asked to be one of the judges. (I'm sure you can imagine how great it was to be able to put two fingers up so publicly at the many in the British circus establishment who said I'd 'never be anything but a tent man'.) I had a great time hobnobbing with top circus magnates from across the world as well as the television executives. As the host, it was my job to show them the delights London could offer, which I did to the best of my considerable ability. However the championships themselves were a total fiasco. Because they were funded by an American television channel, the contest organisers felt it was important that the Americans came out on top. Well, the Americans just aren't good at circus compared to their European counterparts. The TV executives were able to insist that we kept on reshooting until the Americans won. It was a freezing cold wet and windy November day on Clapham Common and after a few hours of this farce the audience just walked out. The Americans were furious but there was nothing I could do about it. We just had to keep moving the audience that was left, to cover whichever camera was filming. It was miserable and took forever. But the final television programme was a great success and it was all wonderful publicity for me. I could hardly complain.

I guess these glorious years in the mid 70s were my heyday. I felt pretty invincible. I even got to meet the Queen. (The first time I was supposed to be in a receiving line I got off at the wrong station and missed Her Majesty. But I had another crack at the whip. Nice lady, very dignified, she reminded me of my mother. Prince Philip had a twinkle in his eye. He looked like he was constantly on the verge of saying something truly outrageous.) I went to loads of parties. Betty very rarely went with me – she preferred to stay at home looking after the children. Instead I often took my other ladies. One was a feature writer for a national tabloid. We met through Mary Chipperfield and I was her 'bit of rough'. I suppose I did look the part. I trotted around wearing a flamboyant hat over long wavy locks, cigar in my mouth, droopy moustache and cowboy boots. She introduced me to her mother who took an instant dislike to me. And then sometimes I would go on my own and meet someone there. On one occasion a friend invited me to the Metropolitan Police's Annual Ball. It was a riot. I met a lady high up in the police force. She was wild. Afterwards she gave me her telephone number. On the way home I threw it out of the car window. I realised she lived just down the road from me. It would be too dangerous to have an affair with someone so close to home. I always kept my home and my play separate. To stray on my own patch would be a betrayal too far, even for me.

Betty found it very difficult after splitting up with John and coming back to me. It wasn't as if we had a passionate reconciliation. We barely spoke to each other for a long time and she was very depressed, but when you look at it what alternative did she have? Betty had nowhere else to go, what was left of her family were travelling with me. The children loved the circus and she felt that no other circus would dare take on my estranged wife.

So Betty went back into the ring with her beloved farmyard act — the grande finale — a small Jack Russell standing on top of a goat, standing on top of a donkey trotting around the ring. But it was always a bit fraught because she had to leave the little devil April unsupervised in the caravan. I say unsupervised, actually my big dog Barney was looking after them. He lay across the door of the girls' bedroom. If a stranger had tried to come in he would have torn them limb from limb. If the girls tried to get out he would bark at them. This had worked perfectly with Sarah, but Barney was no match for the fiend April. Things came to a head when she was found wandering the streets of Clapham in her pyjamas by a passer-by. From then on Betty had to lock the door of the caravan, but used to dread the scene that would meet her when she came back. She'd only be gone twenty minutes to find butter spread all over the furniture, a trail of soap powder or coal dust on her finest red velvet upholstery. And in the circus it was a point of pride for the ladies to keep their caravans as immaculate as possible.

My Wagon's Bigger than Yours

But gradually things got better for Betty. April became more civilised and as you know we had baby Polly. And however miserable I may have made her in other ways, life with me now had a couple of major compensations. For a start Betty enjoyed being married to the boss of Britain's biggest circus and all the perks that involved – the biggest caravan, the best car and the respect she was given. And more importantly Betty knew it was for fantastic for our children. They loved the circus and on their dad's big circus they had the most amazing opportunity to travel and learn the trade from the best circus artists in the world.

The circus is a magical place for children to grow up. It's probably the closest thing to freedom. The girls had lots of playmates and space to run round. They lived outside roaming as a pack. There were always plenty of people around, like one big extended family, in fact most of them probably were family in one way or another. It was impossible to be lonely. Every move was exciting – April and Sarah used to ride in the big articulated lorry with me. April always loved the big lorries. I'd say to her, 'Go and start the Scammell.' She couldn't reach the pedals or the steering wheel, but somehow she'd manage it. In the summer months we'd arrive at the new ground while it was still daylight and if we were lucky we would be by the beach. The children would make for the nearest set of swings. All the horses and elephants would be allowed to wander on the ground and sometimes walk along the beach. The elephants loved swimming. At places like Weymouth the locals were stunned by the sight of the elephants frolicking in the waves. You had to keep an eye on them though because given the chance they'd swim off and keep swimming, probably until they hit France. The summer evening would be filled with the sound of all the different languages of the artists being spoken, the smell of different exotic foods being cooked, everyone sat outside the caravans in deckchairs talking to each other, drinking cold beer. Sarah used to love walking into the empty ring when it was first put up and smelling the fresh sawdust. All the children grew up side by side with the animals, learning how to care for them and love them. Sarah and April spent a lot of time in Sydney Howes' caravan playing with his pet monkey, who wore a nappy and a little hand-knitted jumper. They would sit peeling grapes for him. When they got a bit older the girls took it in turns to ride the elephants for their daily exercise. These were very happy care-free times for the family.

The one difficult thing was school. Betty's first job when we reached a town was to find a school that would take the children for a week – not always easy. She'd march in on a Monday morning and ask to see the Head, Sarah and April in tow, April often in tears. They'd be stuffed at the back of class, if taken at all. Often the teacher would say, 'As we've got a visitor from the circus, let's make this week's special topic the circus.' Great for the class, pointless for my kids. Or even worse, 'As you don't know what we're doing in the class, you'd better just draw a picture. How about drawing a picture of the circus?' The girls were very bored. Worse was usually waiting for them in the play-ground. They were often bullied, called 'gypsy scum' and the rest. Both grew up pretty tough. April in particular was not afraid to defend herself with her fists.

In the end Betty put her foot down. 'Gerry, you have got to do something. The girls can barely read. They're bullied and miserable. It's appalling.' I decided to make our own school. I bought a double-decker bus – the downstairs was the classroom with little desks and chairs, and upstairs was the art room and science lab – and I found us a teacher. In fact I found several teachers. One had to leave because she was too frisky with the tent men. Another left because the travel-ling lifestyle didn't suit. But Pauline came and stayed. There were about ten children in all. She was very good at teaching the basics, but she also got them out and about – every week she would seek out the local swimming baths and take them for a lesson. She made sure his-tory lessons included a trip to the local historical site of interest.

So the family was happy and I was happy. With Bertram Mills' and Smart's retired and Chipperfield's struggling, my nearest rivals were the Roberts – but I was a much bigger operation. Huge high profile shows like Seaside Special and the Circus World Championships had made sure of that. In just five years I had fulfilled my ambition to become Britain's biggest and best circus owner. There's always room for improvement, but I had a show I was really proud of and I had become the best-known name in British circus. Me, Gerry the josser, had taken the closed insular world of circus by the scruff of the neck and given it a good shake. The huge Gerry Cottle's circuses of the mid 70s were the template for circuses for the next twenty years. I had set the standard. It felt like I could do nothing wrong.

Ten things you didn't know about
Circus Around the World

---

1. There are about 1,000 circuses worldwide, with probably over 150 in Italy and at least 100 in Germany. Many are being run by the same families that owned them 100 years ago.

2. Switzerland is a tiny country, but it has over 20 circuses and probably Europe's best – Circus Knie. It still travels by train and they present the best elephants, horses and wild animals you will ever see.

3. Germany also has a great circus tradition. I always like Circus Barum whose proprieter, Gert Siemoneit-Barum, started as a local boy cleaning out the animals, and has become probably the best wild animal trainer in the world.

4. In France many towns have ten shows a year because they cannot refuse a circus visit according to a charter which dates back to the reign of Charles I.

5. South America is a real hotbed of circuses. There are always at least ten shows just around the perimeter of Mexico City itself. The most famous is Circo Tihany, which goes right down to Argentina and up to the Panama Canal and can stay six months in one city.

6. We met the Great Indian Circus in Malaysia. They had been out of India for over 20 years because it was so competitive. They had 70 workers where the equivalent show in Britain would have just 10.

7. China has over 200 acrobatic schools – every major city has one. They all compete against each other in festivals across the country. With the presigious top prize comes the overseas tours.

8. There are probably 2,500 Russian circus performers, of which 1,500 are performing overseas in 30 different countries. There are over 60 circuses which perform in specially constructed buildings.

9. The most elaborate circus building left in Europe is the Cirque d'Hiver in Paris. Absolutely beautiful, it was the setting for the film *Trapeze* starring Burt Lancaster and Gina Lollobrigida.

10. There are large circus festivals all over the world, but the oldest and most prestigious is the International Circus Festival Monte Carlo. I was probably one of the youngest judges in 1985. It is shown on TV in every country in the world except Britain. Why?

Chapter Six

A Big Pie in the Face
1976-81

In 1978 I was summoned to a meeting of Lambeth council. On the agenda was whether the council should let us pull on to Clapham Common. I thought it was just a routine matter – we had been going there for the last five years with no problems at all. I was astonished when they started to ask me some really hostile questions about the care of our animals.

'How do you train them?' an aggressive beardy asked.

I went through my standard answer, that we used whips as an extension of the arm, as a guide, and concentrated on rewarding and repetition. Our trainers were very experienced, took pride in their animals and, I joked, cared for them as well as, and sometimes better than, their children.

'Aren't you demeaning the animals?' the belligerent beardy shouted.

I was taken aback.

'I'm sorry, I don't understand what you mean.'

'To have wild and noble animals caged up. Chimpanzees at tea parties and the like.'

'I don't think our animals are demeaned more than any other pet animal is demeaned. Do you think we should stop old ladies in flats from having pet dogs? As long as the animals are well looked after and happy they are not being demeaned. As for the chimpanzees, don't worry about them. They're basically like naughty children – and the chance to lark about and eat nice food, well nothing could make them happier.'

I thought I'd answered all their questions, but when the officer read out the results of the vote, I had lost by a huge margin. I tackled the chairman of the council afterwards.

'I'm really surprised. What went wrong? I felt I won the arguments easily.'

'You did, but it wouldn't have mattered what you had said. It's Labour Party policy to protect minorities. And no one was going to vote against the party line.'

'I'm sorry. I'm confused. Did you say minorities?'

'Well gay people, black people, small people, women. And animals.'

I felt something really scary was happening.

In 1970 when Brian and I had our first circus, we were constantly asked why we didn't have more animals. If you didn't have at least one elephant and a couple of lions you weren't considered a real circus. Yes, there had always been a few old ladies who wrote letters to *The Times* and there were two councils which traditionally would not allow circuses – Bath and Hove. But it really wasn't a mainstream issue. Now in my heart of hearts I knew where Lambeth led, others would follow. I couldn't bear to think about the consequences. I felt sick in the pit of my stomach. Sure enough next came Haringey, Brent, Islington. Within just a few seasons all the big council sites were closed to us. It is amazing how quickly the tide of public opinion can change.

At the same time we started getting protesters at our gate. At first it was just certain sites in the big cities, especially London and the South East, but then we got to a stage where it was unusual to have a free day from the hairy mob. Generally they were a filthy lot. Lots of unemployed people and students with nothing better to do than stir up a fuss. Some of them were very threatening and used terrible language. I remember seeing one young mum spat at in the face because she was bringing her little girl to see the circus. Disgusting. Imagine what it was like sitting in your caravan trying to relax, watch TV, have a conversation and all you can hear is this constant caterwauling. It really did get to you. And it did have an effect on our takings. Understandably people didn't want their children to be at the mercy of that sort of behaviour. Perhaps worse was the effect on the morale of the artists. The older members felt their whole way of life was being questioned and threatened. The younger members wanted to hit back. Baba and Mike's son, Beau, and his friend, Jan-Erick, were clowns on the circus. They used to walk past them all smiley then throw a bucket of water in their faces. The police did come and clear the protestors away. But then they would go around town taking down our posters and supergluing the locks of shops with our posters in. Our foreign acts couldn't understand it. The animal question just didn't come up anywhere else. They had never seen it before. 'Why do the police not take these people away?' they asked. I couldn't answer.

The problem is when you throw mud, some of it sticks. It became an obsession in the papers, and they were nearly always on the side of the protesters.

We did respond. We changed our travelling methods. We gave the caged animals exercise cages (although it has to be said they never used them. Lions are particularly lazy, and just carried on lying on top of each other like they do most of the time in the wild). But opposition just grew. We offered to take out the caged animals and just keep the elephants, chimpanzees, horses and dogs. But that wasn't acceptable. With these people there could be no compromise, only a total ban on animals would do. I couldn't see where the whole issue was going to end. Or rather I could, but it didn't bear thinking about.

That winter 1976 my old friend Gordon Howes, the son of Captain Syd our lion trainer, came to stay. Things were a bit different from the days we went out looking for girls together on Joe Gandey's circus – we both had three children for a start – but we were still very close. I desperately wanted him to join our circus and do his own animal act.

'Stay Gordon. You know I'll make it worth your while.'

'I'd love to Gerry, but I've given my word that I'll go and do a season with the Duffy's.'

'It'll be bloody hard work. You know they only ever play one night in a town. Imagine what it's going to be like having to move every day in an Irish wet spring.'

'I know. I know. But I really don't want to let them down. Maybe next season.'

'Well, if you change your mind, just let me know.'

But Gordon didn't change his mind and we said goodbye on a cold February morning, Gordon driving off in an appalling old lorry, his three children waving out the back.

Three weeks later I was sat at my desk when the phone rang.

'Gerry? It's Tom Duffy.'

'Hello, Tom. How are you?'

'Not good. Not good at all. Gordon Howes is dead.'

'What?'

'Yes. Gordon's dead.'

'Oh God. No. But how?'

'We found him in the lions' cage this morning. No one saw what happened, but he'd been badly mauled. His neck was broken. He must have had his back to the lion and it jumped him from behind and broke his neck.'

I was totally stunned. It's very rare for a lion to do this. Normally a lion trainer can stop a lion in its tracks by using a loud voice and shouting, 'Back', but you do have to be facing him. As a rule you should never turn your back on any animal. I know Gordon was very tired and working all hours just to cope with the appalling weather conditions. The mud was particularly bad that year. I also know that if an accident is going to happen, it's always in those first few weeks of a season. That's when people fall off the trapeze, mis-throw the knife, trip on the high wire.

Now I had to break the news to Syd and his wife, Jess. I had a terrible walk across the ground to Syd's caravan. Going over and over in my mind was Jess, the way she refused to watch Syd or Gordon in the ring. She always said it was only a matter of time before one of them was badly hurt or worse. I remembered how she had begged Gordon to give up training the lions. It was probably the most difficult thing I've ever had to say to anyone. In the end we organised for Gordon's body to be brought back. Gordon's three young children, Barbara, Paula and Michael, came and lived with their grandparents Captain Syd and Jess and grew up with my children as members of our extended family. They travelled everywhere with us.

The loss of Gordon and the animal question left me feeling depressed. So I did what I always did – put my head down and worked just that bit harder. Took on a new challenge. I decided it was time to put a second Gerry Cottle's Circus on the road. I had to borrow a bit of money but it didn't seem like too much of a risk. One circus would do the usual London, south coast route while the new circus would go to Scotland (as you know, always great for traditional circus) and up to Shetland and the Orkneys – places that had never seen a circus before. My experience with the Channel Islands had taught me that these outposts could be incredibly lucrative. I also sent a circus to Iceland. And at the beginning of the season my gamble seemed to be paying off handsomely. Then my phone rang.

'Gerry. General Shomar's on the phone.'

'Who?'

'He says he's General Shomar.'

'I never heard of him. Ask him where he's from.'

'He says he's a general in the Iranian Army.'

'Blimey. Put him through then.'

General Shomar got straight to the point.

'Mr Cottle. The shah feels it's time Persia had a circus. You have been recommended. We have a 10,000-seater ice rink in our capital Tehran that could be placed at your disposable. For six weeks. At the end of this year. We would pay you a big guarantee. What do you think?'

Need I say what I thought?

Well, I put a lot of effort into getting this circus right. I managed to get a troupe of top ice skaters released from Blackpool, which cost me thousands of pounds. I found the world's only available ice skating chimpanzees in Italy, again they didn't come cheap. All in all it was a class act but the returns were going to have to be big. Things were going to have to go well.

As the day to leave approached there was no sign of the guarantee. Contacting the general was a nightmare. These were the days when you had to book a telephone line to places like Iran. Often you couldn't get a line at all. Then of course, even if you did get through, the man was never in. What should I do? I had merrily gone ahead and booked the acts, the flight tickets had arrived, the posters were stacked up in the office. Surely it was too late to call the whole thing off? Anyway, I was greedy. I kept on thinking of that 10,000-seat stadium – much bigger than anything I had played before. Even if the guarantee never turned up, it didn't matter. We'd make back our money and then some. No problem. I was on a roll and feeling invincible.

So off we went.

First of all, the precious chimpanzees were impounded.

'Mr Cottle, you are going to have to do something about my monkeys otherwise they are going to die. I'm telling you. They are the best animals and they cost a lot of money. I'm not going to find any other in this life, I'm telling you.'

Mr Barbrelli, their Italian trainer and rather excitable, was doing his nut – but he did have a point, they were particularly beautiful animals. The chimpanzees were imprisoned in a tiny container and being fed any old rubbish, if at all. Customs kept on mumbling about bits of paper, which we would produce but then they still wouldn't release them. There was no sign of the general. At this point I was in the Orkneys with Gerry Cottle's Circus so I was having a constant stream of anxious phone calls. Mike Denning (Baba's old boyfriend) was managing the Iranian end. He's a lovely guy but I didn't think he was cunning enough to manage this particular situation. Every afternoon he would jump into a cab and head off to the airport to plead for the chimpanzees release. A complete waste of time.

A Big Pie in the Face

The artists weren't faring any better. They'd put them in the Olympic Village in Tehran. Respectable and appropriate I thought. They hadn't told me it was the village for the Arab Olympics. Conditions were luxurious if you were a travelling Bedouin. Nice holes in the ground for the toilet (no loo paper, obviously). Tiny, tiny beds, one thin sheet on a plank of wood – and I mean plank, roll over and you were lost. Food was standard desert fare served by hand, literally by hand. Well, this may be OK for young Arab men, but nice middle-class ice skating girls were not having any of it. The tears flowed.

Mike's phone calls were getting desperate.

'Gerry. There's something really strange going here. There's no sign of the general. We've got the mother of all stadiums to fill and there's been no publicity at all. Weirder still, there's large groups of protestors marching the streets. Soldiers swarming with guns. All the cabs have bullet holes in them. It's too dangerous to go out at night. There are pitched battles going on outside our bedroom windows. What the hell is going on? And where is the general? Does he really exist? Are you sure this is not just a huge wind-up?'

It was obvious this was not going to be an ordinary gig. I got on a plane to Tehran.

'Have you given customs any money yet?' my first question to Mike.

'No.'

'Ah. Well that's where you going wrong. I think you'll find a few dollars and the paperwork will suddenly all be in order. Call us a cab.'

We went straight over to the airport. On the journey I was feeling nervous. I reckoned it would cost me at least £5,000 to get those chimpanzees out. With no sign of the guarantee I had arrived virtually penniless. At the airport I asked to see the man in charge. Without any further ado I got out my wallet. His face didn't move.

'Now, Sir, these chimpanzees must be costing you an awful lot to feed and look after. Let me give you a little something to help cover their costs.'

I counted out US$200.

'Thank you, Mr Cottle. I will be happy to accept your kind offer. These animals are indeed very expensive.'

He counted the money.

'Well, Mr Cottle, I think the paperwork is now all in order and you are free to take the chimpanzees away with you right now. Let us know if we can help you in any other way.'

That simple. Mike was aghast. I was hardly less so. We got out of there quickly before they could change their minds.

Unfortunately our other problems weren't so easy to solve.

'Listen. It is not customary in our country to serve food with your hands. It is considered unhygienic. We do not know where those hands have been. It's just not the done thing,' I said to the manager of the Olympic Village. He bowed and shouted at the chef who disappeared into the kitchen. He came back wearing a glove and started serving the food with the glove.

How could I put this?

'I don't think that's the answer. For a start you're serving all different sorts of food here with the same glove. What's wrong with a spoon?' The manager shouted at the chef again. He shrugged his shoulders and turned the glove inside out and started serving dessert. I decided we should cut our losses and move into a local hotel. I still hadn't tracked down the disappearing general, all I got was his wife, but Mrs Shomar passed on a message that he would indeed pay the bill.

Mike took me to see the national ice rink. I felt sick. It was absolutely huge, twice the size of Wembley. There was no hope of even half-filling it especially as there were no signs of any publicity, not even the tiniest poster put up outside.

The whole of Tehran worried me actually. The city was controlled by roadblocks and checkpoints. We were told to hide under our beds if we heard gunshots. There were continuous power cuts which sometimes lasted up to twelve hours. Many people seemed to be starving – I suspected going to see the circus was the last thing on their minds.

You see, I had inadvertently arrived in a place gearing up for a full-scale revolution. When you run a circus you really don't have time to read a newspaper or watch the television. So when I got a phone call from a General Shomar of the Iranian Army requesting a circus, it seemed like a good idea. Little did I know the shah had ordered the general to get in some entertainment as a last-ditch (and let's face it ridiculous) attempt to distract the masses from their revolution. The Persian equivalent of 'Let them eat cake,' I guess. Except I was the cake.

I decided that if the general wouldn't come to see me, it was time I paid him a polite house call. The cab pulled up outside a mansion with half an army guarding it. I knocked at the door. Mrs Shomar answered it.

'I'm sorry, the general has palpitations and cannot see you.'

'What do you mean he's got palpitations? I'll give him palpitations if he doesn't come out here and start giving me some answers, or even better, how about the money he owes me?'

'I'm sorry, Mr Cottle. I've told you. He's not a well man. The doctor says he must not move from his bed.'

'And while he's lying in his bed, what is my circus to do? Stop eating until he feels better?'

'I'm sorry, Mr Cottle, there's nothing I can do for you.'

With that Mrs Shomar politely but firmly slammed the door in my face.

I was stranded outside the mansion of General Shomar in Tehran at the start of the Iranian revolution. For the first time in my life I wondered whether I had overreached myself.

That night the show opened to a few hundred people. I was amazed there was anyone there at all.

There's one thing I've learned from these foreign trips. Generals may be able to run an army but they can't run a circus. In Britain we are relatively sophisticated when it comes to publicity and we know the value of it. Often abroad, especially in less developed economies, its a completely undeveloped skill and a circus gets nowhere without good publicity. There's an element of 'God willing' going on in these societies which is not helpful – it certainly does not get bums on seats.

But things were about to go from bad to worse. A couple of BBC technicians I'd met on *Seaside Special* had decided to use their annual leave to come and help us do the lighting. These BBC types are much more gregarious than their circus counterparts and instead of larking about in each other's hotel bedrooms like the rest of the team, they spent a lot of time chewing the cud with the locals in the hotel bar, especially as the local news was so interesting.

We'd been there two weeks when one of them took me aside. 'Gerry, I think you should know. There's talk going around about a curfew.'

'A curfew? Oh God. No.'

'Tonight apparently.'

I felt physically sick. Surely not?

I got straight on the telephone to the general. Of course I got his wife.

'Mrs Shomar, some of my men have just told me there is going to be a curfew.'

'Yes, that is right.'

'I can't believe it. Did your husband not think it might be a good idea to let me know? What time does it start?'

'At six o'clock in the evening.'

'What? Are you serious? You do realise the show doesn't start until eight?'

'I know, Mr Cottle, this will be difficult for you.'

'Difficult? Impossible more like. How is anyone going to get to the show? Can they get special passes?'

'Now you are joking with me, Mr Cottle. Of course this will not be possible. There are bigger things going on in Persia at the moment than the Circus on Ice.'

'I wish your husband had told me that before he invited me out here.'

Mrs Shomar's charm was running out. 'Look, Mr Cottle. I would have thought it would be quite possible for a man as adaptable as yourself to change the time of the show to say four o'clock.'

'Well, I'll try but it seems to me most people will still be at work.'

'You may be surprised, Mr Cottle.'

I bloody well will be, I thought.

A Big Pie in the Face

That night we opened at four o'clock. Absolutely no one turned up. Why would they? Nobody had told them we were there. They were all at work. They were in the middle of a revolution. We were stuck facing a completely empty 10,000-seater stadium. That night the whole circus had to do a midnight flit from the hotel. We had no money to pay the bill and it was obvious the general wasn't well enough to write a cheque. I decided that it was time to call it quits. We left and flew home. A few months later the shah was forced to flee Iran, General Shomar disappeared and Ayatollah Khamenei came to power. We were the last circus to perform in Iran for many years.

I was cheesed off but I thought I would soon bounce back from this little experience. Yes, the debts were the biggest I had ever had. After I had shipped the whole circus there and back at my own expense they amounted to £100,000 (the equivalent of about a million pounds today). Even though I hadn't received a penny from the elusive General Shomar and in the end we were only in Iran for three weeks, I had promised my artists nine weeks' wages. I didn't even consider not paying them the full amount. We always try to keep our word even though we rarely have formal written contracts. I shelled out thousands I didn't have, confident that, in the traditional circus way, we could trade out of trouble.

As part of this strategy I booked big, all-singing all-dancing Christmas runs for both my circuses – one at Cardiff, the other at Alexandra Palace. We started well. Takings were good at both circuses. New Year's Eve at Ally Pally, I finished my accounts and lit a cigar. I felt confident we were getting out of trouble. I was looking forwards to driving down to Cardiff that night for a party with all my staff and the family. Thinking about the long drive down the M4 I walked to the window to take a look at the weather. To my horror the whole world had gone white. While I'd been happily counting my money, a deadly silent invasion had taken place outside. I turned on the radio.

'This is an extreme weather warning. Heavy snow is expected to cover the whole of the south of the England and Wales in the next few hours. It will be the start of a big freeze.'

Of all the terrible luck. The winter of 1978–79 turned out to be the worst of the decade. The last thing people want to do when there's snow on the ground is venture out and sit in a tent. We spent a fortune in extra heaters, generators, hot dogs etc. The toilets froze over and couldn't be moved. It was miserable. In fact it was a miserable time for everybody. It was the Winter of Discontent with strikes, power cuts and rubbish piling up in the streets. Imagine trying to run a circus with petrol and paraffin rationed. It was not only the circus that felt doomed, the whole country felt like it was falling into the abyss. Where would it all end?

A fight started in a garage when I tried to fill up one of the lorries with petrol. I was accosted by the large lady running the forecourt. 'What do you think you are doing, you greedy swine?'

'I'm sorry, I don't know what you mean?' I said, pretending I hadn't been watching the dials.

'You selfish bastard,' joined in an aggressive lorry driver.

I beat a hasty exit.

Then I was hauled up in Tesco's trying to make off with twenty bags of sugar for the candyfloss machine. 'What on earth do you think you are doing with those?' asked an incredulous lady behind the till. It's almost unbelievable now to think that sugar was actually rationed that winter, and you know how important candyfloss is for circus profits.

I realised I was in trouble when I couldn't pay £20 for the hot dog buns. I tried my bank account, my desk drawer, the boot of my car – nothing. I had quite literally run out of money. But ever the optimist I went to see Ken Morgan, my accountant, to see what he could suggest.

'You are going to have to liquidate.'

'No!' My jaw hit the floor. I had no idea it was that serious. I didn't really know what it meant, but I didn't like the sound of it.

'What does that mean anyway?'

'It means your company is going to have to be declared bankrupt.'

There was a real stigma attached to going bankrupt in those days. Of course it's not great today, but I think our whole attitude to credit has changed. In those days it was really difficult to borrow money or get credit. These days many circuses go off on the road at the start of the season with everything paid for on a credit card. In those days a visit to your bank manager was the only way to raise some cash. In 1979 I was appalled at the idea of going bankrupt. It was truly shameful. My mother's face asking, 'What would the neighbours say?' came into my mind. Just six months ago I had been hosting the Circus World Championships. Now I felt like a feckless character in a Dickens' novel. How had it come to this, so quick?

'Don't be daft, Ken. You're pulling my leg, aren't you?'

'Look, Gerry, your debts are a quarter of a million pounds.'

I hadn't realised it was quite that bad. That would be over £2 million today. Keeping the books was never my strong point.

Ken couldn't advise me about liquidation, but he passed me on to a company who could. They were very sympathetic to my situation.

'I think we can do something better than liquidate. Have you heard of a moratorium, Mr Cottle? We could offer your creditors the option of putting your debts on hold for a few months, trimming down your business and allowing you a few more months to trade with the hope you might be able to pay off at least a significant amount of your debts at the end of it.'

'I like the sound of that a lot. I am sure it's still possible to make serious money in the circus. I've just been terribly unlucky in the last few months.'

'Well be warned, Mr Cottle. The decision is in the hands of your creditors. You may have to work very hard to make them see things the way you do. Good luck.'

The creditors would take this decision by voting at a creditors meeting. We set the date. The night before I couldn't sleep. My fate was in the hands of others for the first time in years and I didn't like how it felt. I knew I was going to have to put on the performance of my life. My aim was clear – to avoid bankruptcy at all costs.

We had tried to be clever and fixed the meeting for a Friday afternoon in the hope people would have better things to do than turn up. But we forgot to locate it in Outer Siberia. Instead we chose central

London, the Bonnington Hotel in Russell Square. Masses of people were there, including the national press. It was a horrible freezing, slushy, grey February day which will forever linger in my memory like a bad smell. When we arrived the press was waiting for me. A few months ago I would have welcomed them with open arms. That day I turned up my collar, pulled my hat down and with a strong arm around Betty pushed past them growling 'no comment'. I walked into the room and was shocked by how many people were there and the hostility in their faces. Many of them were close friends I had worked with for years.

I was put on the spot straight away:

'Why did you go to Iran?'

'We were offered a good guarantee.'

'Why did you come back with such bad debts?'

'They never paid the guarantee.'

'So why on earth did you still go then?'

'We had already spent so much money on the tickets to get there. Look, I had hundreds of posters already printed and paid for sitting in my office. I thought it was a risk worth taking.'

'Even when there was a revolution about to happen?'

'Well, I didn't know about that, obviously.'

'So why did you carry on trading when you got back and you knew you were in such a bad position?'

'In circus it's usually best to try and trade out of bad patches because business is always very up and down. May and June are nearly always pretty bad but July and August are always really good. As they were this year.'

'So why didn't you stop when you had money in the bank in August?'

'We still had to feed the animals so we had to keep on trading.'

'Shouldn't you have paid your debts first?'

'Well maybe. But if every circus sold its animals when things got a bit rough, there would be no circuses left. As I said business is up and down from one week to the next. It's impossible to predict how it's going to be and it takes a long time to sell an elephant, you know. And buying them back takes even longer. It's not something you can do at the click of your fingers.'

'Why did you keep going into Christmas?'

'Sometimes you can do really well at Christmas. We were on course for record takings until it began to snow.'

I did my best but a lot of people looked unconvinced. It was an ugly meeting. After an hour and a half the questions finally dried up. Ken proposed the vote.

There was a show of hands. I narrowly won my moratorium. But there was one condition attached – they insisted I appoint a financial controller to do the accounts. We drove home in silence. The weather was so bad, it took five hours to travel the twenty miles back to Addlestone. Cars were skidding all down Tooting High Street. Betty seemed amazingly undaunted by the whole episode. But I was feeling very bruised. I think I had gone so far, so fast, people felt I had got above myself and were particularly vicious when I fell.

I learnt a few important lessons from this experience:

1. The press keep files on you. The next day on the front of the *Evening Standard* they'd dragged up an old photo of me with a big fat cigar in my mouth outside my circus on Clapham Common looking unbearably smug. The headline was 'Circus Owner Gone Bankrupt'. Other papers went along the same lines. One paper had a picture of Betty's uncle Sonny Fossett sat at my desk dressed as a clown with tears rolling down his face.

2. Just because people are mates, doesn't mean they won't be ruthless if you're going to lose them money. People I thought were my friends, who had profited from my success for nearly a decade, were now questioning me as if I was a criminal.

3. I decided in future I would pay my friends first and the government last. Most of my creditors did work with me again, but a few key relationships could never be repaired. The taxman on the other hand would never desert me!

4. That old cliché – you learn who your friends are. I couldn't believe how people I had employed for years, as soon as the going got a bit tough, just upped and left. People who had been happy to take my money and tug their forelock when I was the boss of the up and coming circus fled to my rivals faster than you could blink. OK, so they had to earn a living, but they were going around saying: 'We knew it wouldn't last,' 'It was only a matter of time,' 'He had it coming to him.' I felt like they were giving me a big pie in the face. Worse, a lot of my equipment went 'missing'. For example I had bought a job lot of military-style uniforms from an outfitters in Hammersmith. I kept seeing them appear in circuses across the country for years. I had some fantastic Second World War allied bunting I used to rig round the Big Top. Some strangely familiar-looking bunting turned up a few months later on a circus set up by my old German high wire act. People are unbelievable.

Now I had to frantically get a new circus together on very limited funds. Difficult when every single sledgehammer has been nicked. Difficult when all my staff are busy defecting to Mary Chipperfield's new circus. I was furious. Mary and I have always had a bit of a love-hate thing going on. Well this year, with me down on my uppers, she saw an opportunity to step into my shoes and set up her own circus. I found out they were starting the season at Newbury racecourse. I immediately started hassling the council to give me a site in the town centre for the week before – the old classic spoiling tactic. The council took a lot of persuading, a lot of financial persuading that is. On the promise to pay the most enormous rent, we set off for Newbury very early in the season. Boy, did we pay the price for trying to be too clever. We were totally snowed in. Nobody came and we lost a fortune. We struggled on.

In April 1979 there was the groundbreaking general election when we got our first woman prime minister, and the Conservatives for the next eleven years. I voted Conservative, of course, and was over the moon when Margaret Thatcher came to power. But when she announced the very next day a rise in VAT to fifteen per cent, I knew

A Big Pie in the Face

I was finished. When they first put VAT on in 1973 it had been difficult enough – a lot of circuses had gone out of business. (Some had
just cheated. But it was tough when they came knocking at your
door. One of the biggest circus families were made an example of,
paying a huge penalty and never really got over it.)

I knew immediately there was no point in going on. I took the circus back to the farm and we called another creditors' meeting. It was
obvious this time we couldn't escape liquidation, but I'd had a few
months to get used to the idea. My skin had thickened and I was
looking at things more practically. I also had a plan. I sold the biggest
caravan in the world to the Hoffman family for £20,000 and my car.
But the farm was owned privately so it was safe. I worked out that I
had about £40,000 to buy back the circus from my creditors.

The meeting was at the Thames Hotel in Staines. There were fewer
people than last time, and it seemed a lot more good tempered. I was
going to offer £40,000 for what was left of the circus, but looking at
the people in the room I suddenly had a hunch I could do better. I
got up to say my piece.

'This is a very sad occasion. We've tried our hardest to make this
circus work, but events have conspired against us this season. Yes, of
course we can liquidate the business. But it strikes me that while we
wait for the assets to be sold, and many of you here know how long it
will take to find suitable homes for the animals, I will have to charge
the administrator for their stay at my farm. I've got to make a living
and animals have to be fed. The cost will be £1,000 a week. Now if it
will make it any easier for you I've sold my big caravan and my car,
and I have raised some money. I could buy the circus back from you
and go out on my own, but without any limited protection of course.
I'm not sure I want to do this. In fact I'm totally fed up with the circus, but it would be one way of keeping a few loyal people employed,
the animals fed and the family in business. I know it's worth a lot
more, but I can give you £20,000 for the lot.'

There was a gasp of astonishment in the room. Ken looked at me
as if I had completely lost the plot. Betty was frantically picking non-
existent fluff from her skirt. I nodded at the startled Ken.

'Gentlemen, shall we take a vote on Gerry's offer then?' Ken said. 'Raise your hands if you would like to accept . . . and those against?'

'Gerry, if you can raise the money, you have yourself a circus for the sum of £20,000.' For a brief second I was elated in the way that you always are when you've pulled off a deal.

Afterwards, Jimmy Chipperfield cornered me in the corridor. 'I was so f—ing shocked at your nerve, I went along with it. You were good today, really good.' He walked off shaking his head.

The elation didn't last long. Now I had to do something with the wretched circus and my heart really wasn't in it. I was feeling weary. And of course this time I would be personally liable. Our home, my car, everything would be at risk if I couldn't make it work. It did strike me around this time that while I kept on losing my shirt, Brian Austen and his brothers had trundled along with a tried and tested formula and was doing good steady business. I suffered terrible jealousy at this time. All my rivals seemed to be making it and I was just overstretching myself, gambling and losing. I had fulfilled my ambition of having the country's biggest circus, but I had just thrown it away so quickly. I was in a state of shock. Just how had it happened?

In the absence of any real inspiration or enthusiasm, what was left of my circus crept down to the West Country. I had to go back into the ring as ringmaster. I hated it. I really had grown out of performing and worse it tied me to the show – I had to be there to perform every day for twice a day. I was grounded. No more trips hunting for grounds. No more visiting girlfriends. This was not the life for me. I started working on a plan.

There was one person in Europe who had dared to be different and succeeded. Bernhard Paul was a graphic designer from Austria who had put together a retro nostalgic non-animal circus centred around a cabaret which travelled around Germany – Roncalli was the circus everybody was talking about. I went to see it in Munich and I was amazed. It was ironic, funny and decadent. There were girls dancing with snakes, gay blokes on the trapeze dressed in pink feathers, in the finale he got all the audience up on their feet dancing. Circus sites are a closed shop in Germany, so Roncalli toured around all the university campuses and was a huge hit. I decided to try something similar. I set up the Rainbow Circus – a hippy trendy thing with a big band dressed in military jackets playing the music to *Flash Gordon*.

I was excited because my girls could go into the ring for the first time with their very own act. Just by growing up on the circus, all children pick up the basics effortlessly. They really do learn to ride elephants before they can walk and tumble before they can run. Juggling is just something they all do with their cutlery while they wait for their tea. It's all around them. There were always lots of children on my circuses, and if one of them was learning the trapeze then they'd all have a go. None of my girls can remember actually being taught to ride horses – as far back as they can remember they could just jump on any horse and ride it bareback. But there does come a time when, if they want to perform in the ring with their own act, they need to get some proper training.

Often children are taught by their parents. You find the Eastern Europeans nearly always do it themselves, and they are really tough with them. Sometimes parents hire other artists on the show to do it. Neither Betty nor I had the time to train the girls ourselves, so we asked Willie Cottrelli to start training Sarah and April. I had first met Willie years ago on Roberts Brothers Circus. Together with his wife, Joanna, they had a balancing act which included Willie touching the roof of the Big Top at the top of a stack of wobbly chairs. Great fun. For some reason, and I can't for the life of me remember why, we decided it would be good for the girls to spend their summer holidays learning the 'Globes' – doing tricks on top of huge rolling balls. Sarah was eight and April was five. We agreed they'd spend around five hours a day practising.

How can I say this politely? The girls were not always over the moon about the training. Willie was hard, he'd scream and shout and make them do it over and over again until they got it right. As Sarah was the biggest she had to carry April on her shoulders as they walked the huge ball up different ramps. April spent a lot of time crying. The wicked child used to pull Sarah's hair, kick her ears with her heels and dig her toes into the small of Sarah's back, but there was nothing Sarah could do – one move and they would both tumble. It was a long way to the ground and then there would be Willie's stick to face. Looking back it was very hard, but it was just the traditional way the circus children were trained. Some days, when the weather was warm, Willie would let the girls take the mats outside and they'd spend the afternoon tumbling in the sunshine, which they loved. I guess it was his unpredictability they found difficult. One day he would be smacking them, the next giving them lollipops.

The BBC were making a circus documentary and filmed the girls training. April was late and we found her sobbing in a wardrobe because she didn't want to practise. This was all caught on camera and, amazingly, when the programme was broadcast, we had not one letter of complaint – but there were dozens about a dog jumping through a hoop! The British public, they never cease to amaze me. Later on that year the girls joined together with Baba and Mike's son, Beau, and Gordon Howes' children and formed the Superkids – a jolly trampolining tumbling act. Willie had long canes to reach the children and to give them little taps if they weren't pointing their toes. April reckons Willie changed the course of her life – she took up juggling just to get away from him. But Willie was excellent. He taught the girls the real discipline you need to be a performer. Not many children have that opportunity and all the girls went on to have successful careers in the ring. They never would have done this without Willie's disciplined coaching.

Are circus skills inherited or taught? Some things, like juggling, it is possible to teach yourself – other things not. You need to learn young, only hours of practise for years will take you to the top of your profession. But all my children were trained in the same way and yet they have completely different talents – Sarah was always a fantastic rider, April a natural juggler, Polly an aerialist. There's nothing I like more than seeing my girls in the ring. I always wanted to have the biggest and best circus, but really seeing my children perform so beautifully and enjoy the circus so much has given me much more pleasure. I am very very proud of them.

A Big Pie in the Face

Betty always says I am ahead of my time. I think on this occasion I was. The public weren't ready for a circus without animals, despite what the councils were saying. Maybe if I had done the same as Roncalli and gone to the university campuses I would have had more success. Instead I stuck to London and did a deal with *Time Out* where they would offer cheap tickets for the circus in return for loads of publicity. Unfortunately this deal coincided with the only strike in *Time Out*'s history. After only a few weeks the circus was dying on its feet, but luckily I was already making new plans.

I watched Gary Glitter prancing across the stage at the Dominion Theatre. He was strutting his stuff dressed up like a Christmas Turkey, all wrapped in silver foil. He was like an outrageous toddler shouting, stomping, strutting his stuff. He'd hired my chariot to come bursting through the scenery as his grand finale and I had decided to deliver it personally. It struck me that there was far more performance in his act than music. He was the pantomime dame of the music world, the biggest clown in pop. I wondered what he'd look like in the ring and then I wondered what he'd look like in my ring.

'Has Gary ever thought about circus?' I asked his agent.

Steve laughed.

'No. I'm serious. We could do a Gary Glitter Rock and Roll Circus.' Talking off the top of my head as usual.

'You know, that's a great idea. Let me think about it and give you a ring.'

Well, a week later he rang me back. Gary was totally up for it.

I sat at my desk with a pencil and paper. How could we do this? We could have him arrive in the ring sitting on a trapeze hanging from a motorbike riding along the high wire. Cool. Must find out what Gary feels about heights. Then he could perform his big old favourites punctuated by my faithful favourite core acts – Barry Walls on his dagger ladder, my sisters-in-law looking delicious on the trapeze, the children doing their trampoline act – as long as April didn't burst into tears! Maybe we could send him off at the end in a rocket, lots of smoke and a countdown then shooting off into the darkness of the Big Top. The dramatic possibilities of the Glitter package kept me chuckling to myself. I was on to something.

Next I rang some key venues to sound them out. There was over-whelming excitement. I kept going. In two weeks I had managed to book thirty prime sites across the country. I couldn't believe my luck, none of my little extravaganzas had ever been so well received. If it was that easy to sell to the councils, the public should be a piece of cake. I quickly brought the Rainbow Circus back to Addlestone and painted over all the wagons with Gary Glitter's Rock & Roll Circus. Gary arrived with his band to begin rehearsals. We were all impressed with how up for it he was. The consummate entertainer got the gist of the circus straight away. He seemed to relish dangling from the trapeze, fist raised in triumphant salute; flying up in a rocket; hanging like a fairy on wires, flying over the ring in his excruciatingly tight shorts and huge hair. Yes, Gary Glitter was a natural in the ring.

The problems came from the band – they were *so* noisy. The music was unbelievable. Poor Barry the fakir lost concentration and cut himself, Willie screamed at the children, 'I can't hear you, I can't hear you.' Sarah kept dropping April, Beau started to cry. There were complaints. I went to talk to Gary. He was sunbathing on the top of his caravan. I shouted up.

'Gary, can I have a word?'

'Of course, Gerry, my son,' Gary rolled over and looked down. I realised he was totally naked.

'Gary. It's sounding very good. A bit too good really. Any chance you could turn it down, at least in rehearsals?'

'Yes, of course. I'll talk to the band.'

Well, it just got louder and louder. By the time we had reached our first site in Reading, although the nearest resident was a quarter of a mile away, the complaints were immediate. The police came round three times.

I went to speak to Gary again. I knocked on the door of his cara-van. A window opened. I went over and Gary stuck his head out.

'Hiya Gerry. How can I help you?'

A Big Pie in the Face

I had to blink. Gary was talking to me while being serviced by two young women. Let's face it, I'm no Mother Theresa, but even I didn't know where to look. He looked me straight in the eye as if he was doing nothing more than making a cup of tea.

'Shall I come back?'

'No, why?'

'Well . . .' At this point I decided to take his line and pretend nothing was going on. 'It's the noise of the band, Gary. You really must keep it down. The police have been here three times now.'

'Yeah right, Gerry. No problem.'

He closed the window in my face.

The band continued doing exactly as it pleased. The next time the police arrived, I hid and got my manager to give them a made-up telephone number.

I used to like Gary's music but now the merest hint of 'D'you wanna to be in my gang' now sends shivers down my spine.

Then I hit another little problem. Nobody in the press was interested in Gary. It was difficult getting him any radio interviews or local paper publicity. I think he'd been a bit unreliable in his heyday and not turned up to one too many interviews, nobody wanted to know. I started to worry.

The night before we opened we all went out on the razz. There's a pub where circuses are always welcome when they stop in Reading. We took Gary down there and he got totally smashed. I was, of course, not drinking. I watched with concern. But the next morning he went jogging with his roadies right as rain. He was nervous, though, as we all were. We'd got the circus together in a real hurry and it was very rough round the edges.

As I blew the whistle for the artists to get ready, I went to see how the tickets were selling. There was a queue – a sorry straggle of forty groupies. This left just 1,460 seats to fill. This was worse than the Rainbow Circus, worse than the wettest Monday afternoon in the smallest dingiest town.

Everybody put on a brave face. Glitter's enormous ego protected him from getting too down, or at least showing it. But I was feeling it in my wallet – at this rate we were going to lose thousands of pounds a day. Two more nights in Reading were just the same – the word of mouth thing wasn't happening. We packed up early and decided to try our luck in Swindon. The same story. I calculated there were more people in the ring than in the audience. I had learnt my lesson not to flog a dead horse. I decided to call it quits quick. But I needed some cash to pay off the band – Gary didn't even have enough money to do that. I called up my mate Davey from Brentford who had access to ready cash and owed me a favour. He came that night with money in his pocket. Gary Glitter's Rock & Roll Circus ended as the shortest circus in history.

With the benefit of hindsight I should have advertised in places like the *NME* and *Melody Maker* and played down the circus element, and then if we had tried the circus five years later when Gary was in the middle of a very successful revival, I'm sure everything would have been different. But then I guess he wouldn't have agreed to do the circus anyway. Now as I write this Gary has been convicted in Vietnam of sexually abusing two very young girls. When he was with us there was no sign of his problem. Gary was always pleasant, and while he was an exhibitionist and was, shall we say, a bit adventurous sexually, he never struck us as liking jailbait. He seemed to be simply displaying characteristics that a lot of people in show business display. We were shocked to hear of his arrest and conviction.

We retreated with our tails between our legs to Addlestone. I didn't have a clue what to do next. There was only one thing of which I was certain – it would have nothing to do with the circus. Too much hard work, too much money lost, too much hurt pride. I still adored the circus but it was like being in the middle of a destructive love affair – I couldn't live with it and couldn't live without it. I had to stop this fatal attraction.

Ten things you didn't know about
P T Barnum and Circus in North America

1. P T Barnum was born in 1810 in Connecticut, the son of a storekeeper. His first adventure in show business was promoting a 161-year-old lady called Joice Heth, said to have been George Washington's nurse.

2. Barnum was 58 when he started his first circus. In 1880 he partnered with James A Bailey, creating the world famous Barnum & Bailey Circus and using the unique slogan: The Greatest Show on Earth.

3. In 1900 there were 150 shows of all sizes in the States. Unlike the UK, nearly all the shows in America were operated by businessmen – only the artistes were from generations-old circus families.

4. Barnum claimed that a third of his expenditure went on publicity. When Jumbo got killed by a train he even exhibited his skeleton on tour.

5. The five Ringling Brothers were sons of an immigrant Milwaukee saddler. In 1919 the Ringling Brothers World's Greatest Shows and the Barnum & Bailey Greatest Show on Earth combined to form one circus. Today it still plays large 40,000 seat arenas across the States.

6. The most famous bandleader was Merle Evans. He never finished high school and played the cornet on Ringlings from 1919 to 1969 – 50 years without ever missing a single show, sometimes two shows a day.

7. Americans always had celebrated wild animal trainers. Between the wars Mabel Stark was probably the most famous big cat trainer. A rare woman trainer, she allowed lions and tigers to jump on her from behind.

8. Originally a troupe of street entertainers, in just 20 years Canada's Cirque du Soleil have grown beyond belief, employing over 3,000 people. They mix circus skills, theatre, dance and music to create a very unique style of show. I love them.

9. My favourite circus school is Cirkus Smirkus in Vermont, started by Rob Mermin, 20 years ago, after his years in Europe as a top professional clown. They have a great team spirit and great comedy.

10. Sarasota is the circus city in sunny Florida. In the mid 1920s Ringling Brothers moved the whole winter operation to Sarasota to take advantage of the weather. Now the city is absolutely full of circus families, including many Fossetts. They have gold paving stones dedicated to the world's greatest acts.

Chapter Seven

A Brush with the Orient 1982-83

'Watch my finger, Boris. Watch it very carefully.'

I was sitting with a borrowed turban on my head facing the enormous jaws of Boris, the beady-eyed crocodile. He blinked very slowly. Everyone held their breath. 'Good boy, Boris. Good boy. Just you keep watching Uncle Gerry's finger.'

Dicky Chipperfield was giving me a crash course in how to hypnotise a crocodile – the same way you hypnotise any animal, apparently, from chicken to rhinoceros – you bring your finger down very slowly in front of their eyes and then move it in towards their face. Boris was looking distinctly cross-eyed at this point. I decided to seize my chance. Before poor Boris could blink, I had grabbed his jaws and held them open at their widest point. If you hold a crocodile's mouth wide enough apart, the jaw locks and can't snap shut. Hey presto! You can stick your head in the crocodile's mouth without any risk of him biting your neck off. In theory anyway.

'Go on, Gerry, old boy. What are you waiting for?'

Dicky jeered. He knew exactly what I was waiting for. Crocodiles are renowned for having the worst breath in the universe. They live in swamps and eat dead things, for goodness sake.

I took a deep breath and stuck my head in. Horrible. It was all I could do not to throw up. They really are vile nasty creatures.

Why on earth was I doing it?

A Brush with the Orient

We had finally settled down to a life of respectable middle-class normality at the farm in Addlestone. My mother was pleased. The girls were going to the local school. Betty was pregnant with our fourth child. She was totally convinced she was having a boy. She had bought a blue dress to wear to the hospital. The nursery was full of blue Babygros. I was very afraid. After all the tears last time, what on earth would happen if it was another girl? I wasn't sure I could handle the grief. I awaited the day of reckoning with fear and trembling. She woke me up at two on the morning of 8 September.

'Come on, Gerry, it's time to go to hospital to have this son of yours.' I didn't know what to say. I was so nervous that I got into the wrong car – the one that had no petrol. Luckily there was an all-night garage on our way to hospital. As we pulled into the forecourt there was one other car sat at the pumps.

'See, Gerry, that car is blue. It's a sign. We're having a boy.'

I said a silent prayer.

This time Betty had an epidural and the labour seemed far too easy. 'Aren't you feeling any pain?' I asked.

'I can't feel anything at all.'

'Well, that can't be right, I'll get the midwife.'

'No, you won't. That's the whole point of having the epidural, you idiot.'

Betty was reading a magazine and cackling with laughter. It was so unlike my other two experiences of childbirth I ignored her and collared the midwife.

'Shouldn't she be feeling something, sister?'

'For sure your wife shouldn't be laughing like that, Mr Cottle. She needs to save all her energy to push.'

'Oh, don't you worry about that,' Betty shouted. 'I'll push when I'm ready. Nothing's going to stop my boy coming out.'

I bit my nails. Had the hormones gone to her head?

But Betty was right. One push and the baby came flying out. The midwife caught it. All I could see was a mass of long black hair. The midwife said, 'Mr and Mrs Cottle, you have a beautiful baby boy.'

Betty grinned from ear to ear and said, 'See Gerry, I told you you would have your son.'

Apparently I literally leapt in the air. I was absolutely over the moon. Holding my son, Gerry Junior, in my arms, I vowed I would never go on the road again. I would build a stable home and business for my family. There would be no more circuses.

So I was sat at my desk wondering what to do with the rest of my life when the phone rang. It was my old friend Fred Pittera, an Italian-American who was making a nice living as a fixer in the United Arab Emirates.

'Gerry. What are you doing at the moment? I'm organising a little expo in the exhibition halls in Sharjah. I need a small circus.'

'Well thanks for thinking of me, Fred, but I'm looking to get out of circus. I really feel like trying something new.'

'That's a shame. The money would have been very good, and as I said we're only looking for something very small, just for a couple of weeks.'

'Oh yes?'

It had been a long time since any money had gone into my bank account. After our Glitter fiasco I was down to selling the trucks and trailers just to feed the family.

'Yes. We're offering a good guarantee and a percentage over and above.'

That was good. Too good to refuse. A definite guarantee with no risk attached.

'Well in that case I'm sure I could sort you out with something. Especially as it's only for a week.'

'That's great, Gerry. There's just one condition.'

'Oh yes?'

'We need a man to put his head in a crocodile's mouth.'

'Right. Any reason in particular?'

'It's the emir of Sharjah's express wish and, as you can imagine, if the emir has expressly wished it we have to expressly provide.'

'No problem. The emir's wish is my command,' I trilled flippantly. I couldn't put my head in a crocodile's mouth, but I knew a man who could.

Crocodiles are a bit of a niche area in circus.* They are dangerous, nasty creatures who will snap at you if they are disturbed, and they've got eighty teeth in those jaws. Get it wrong and your head is bit clean off, as easy as biting the top off a banana. Then you also have to stand well out of range of their tails, which are incredibly powerful – one whack and you are knocked out, then they quickly whip round and before you know it, your head is snapped from your neck like a twig off a branch. They're not very loving creatures either – it's very difficult to get close to a crocodile. You couldn't cuddle up to them at night like old Jock used to with his elephants. But then the fight they've got in them does mean they always put on a good show. They stalk into the ring, tails thrashing jaws gnashing, and the little ones can move quite fast. Then you hypnotise them and put your head in their mouths. Then pop a beautiful girl in a tiny bikini in a tank with a few – that wakes up the dads!

In fact at this time there were only two men in the world who could do it – the Karah Khavaks. A father and son. I knew them quite well and thought it should be easy to get them on board. But when I rang them, disaster. They both had a special appearance on television lined up for that week and nothing could persuade them to pull out. I was stuck. But how difficult could it be? I borrowed a turban and a couple of alligators, Boris and Doris from Longleat. Dicky Chipperfield was playing just down the road and agreed to pop over and give me a quick lesson in crocodile psychology. There's nothing a Chipperfield doesn't know about animals.

Although I did manage to put my head in Boris' jaws, it was apparent to all that sparks weren't flying between the crocodile and me. Luckily Barry Walls, our resident wacky fakir and top showman,

---

* We call them crocodiles but actually circus people always use alligators. Crocs have more pointy jaws whereas the alligators' rounded jaws are easier to play with, but I guess the word crocodile has more of a hold on the public's imagination. *Peter Pan* might have a lot to answer for.

took pity on me and offered to reincarnate himself once again as El Hakim and do the honours with Boris, which he carried off with his customary style and panache. I guess for a man who climbs ladders of swords barefoot, lies on beds of nails and eats glass, putting your head in a crocodile's mouth is all in a day's work.

Who else did I find? An exotic lady dancer from a Bournemouth nightclub called Melanie, who could do interesting things with a boa constrictor. She was very excited at the prospect of life with a circus. She toned down her act and joined us.

My children came out of the local school in Addlestone and joined us as the Superkids. Uncle Sonny Fossett was free to be our clown. My one investment was a brand-new tent from Italy, but I was pretty confident of getting a good return so I didn't mind and we set off for Sharjah in high spirits.

And everything was looking good until I received a threat from the Palestinian Liberation Organisation (the PLO).

'Unless you take down the sign of the infidel from your tent it will not be left standing,' an Arab voice said down the phone.

The phoneline went dead. I didn't like the sound of it. The man sounded rather specific to be insane. I ran down to Fred Pittera's office. He looked relieved to see me.

'I was just looking for you, Gerry. We have received a complaint from the PLO about your tent. They say it's full of Stars of David. What on earth are you thinking of?'

I was thinking the whole world had gone mad.

'Can you get back to your mate in the PLO and ask him exactly where these stars are supposed to be, because I haven't a clue what he is talking about.'

Five minutes later Fred had the explanation. The PLO had a stand at the expo and one of their representatives in his lunch break had decided to come and check out the Big Top. Wandering in he had been incensed to find a Star of David at the top of every tent pole – thirty in all – and the Star of David being the national symbol of Israel and Judaism, well you can see the problem. In reality, the star was simply two bright red triangles of fabric put on the tent to reinforce it. It was a

complete coincidence. But in the early 80s the PLO was hugely powerful throughout the Middle East – not just in the realm of high politics,
but on the ground in the day to day lives of ordinary people, much like
the power of the IRA in Catholic communities in Northern Ireland at
the same time. If they made a complaint you treated it with the utmost
respect, otherwise consequences would most definitely follow. I did not
have this local knowledge and I tried to reason with Fred.

'The show opens tomorrow. We haven't time to do anything
about it.'

'Buy another tent.'

'It's far too expensive. Where are we going to get a Big Top with
twenty-four hours' notice?'

'You'll just have to take the whole thing down and go home then.'

Fred was adamant. The show could not open if the Stars of David
were still there.

'What's stopping you from just covering them up?' he asked.

'It will ruin the tent. The sides will be stretched.'

'I will buy the tent off you afterwards.'

I could hardly refuse that offer. Our carpenters worked all night
erecting pieces of plywood to cover each star. It did stretch the tent,
but now Fred had offered to buy it that was hardly my problem. First
thing in the morning half a dozen serious bearded men walked into
the Big Top. Fred treated them with the utmost respect and they
slowly walked around the tent staring hard at the ceiling. When they
had walked all the way round, there were smiles and handshakes. The
tent had passed the PLO test.

We had a great two weeks and made a tidy profit. My appetite for
circus had been restored. But where could I go next?

The answer lay in the Far East. There was word on the street about a
fantastic opportunity to take a circus to Hong Kong. It was my
absolute dream to take a circus to the Far East. Remember, even in
the early 80s people didn't travel the way they do today. Backpacking,
cheap flights, package holidays to Thailand didn't exist. These areas
were really only open to the very rich, senior businessman or the

most intrepid travellers. The Far East to me conjured up images of ancient temples, tropical flowers and exquisite ladies. And money of course – it was virgin territory for Western circuses. Although these cultures did have circuses of sorts, they were concentrated on acrobatics in theatre and there was no tradition of any performing animals. The only Western entertainment to make any inroads out there was Holiday on Ice, who regularly toured and were doing very nicely, thank you. I reckoned there was a great opportunity for someone brave enough to take the risk – someone like me. For several years I had been sending off my CV to an exotic array of countries and potential backers in Singapore, Thailand, Malaysia and Japan, to name just a few; and got absolutely nowhere. One cold winter's day I put some photos, programmes and my CV into a brown envelope and addressed it to Hong Kong. It sat on my desk for a week. I felt so jaded from sending off these things and never hearing back. I sat looking at it thinking, 'Why am I bothering? It's a complete waste of time.' But with nothing else to do on a Friday afternoon I went for a stroll with the dogs into Addlestone village and popped it into the post box.

I heard absolutely nothing for ages. Then the week we got back from Sharjah I got a telex (no faxes in those days of course) from the Royal Jockey Club of Hong Kong.

Dear Mr Cottle,

Thank you for sending us information about your circus. We are currently looking to bring an English circus to Hong Kong for eight weeks at the beginning of 1982. It will be based in Ocean Park, the world famous amusement park on Hong Kong Island. The Gerry Cottle's Circus appears to be very much what we are looking for, particularly your beautiful animals, something which we have never seen in Hong Kong before. We would like to invite you to Hong Kong to discuss this further.

Yours sincerely,
Peter Hulm
Marketing Director

A Brush with the Orient

My heart missed a beat. I punched the air and danced a little jig. I could sense my luck was about to change. There was one problem. I no longer had any animals, having sold all of them to pay the bills. However I knew a man who did. I gave Dicky Chipperfield a ring. I was a bit hesitant. Dicky and I, well how can I put this? We'd had our ups and downs since those early days when Brian and I walked out on him and ended up sitting in a lay-by.

Dicky and I had been clashing throughout the 70s. At one point it got so bad Betty's sister Julie went to pay a visit to Dicky's show in Bournemouth but was told, 'Get lost. I'll have no relation of Gerry Cottle's set foot in my circus.' Amused I put on a wig and some sunglasses, borrowed Barry Walls' children and popped down to see it for myself. I slipped in unnoticed and in the interval even managed to get a Polaroid taken holding a lion cub. As I left I handed in my photo to the musical director who used to work for me, 'Give this to Dicky and tell him Gerry Cottle really enjoyed the show.' That must have really wound him up, I'm chuckling again just thinking about it. But whatever our past differences, Dicky was a pragmatist. He'd helped me out with the crocodile. He'd also heard about this Hong Kong job and it wasn't difficult to persuade him to fly out with me and present ourselves as a team.

My first experience of Hong Kong was the spectacular descent into the old airport, Kai Tak. As we wound between the skyscrapers, I could see little Chinese people watching TV in their living rooms and cooking in their kitchens. The runway was built on a piece of wasteland stretching out into the sea. If you overshot you would definitely end up with wet feet, so my adrenaline was flowing before I even stepped off the plane. And then there was the city itself – a hive of intense activity, overwhelming hustle and bustle like an enormous ant colony which hit you straight between the eyes as soon as you walked out of the airport. It was much more frenetic than 1980s London. There were red taxis, yellow double-decker buses and dilapidated old British BMC lorries everywhere. The streets were lined with people eating and old men playing mah-jong. Everywhere there were cranes and building sites working twenty-four hours a day on bamboo scaffolding tied with string. A lot of the Chinese didn't have fridges so people were always out shopping, sometimes they would go out three times a day. Their food was incredibly fresh – you'd pick your fish which would be swimming in a tank. It still had a colonial feel – the police wore immaculate white uniforms and Rolls-Royces were everywhere, carrying government officials (and maybe the odd triad boss). There were big white buildings built by the British filled with dark mahogany and Indian servants in turbans. The city was schizo-phrenic, with polo games on the one hand and this incredible Chinese work ethic on the other. It was a twenty-four-hour city. At eleven at night they'd still be shopping for their groceries in bustling street-market stalls lit by one light bulb and protected from the typhoons by an old sheet of tarpaulin. It was love at first sight.

We were met at the airport by a posse from the Royal Jockey Club led by Peter Hulm. We immediately got on. Horse racing is huge busi-ness in Hong Kong. The Chinese of course love to gamble, so the Royal Jockey Club made vast amounts of money. But it was also expected to put some back into the community. They funded great charitable works in Hong Kong but they had also built a beautiful amusement park in the hills of Hong Kong Island. Amusement parks all over the world billed themselves as 'World Class' but not many really were. Ocean Park was exceptionally scenic. There were tiers of fragrant tropical gardens cut into the steep hillside overlooking the South China Sea – a perfect antidote to the madness of the city. They had a terrifying cable car down to the bottom where there were small tasteful rides for the chil-dren, and an aquarium and ocean show with sea lions and dolphins. Every year they liked to host a special attraction. One day some old colonel expat at the club had said, 'Why don't we have a circus, old boy?' The Royal Jockey Club did like to do things in style, so they wanted a big, beautiful, ambitious show with no expense spared over the Chinese New Year. We could live in the park and all their resources and staff were at our disposal. They would do all the publicity and sell the tickets. It was a great deal. I shook hands on it without hesitation and rushed back to England to get the circus ready.

It was relatively easy to find the artists – it was winter, when most

top: My parents, Jane and I, on holiday in Devon. 1960
bottom: At Joe Gandey's circus. Back row (left to right):
    Bob Gandey; me; Roy Rama; Bob del Rio; Peter Featherstone.
    Front row (left to right): Michael, Julie, Mary and Phillip Gandey;
    Janet; Joe Gandey. 1963

above: Betty at her dad's circus,
      James Brothers. 1964/5
left: Me on the rola rola at
      James Brothers. 1968
below: My wedding day.
      From left to right: Baba, Mike
      Denning, Betty, David Weeks,
      me, Uncle Sonny Fossett, my dad.
      7 December 1968

right: Our big break. From
left to right: Brian
Austen, me, Betty,
Michael Austen, May
Austen, Trevor
Philpott. May 1971
*(Photo: Gordon Moore/
Radio Times)*

below: The crowds in
Kingsbury when we
first came to London.
1973 *(Photo:
Doug McKenzie)*

Oman, 1976
left: The elephants walking
   on to the plane.
below: The Big Top in
   the desert.

left: Her Majesty
   the Queen
   hesitantly
   profers a snack
   to a member of
   the elephant
   guard of
   honour at
   Hyde Park.
   1977

top: Uncle Sonny Fossett and I (as I'm just about to go bankrupt). 1979
(Photo: Mirrorpix)

centre: The visit from the feng shui priest, in Hong Kong. From left to right: the priest; Marcel Peters, tiger trainer; Peter Hulm, Ocean Park's marketing director; me about to cut the roasting pigs; Polly; Sarah; and Betty. 1982

right: Sarah, April and Polly on the rolling globes. 1982

above: Elephant relaxing off the
    South Coast. 1988
left: A great circus fan, Jeremy
    Beadle worked with us at
    Wembley 1991–92.
below: Leaving Chertsey
    magistrates' court after
    receiving a £500 fine for
    possessing cocaine, with
    Mark Borkowski (left) and
    Henri Brandman my
    solicitor. 15 January 1992
    (Photo: David Rose,
    © Independent*)*

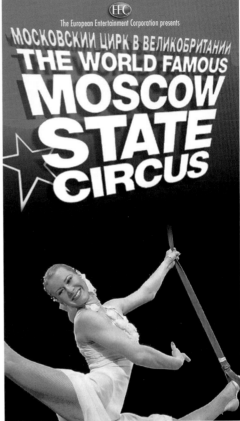

bove: The Chinese State Circus, thirteen on a bike!
2000 *(Photo: Linda Rich)*
ight: A Moscow State Circus poster.
2004 *(Photo: Richard Balmforth)*
elow: Our record-breaking human mobile, with the
Circus of Horrors in Buenos Aires. 1997

top: Cottle and Austen's Circus. 1999
bottom: Gerry Junior, April, Polly, myself and Sarah at a recent wedding.

of them struggle to find good well-paid work. I assembled probably my most successful line-up ever.

I found the programme the other day and it includes:

The Podeszwa
Gifted Gymnasts and Amazingly Agile Acrobats from Poland
(Now we take Polish decorators for granted but in the 1980s Poland was still part of the Eastern bloc, so these were one of the first troops to be let out. Consequently the young men were incredibly polite and diligent. Most of the money we paid them had to go into the state kitty to fund the circus school back home, so they had virtually nothing to live on, but they were still very cheery – just glad to be out I suppose. They had just won the Monte Carlo festival.)

The Swinging Cottrellis
Australian Artistry at Harrowingly Heady Heights
(Willie Cottrelli, our children's trainer, and his beautiful wife Joanna. He had a simple act which he'd being doing for years, but he was a great showman. He'd do a one-handed handstand on the top of a pile of chairs and always do a great wobble at the end. On our opening night as he was levering up into a handstand on crutches on a pile of chairs, stretching to the top of the tent he paused, looked at the audience and with a big grin shouted 'Kung hei fat choi!' ('Happy New Year!'). They erupted in appreciation. That little touch was supreme showmanship.)

Ivan Karl
Unbelievable Feats of Endeavour by the World's Smallest Strongman
(Our pocket Hercules was a bit down on his luck. He'd had a cracking job dressing up as the Hofmeister bear in the adverts until he got sacked for being blind drunk once too often. But even with a drinking habit, he was a great showman.)

Jungle Fever and Gentle Giants
The London Showgirls Introduce Chipperfield's Famous Indian Elephants

(Our three elephants were very beautiful. We dressed them with lovely glittery jackets; they pirouetted and danced, and ended up in a pyramid with some beautiful showgirls on their backs.)

Ape Activities

The Greatest 'Little Monkey' Show on Earth

(We had a great spoof gorilla moment. Sonny Fossett in a gorilla outfit would run into the audience and steal a lady's handbag. She would run after him, but he'd climb to safety up the top of a pole and proceed to show the contents to the audience – find her spare bra, put her talcum powder under his armpits, put a cheeky pair of knickers on his head. Of course she was a stooge, but I think most of the audience never realised. Stooges work nearly every time. One of the best is the lady riding the bucking bronco and her skirt being pulled off. I saw an act with a stooge at Cirque du Soleil only the other day.)

The Flying Carrolls

Direct from Circus Circus, Las Vegas, the Renowned Female Stars of the Flying Trapeze

(In reality two sisters with poor Bobby catching them. Bobby was bald and the girls were horrible to him. They made him wear a wig, which in the heat and humidity of Hong Kong would fall off as he hung upside down, and float elegantly down to the ring floor to the absolute hysteria of the Chinese audience. The poor man begged to be allowed to leave it off but the big sister wasn't having any of it. Although it must be said the girls were great performers – Gaynor was one of the few women to perform a triple somersault.)

Richard Chipperfield

In the Steel Arena in a Striped Presentation of the Royal Bengal Tigers

(They really were magnificent and Dicky was an excellent trainer. You have to be careful with tigers. They are quite crafty a lot, more dangerous than lions. A few years later Dicky's son was attacked by a tiger on the Ringling Brothers Circus in the States and will be suffering for the rest of his life.)

A Brush with the Orient

Michelle Duo
Astounding Mid-Air Manipulations
(A couple of female aerialists who did the most unusual things in the air. Usually one person in this sort of duo would be a man doing the heavy work. But both these girls were quite butch and managed to perform a most spectacular and dangerous act.)

The Man Who Fear Forgot
Richard Chipperfield, Winner of the Circus Festival Prize Monaco 1980 and His World Famous Lions
(Dicky's pièce de résistance. He specialised in what we call 'bouncing' lions, where the lions prowl around looking as if they are about to kill the trainer, snarling and roaring. These days the fashion is to have them much more controlled but I liked the excitement of Dicky's act. It made it especially impressive when at the end of the act he had them all lying down and he'd jump on top and roll around with them!)

Gene and Eleanor Mendez
Unique High Wire Drama with No Safety Devices Whatsoever Culminating in the Death-Defying Walk over the Top of the Lions' Cage
(This aerial act was so dangerous. In those days no artists worth their salt wore a safety wire. Nowadays nearly all acts like this are performed with lunges. It all changed when the Russians came over in large numbers in the early 90s – they had always performed with a safety wire. It's OK and completely understandable, but you do lose that extra frisson.)

Gerry Cottle's Superkids
The Circus Stars of the Future, Leaping, Somersaulting and Tumbling on the Casting Trampoline
(The Chinese seemed particularly tickled by the girls' performance. They always got a great round of applause, which of course gave me a special thrill.)

Sonny Fossett and Company
The Clowns in a Merry Madcap Frolic of Painting Problems
(A dose of good old-fashioned slapstick, which seemed to appeal to the Chinese sense of humour as much as it does the British.)

Sensational Dive of Death
From the Roof of the Big Top
(Gaynor Carroll would dive from the top of the tent – fifty feet at least – into a blow-up mattress. She did it every night and never missed.)

Now we had to sort out what to call the circus. Dicky was adamant that it should be called the 'Cottle Chipperfield Circus'. I didn't like that at all. He thought we were equal partners in this little enterprise. I didn't. I believed I'd introduced Dicky to the Jockey Club and I'd organised the whole damn thing. I very carefully mustered support. But it was his dad, old Dicky, who finally made young Dicky see sense. 'One person has to be in charge, Richard, otherwise it will never work. Let Gerry be the boss, you concentrate on your act and charge him extra for it.' So Dicky bowed out in return for a bigger pay packet and the circus was called: Gerry Cottle's Circus starring Richard Chipperfield.

Then all we had to do was get the circus there. Imagine trying to ship a whole circus including sixteen lions, six tigers and three elephants across to the other side of the world – that's at least three weeks at sea. OK, so we had put a circus on an aeroplane before, but this time we had to pack a massive 5,000-seater tent, all the equipment that goes with it and all our accommodation too.

There was a constant stream of telex messages going to and fro. Because Hong Kong was nine hours ahead, my shipping agent John Smith would walk into his office in the morning to find ten-foot-long telex messages covering the floor. Because hotels were so expensive we had to put our caravans on containers and ship them out. Shipping a circus of animals to Hong Kong had never been done before. There were the most incredible number of bureaucratic hoops

we had to jump through – special licences and health checks – before
the animals could board the boat. We built special cages and then we
had to find a couple of people willing and able to feed, clean and
exercise them for the entire journey. With a lot of hard work we managed to get everything ready just in time.

Then the Union of Seamen called a strike at Southampton where
we were due to board our ship, *The Merry Widow*. We frantically called
Hong Kong. They insisted we had to open as promised for the
Chinese New Year. The circus was already sold out. We had no alternative but to get on that damn boat, but there was no way we were
going to be able to load at Southampton. John came up with the idea
of getting the whole lot to Le Havre, *The Merry Widow*'s last stop
before sailing off to the Far East. This meant driving the whole circus
from Southampton to Dover, catching the ferry to Calais and then
driving down. We had two days before *The Merry Widow* was due to
leave Le Havre – enough time surely? Our huge convoy of trucks and
trailers set off for Dover, nervous but confident. As we crossed the
channel it got colder, then began to snow. I stood shivering on deck
with the men, none of us talking, all of us smoking, it looked grim out
there. The coast of France was completely obliterated by dense grey
cloud with that ominous purple tinge. I couldn't believe my bad luck.
I silently prayed, 'Please God, don't let us miss this boat.' I racked my
brains but I couldn't think of any other way we could get to Hong
Kong in time.

As the ferry touched the quay, the ropes were thrown overboard. I
checked my watch for the umpteenth time. We were all knackered,
none of us had slept, but it was just possible, just possible that if we
drove very fast we could still catch that boat. I couldn't see what other
option we had. The captain made sure we were first off the ferry. I pity
any poor French drivers who got in our way that day. Our huge convoy went hurtling down the roads of Northern France with
unstoppable momentum in a terrible blizzard. The boys did me
proud. All the trucks, animal containers and caravans went from Calais
to Le Havre in record time. As we rounded the bend into the harbour,
I could see *The Merry Widow* still alongside the quay. The sense of

relief as we joined the end of the queue was enormous. Five minutes after seeing the last elephant walk up the ramp into the bowels of the boat, *The Merry Widow* pulled out of the harbour and started its long journey to the Far East.

All the artists and the family flew into Hong Kong in time to see the boat arrive. We took a trip to the docks to watch the animals disembark. It was quite a sight to see our beautiful elephants walk out of the boat in a line, holding trunk to tail, all safe and sound in this amazing setting. Betty wept. Unfortunately our caravans had not had such a successful passage. *The Merry Widow* had hit some terrible storms and because we were last to board the boat, the caravans caught the full force of the waves buffeting the bow. They were completely smashed up and we had only a week to get ready before the circus opened.

We worked all hours like devils building the circus – the seats, the rigging, the props. All the caravans had to have new glass fitted. Luckily we were in the hands of some excellent local contractors, Mr Nye and Mr Wong, who drafted in dozens of Vietnamese and Filipinos to do the hard work. I was swept off my feet in the most amazing round of publicity. Every media outlet wanted an interview with the British circus boss of the latest and most novel show to hit town.

I had the ultimate publicity stunt handed to me on a plate. According to Chinese tradition any new venture, be it a new business, house or brothel, has to have a visit from the feng shui priest. I was game, especially as I could invite the media along to observe. I was told not to be tight about his fee and his advice would not be too disastrous. The priest arrived in his billowing red silk robes accompanied by an interpreter and the press. I slipped a wad of Hong Kong dollars in his hands. He walked around with a deep frown on his face, closed his eyes and breathed deeply. I tried very hard to suppress a smile, he was good, very good. After ten minutes of suspense he spoke. Miraculously the feng shui priest agreed that the Ocean Park car park was indeed the most propitious spot to erect the tent. (Where we would have put it otherwise, I don't know, unless it was half way up the mountain slope.) The door would have to be facing west so the rays of the setting sun could see the show. There was a polite round of applause from the press and a bit of bowing. I realised I was not just on the other side of the world but on another planet. We roasted some suckling pigs (it was the best crackling I have ever tasted), burnt some incense and said some prayers. The circus was open.

The Chinese loved us. After years of the red and gold costumes, plate spinning and twanging strangled-cat music that was their usual circus fare, we were a sensation. The press interest was insatiable. I became a star overnight. My dodgy moustached face popped up everywhere. The Circus was coming to Town, Oh Yes! From the opening night onwards our 5,000-seater Big Top was full. In fact we could have filled it ten times over. I loved the Chinese people, they were very warm and welcoming. Our original contract was for eight weeks. I immediately extended it for another eight weeks.

I noticed a few differences between the Chinese and European audiences. The Chinese were a lot more polite, applause was on the whole restrained, they didn't call out, except when poor Bobby lost his wig. We were advised never to throw water at them – the Chinese take getting splashed very badly. We were also warned not to bring children into the ring – the parents would not appreciate it. But the clowns did it anyway – every night we got a full complement of kiddies to march up and down as a comedy band. They loved it. They also had an insatiable appetite for candyfloss. We made the most phenomenal amount of money. We joked for years afterwards that the money given to the feng shui expert was the best I ever spent.

Looking back now it was probably the best of times. After a few pretty lean years, we had money in our pockets, a very successful show and an audience that loved us. We were together as a family. Sarah was eleven, April eight, Polly five and Gerry Jr a toddler. They had the whole of Ocean Park as their playground during the day and the girls performed in the ring at night. It was so good for them, they were seeing the world.

And I was extremely well behaved. Success seemed to curb my urge to wander. Every night we went out as a family. We were warmly embraced not just by the expat community but by the Chinese we worked with, and shown the whole island. We used to hire a coach and take the circus sightseeing. I remember going to the Jumbo Floating Restaurant (famous for burning down in a James Bond film), the manager welcomed us with open arms so I got the girls to juggle plates for his customers. Wee Bean the midget had a whale of a time. He used to spend the evenings in dodgy bars, sitting on bar stools, being fussed over by the working girls. They loved him and bought him loads of drinks, until he fell off the bar stool. One night he was so tipsy he took them home.

'Where do you live?' they asked.

He pointed to a container, which had been converted to house two families. Unfortunately he got the wrong end of the container and crawled into bed with Old Dick Chipperfield and his wife. Poor Bean ended up with a right royal flea in his ear and the ladies of the night on the street.

We were working our socks off – four two-hour shows, all of them completely sold out. In the middle of this I got a call from a Mr Stanley Ho of Macau. That name rang a bell. I made a few discreet enquiries. The mere mention of his name brought raised eyebrows and looks left to right. Voices sunk to a whisper. Mr Ho was apparently the highly respected and feared boss of Macau's casino and gambling operations. Not a man to be messed with. It would hardly be wise to refuse his invitation. With my shipping agent, John Smith, and my solicitor, Malcom Clay who had flown over from the UK specially, as moral support, I boarded the ferry to Macau.

Let me describe Macau to you.

Whereas Hong Kong was run by the British, Macau was still a Portuguese colony. It was like Hong Kong's dishevelled, down at heel, decadent younger sister. A prodigal, black sheep of a younger sister. Things were allowed in Macau which were not deemed appropriate in relatively uptight Hong Kong. It was filled with crumbling colonial buildings and many people still lived in shacks. The streets were filled with people crouched by the roadside talking and eating. It was friendly and tropical. Business was dominated by a few extended loyal families and their followers. I fell in love with it instantly. It had that sort of Wild West feel about it. These families, of which Stanley Ho headed the largest, were in charge of everyday life, but they knew that they also had to keep the Portuguese governor sweet. Now when we opened in Hong Kong, the governor expressed a belief that this marvellous circus should visit his patch too. Mr Ho, knowing what was good for him, immediately went into action.

We were ushered into his penthouse at the top of the Hotel Lisboa. It was like meeting the Chinese version of the rat pack – there were six men sat round the table in smart suits and £200 crocodile shoes. Round the edge of the room were Sikh guards wearing turbans and carrying Kalashnikovs. Mr Ho was obviously no pussycat. He spoke no English but his older brother, Mr John, had been British Leyland's representative in Hanoi. He spoke perfect English and acted as interpreter. The negotiations were long and hard. After several hours of going round in circles Mr John suggested a gentleman's break. He came and stood next to me in the toilets.

'Look, Mr Cottle. You know we really want you to come to Macau. We need to do a deal. The problem is you are being too hard. Let me explain a little about our culture. Face is everything to the Chinese. If you bargain too hard we will never come to an agreement. We cannot be seen to be losing face. We will pay the money you are asking, but you need to give us something in return.'

'But we've been through this. I can't give you anything. After I've paid for the tent, the artists . . .'

'No, no, this we have talked about. You are getting too complicated. How about if we asked you to do a couple of charity shows for us? Perhaps one for the governor's favourite children's home?'

'Absolutely no problem.'

We went back into the room and struck a deal straight away.

I had a devil of a time keeping the artists. Originally I had only contracted them for eight weeks, then we stayed for another eight. By now it was April and the European circus season was getting under way. Another four weeks and all that would be left for them would be a week on the end of a pier in Bognor. I had to do all sorts of deals. 'I'll throw you in a new trapeze.' 'We'll build you a new set of magic props.'

Then, how were we going to get the circus there? In the end we loaded it piecemeal on to flat-bottomed barges and floated it up the Pearl River to Macau. There were animals here, there and everywhere and a barge filled entirely with the hay and straw we needed from mainland China. Hundreds of people lined the banks of the river, waving as we went past. It was quite spectacular to see the elephants standing on the barges, the sixteen lions looking out of their cages. Looking back I can't quite believe we did it. But they all reached shore safe and sound. The circus was erected on a football pitch right in the centre of town and we were staying in the Hotel Lisboa next door. Everyone was on the sixth floor which was a bit of a pain. At the first opportunity I cornered Mr John.

'Is there any possibility we could move closer to the ground floor? We are wasting a lot of time waiting for the lifts.'

'Let me take you downstairs,' he said smiling.

We got into the lift and went down to the second floor. The door opened to reveal a corridor. Along both sides was a sheet of glass. As we walked along, behind the glass were dozens of girls, scantily clad, posing with numbers round their wrists. We were living above an enormous brothel!

'As you can see, Mr Cottle, I did not think it would be suitable for your family to be living close to our other business.'

I nodded agreement and said no more about it.

Strangely enough we still managed to shock the establishment. Barry Frost, the leader of our band, was sharing a room with the drummer, Vic Coleman. Both of them enjoyed fully all the alcoholic revelling delights Macau offered, and there were plenty. They got to bed in the early hours one morning. Later on, Barry had a desperate need to relieve himself and in his alcoholic haze, instead of going to the bathroom, walked out of the door to the room. It slammed behind him, and he found himself stuck in the corridor stark naked. He banged on the door but the drummer was away with the fairies, so he went and got into the lift. Unfortunately it was full. Someone immediately called the Kalashnikov-clad guards who were on hand to arrest him as soon as he walked into the foyer. The next day I was summoned to see the manager, Mr Simon, who was in a right state.

'Your Mr Barry was drunk last night and he was running around the hotel in the nude. He embarrassed the guests and he embarrassed the hotel.'

I obviously had to make reparations. I went to see Mr John. This big gangster type surrounded by his obligatory Sikh guards had been a real friend to us. If he ever bumped into me in the morning he would invite me up to his penthouse for English tea and toast. We'd have lovely polite conversations. Or if he ever bumped into the children he would take them to the hotel swimming pool and buy them ice creams. Contrary to my first impression, Mr John was an incredibly gentle man. I really did not want to upset the Hos or abuse their hospitality.

'Mr John, I've come for two reasons. Firstly I would like to apologise for the unfortunate predicament my bandleader found himself in last night. I am sorry for any embarrassment we may have caused you, your hotel or your staff. Secondly I would like to tell you that we have named the two lion cubs born here last week Stanley and John, in honour of all the kindness and hospitality you have shown us in Macau.'

Mr John's face cracked into the widest smile.

'Mr Cottle, your stay in Macau has made history for many reasons. This is the first time we have had a streaker run through a hotel in Macau. Secondly this is the first time we have had lion cubs born in Macau.'

Diplomatic relations were restored. At the end of our stay we gave the lion cubs to Canton Zoo in China to help their breeding programme.

The heat was intense in Macau, and then we were caught up in a typhoon. In the middle of the night we were woken by the noise of a torrential downpour. It was like nothing I'd ever seen before. I ran down the hotel corridor getting everyone out of bed and we struggled out in the rain in all our nightclothes. Cars were floating down the street, we had to push them out of the way to cross the road to the football pitch. The tent was about to collapse under the weight of the water. Already the circus was two-feet under. The animals had to be led to safety on higher ground – luckily all the hotel staff came out to help as well.

Then the rain stopped as suddenly as it started. Obviously they are used to tropical downpours in this part of the world and there seemed to be some confusion as to why everything had flooded quite so badly. Divers were sent down to check the drains. They found just a single sheet of plastic blocking one of the pipes. They removed it and within a couple of minutes the water had disappeared, but the tent was quite badly damaged. Before we could say anything a team of thirty Chinese workmen turned up, took the tent down, loaded it on to a wagon and took it away.

Now all the artists sprung into action. When the chips are down the circus community is a wonderful thing. No matter how grand or precious the performer, everybody gets together to help out. We worked non-stop for twenty-four hours, right through the night and the next day, to clear up the mess the floodwaters had left. Have you ever seen the Cecile B De Mille film, *The Greatest Show on Earth*, where everybody risks life and limb to save the circus from a terrible fire? Well the level of personal bravery and sacrifice wasn't quite on that scale, but you get the idea . . .

Courtesy of Mr Ho the tent arrived back in time for the last show of the next day repaired completely free of charge. We had missed just three performances. One thing that couldn't be saved was my accounts, which I had just finished that afternoon. All my books were neatly laid out in my caravan, perfectly positioned for the floodwater to come in and take them away. I was so cheesed off. I hate doing the wretched things at the best of times.

By the beginning of June we had finished our Far East tour. With another visit to Hong Kong already booked for the end of the year, my accountant advised me to stay out of the UK for tax reasons. I'd never been to California, so I decided to treat the whole family to a summer touring the West Coast of America. We flew into Los Angeles and I bought a huge touring Winnebago. Of course there were loads of Fossetts and Fossett relations kicking about that we could go and visit. Our first stop was with our old animal trainer Marcel Peters and his family who were touring with Circus Vargas. We ended up staying two months. It was great fun being part of a huge show, watching how it operated, and for once not being the boss. In fact we didn't do anything but help a little with the publicity. I couldn't believe the gossip and politics of this huge outfit. Everybody was having affairs. It was great, I could watch the dramas unfold and none of the fallout was my responsibility.

I couldn't sit still for long though and I had a perfect excuse to go walkabout. The Royal Jockey Club had insisted that we brought a completely new set of acts back to Hong Kong. Dicky had already decided to take some polar bears and crocodiles. I flew to Europe to hire an unusual human aerial act – Gerry Sebastian the human rocket, otherwise known as Supernova. He'd built a rocket that went up into the air and circled around the ring at high speed. He climbed out of the top and his daughter, Alison, fell out of the bottom on a trapeze. It was all laser lights and *Star Wars* music, which climaxed with Gerry hanging upside down from the whirling rocket while his daughter hung from him with a neck loop. Sebastian was working at a circus in Paris and was terribly popular. They really didn't want to let him go. On the day he was due to leave Paris, the circus hands had parked their caravans in front of his caravan so he couldn't leave. I had to send my solicitor, Malcolm Clay, to Paris to get a court order to have him released, and then a posse of men to physically remove the caravans and make sure he caught his flight.

I also thought the Chinese would really appreciate some naughty chimpanzees. Let me say right now, of all animals (crocodiles aside) I dislike the chimpanzees the most. Despite appearances, they're not cute, they're not cuddly – they're intelligent and devious and very strong, and quite capable of being very malicious, but they can perform in the ring. If I was to compile a list of the most dangerous animals to work with in the circus, at the top would have to be bears, particularly polar bears. The thing is their eyes are pitch black. It's impossible to read what they are thinking. You know when a horse is agitated. A bear will take you completely by surprise. Next I would have to say elephants. They are beautiful noble creatures, but one in ten will be a rogue. And they do indeed have very long memories. If you make them do something they don't want to do, they will get back at you – not immediately, but they'll bide their time and as soon as they have the opportunity they'll squash you like a flea. Old Jock was completely safe sleeping night after night with his elephants, often totally off his head, because the elephants saw him as one of them. But a young trainer who tries to bully them, well I don't rate his chances. I've also observed elephants don't like clowns much. When I was in the ring as Scats, one of the elephants had it in for me and would take every opportunity to squash me or flick me with his trunk as I walked passed. But after the elephants come the chimpanzees. Dangerous for completely different reasons. They are very strong and very intelligent. Imagine a beast with the temperament of a naughty toddler and the strength of ten men.

Willi Kubler was an Austrian who had a whole colony of chimpanzees living in his castle in the Alps. I arrived in Austria with my agent, Billy Arata, who felt the same way about chimps as I did, but was a bit more – how shall I say? – highly strung. I was dreading going to the castle. It was way up high in the mountains at the end of a long road, like something out of a Dracula movie. Betty came with us and managed to put Billy on edge before we'd even arrived. Driving along, he was playing the best of Shirley Bassey over and over on the clapped out hire-car stereo.

'Billy. Could you please change the tape? This Shirley Bassey is driving me mad,' Betty asked.

'It's the only tape I've got.'

'But we've listened to it ten times already.'

'One can never tire of a classic.'

Five more minutes went past as we climbed slowly up the mountain pass.

'Billy. I'm serious. I can listen to no more of this. I am going mad.'

A Brush with the Orient

'How can you say that about Miss Bassey? She's a star beyond compare.'

'No one is that good, Billy.'

At which Betty snatched the tape out of the car stereo and flung it out of the window. It clattered down the mountainside. Billy nearly drove straight over the edge of the cliff. A huge row erupted which would have been quite amusing if we hadn't been driving round the most hair-raising single track roads complete with hair-pin bends and sheer drops.

We survived that only to have the door of the castle opened to by a four-foot high male chimpanzee in his prime. He beat his breast.

'I don't like this one bit, Gerry. I'm not walking past *that*,' Billy said.

Betty said nothing but raised her eyebrows at me as if to say, 'OK Big Boy, what are you going to do now?'

My male ego was feeling the pressure. I looked Mr Alpha Primate in the eye and slowly but firmly edged past him, taking care to keep looking him straight in the eye (remember never to turn your back on an animal, not even a bunny). As I suspected, Herr Kubler was hiding behind Mr Hairy having a laugh. Cruel sense of humour, these Austrians. Betty followed me straight in, but Billy edged into the hall and headed towards a side room.

'Herr Kubler ... Herr Kubler ... I think I'll wait in here until you can perhaps put this animal in another room.' He tugged my coat and we backed into the side room and closed the door. Like an episode from *Scooby-Doo*, we turned round to find three new adult chimps glaring at us.

'Oh bloody hell, Gerry, let's go back to the hotel, I'm not staying here a minute longer.'

'Just stay still, Billy. STAY STILL!'

This was a man who regularly did a head stand on his brother's head while he walked the high wire. (Known as going head to head.) I guess we all have our weak spots.

Eventually we managed to persuade Herr Kubler that the joke was wearing thin, and he locked the chimps away for long enough to hammer out a deal.

We opened in Hong Kong at the beginning of December. Business was good but not as good as the year before. It was a shame because I had spent a lot more money on it. It was a classic example of something I have learnt over the years – spending more money on a show does not guarantee a better audience. It was difficult to persuade the Chinese that this circus was different to the one they had all seen the year before.

It wasn't as relaxing either. I was very busy trying to realise another lifelong ambition – to do a Round the World Tour! I flew here there and everywhere desperately trying to make it happen, Australia, Japan, Indonesia. But I had been badly burnt by my experience in Iran and I was probably quite rightly not prepared to accept a contract without any real money in my hands.

One place I had success was in Singapore, although it wasn't to be as straightforward as it first seemed. I met Mr Edwin Chan, a shipping agent who expressed an interest. He asked me to compile a list of everything we needed in order for a deal to be done (known in the business as the 'OK Sheet'). John Smith and I wrote a seven-page document detailing the food for the animals, the accommodation, the publicity material etc. He never got back to us. In the meantime, the Holiday on Ice rep in Singapore had introduced me to a man from Isuzu trucks. They came up with a sizeable guarantee so after Hong Kong we shipped the circus to Singapore for an eight-week stay. We did fabulously well. Mr Chan even came to visit the circus with his family. He was very polite and said how much he had enjoyed the show.

The next day a man rolled up on a motorbike and handed me a court summons. Mr Edwin Chan was claiming we had broken his contract and he now wanted a percentage of the circus takings. I was totally dumbfounded. There is no way he could have truly believed we'd had a deal. He certainly hadn't mentioned it the night before. He must have seen how well we were doing and decided to chance his luck. I was worried though. I had no idea how Singapore courts operated or how fair they would be to a foreigner. We spent a week in court. I spent a week staring anxiously at the judge's face. He wasn't giving anything away. I was making good money in Singapore, but by

God I'd worked hard for it, I couldn't bear to see it all dribble away in lawyers' fees and end up in a scoundrel's pocket. I made lots of vows only to stay on England's fair shore in future.

At the end of the week the judge had heard all the evidence. He was ready to pronounce. I was led into the room with Mr Edwin Chan. I couldn't believe the nerve of the man. I looked at the judge anxiously. His face was totally inscrutable.

'After considering all the evidence before me, I find in favour of the defendant.'

That was all he said. Was that me? Had I won? It took me a second to realise he'd thrown the case out. I was delighted there was justice after all. That was the last of Mr Chan, I thought. I started making preparations to take the circus to Malaysia. Nestlé had agreed to sponsor us and had paid a generous amount up front.

There's a famous train journey down from Singapore to Kuala Lumpur. Romantic devil that I am, I liked the sound of it, so instead of doing the simple thing and taking the ferry, I bought tickets for the whole circus. This was a big mistake.

The huge steam train had barely got out of the station when there was the most almighty crash and terrible scraping sound. We were all thrown from our seats.

'God Almighty, what was that?' I shouted.

There was screaming and chaos as everybody clambered over each other to get outside to see what was going on. The roof of the front three carriages had been totally taken off by a low-level bridge. Some of the animals had escaped, there was chaos with ponies and chimpanzees running amok. Hundreds of people came running down the tracks to see whether we were all right. Then they started chasing the animals. I watched the whole fiasco in astonishment. Surely I would wake up and find this had all been a bad dream? How could they crash into a bridge? How could they misjudge the height of the wagons? Surely they did this journey every day? It took an age to get the llamas back. New lower carriages had to be found. Six hours later, now well into the heat of the day, we started to move off again. This time desperately slowly – the driver was petrified of hitting another bridge, I suppose. The views were magnificent, but all I could look at was my watch. The journey was only supposed to take twelve hours, at this rate it was going to be more like twenty-four. I wasn't worried for myself or the artists, but the poor animals – we had polar bears who needed to keep cool and lions who needed to eat. Malaysia had water shortages so after a certain time of day there was a water curfew. We should have been all right because the railway company had arranged for four-hourly stops to get water, but with the delay the schedule was thrown and we were arriving at stations during the curfew. When we'd be going for twelve mind-numbingly slow hours we stopped yet again at a little station in the middle of nowhere. For what purpose I couldn't see. I decided to try and get some water for the polar bears. I got into a huge row with the station master who just wouldn't budge. I called for the mayor. Someone went and got him out of bed. He was charm itself and agreed for the water to be turned on specially for us.

In the end it was all worth it. We had a fantastic six-week run. The circus went down a treat. I was really enjoying myself, the tropics suited us all. That is until I heard from my friend Mr Chan again. I thought there was some international law called 'Precedent' which meant that once a ruling had been made it was final whichever country you were in. Obviously the legal system in Malaysia didn't believe in 'Precedent'. Incredibly, within a few weeks Edwin Chan brought another case in Kuala Lumpur about the Singapore trip, which you'd think was a ridiculous move. But of course he knew the patch better than I did. Instead of throwing it straight out of the window, the Malaysian legal system decided there was indeed a case to be heard. Instead of manag- ing the circus I had to spend the next four weeks going backwards and forwards to court. After four weeks we had done our final performance in the ring and we were still awaiting the decision of the judge. It had been a huge pain in the derrière but I was confident of victory – if Mr Chan couldn't even win on his home turf, I couldn't see the judge find- ing against us here. I was summoned to see the judge in his office.

'Mr Cottle, after hearing all the evidence, it seems to me that Mr Chan may well indeed have a case. However I am only qualified in fam- ily law.' He grinned from ear to ear, 'I am normally hearing divorces.'

Did he expect me to laugh along with him? I didn't like the turn this conversation was taking.

'Our commercial judge is currently on holiday, so I have decided to put an injunction on your circus until he gets back.'

I couldn't believe it. It was said so casually, like this wasn't really my business about to be ruined.

'What do you mean?' I asked as respectfully as I could muster.

'I mean, Mr Cottle, that you and your circus are not to move until the commercial judge can hear your case.'

Not being able to contain myself any longer I blurted out, 'So it's taken you four weeks to decide . . . nothing?'

'No, Mr Cottle. It's taken me four weeks to decide there's a case that you have to answer and should you go against my judgement, you will find yourself in jail.'

The grin had disappeared.

'Of course, Sir. I was in no way implying that I would go against your ruling. But may I be permitted to make the point that my business here in Malaysia is finished. We have engagements back in Britain and if we wait for the judge to come back and then presumably another few weeks while the cases are put all over again, not only will we lose any earnings from other engagements but I will still have to find food and shelter for the artists and animals. It would not be an exaggeration to say this could be financially terminal for me.'

'Perhaps it is different in the United Kingdom, Mr Cottle, although I would be surprised, but here in Malaysia a judge's word is final. And now it is time for you to leave, otherwise I will have to have you taken away.'

On the taxi ride back my mind was working overtime. The case could drag on for weeks. I'd made lots of money out here but circuses are horrendously expensive if there's nobody buying any tickets. Just to keep everyone fed and paid cost thousands a week. I did a quick calculation on the back of an envelope. By the time the judge came back I would have lost all the profit from this year in the Far East. And then how long would he take to come to a conclusion? How long is a piece of string? Even if the judge found in my favour would Mr Chan ever pay my costs? It was lose-lose all the way. I called a meeting of the whole circus in the tent.

'I know you are all wondering when we're going home. I know many of you have new jobs which start very soon. As you know we would be halfway home by now except for this legal problem I have had. Today I was summoned before the judge, I thought because he had reached a judgement. Well it seems he had come to a decision of sorts but not the one I was hoping for.'

I went for the dramatic pause. Everybody looked very solemn.

'He's decided that because he's only a family judge, deciding on divorces and the like, he can't decide about us. The commercial judge is on a very long holiday, so in the meantime he's put out an injunction on us so we can't move.'

There was a gasp. Everybody looked at each other horrified. I put up my hands.

'Don't worry, I know this will be very bad news for most of you. It's catastrophic for me, I can tell you. That's why I'm proposing that we stick to the code of international law, view this as a travesty of international justice, and get the hell out of here as quickly as possible.'

Everybody cheered.

'We need to start packing straight away. I think time will be of the essence. I've made arrangements for everyone to be shipped out of here on a boat that leaves at 4 am. This means we can get to the port under cover of darkness and hopefully through customs before news of the judgement has spread that far. Only when everyone has left the country will myself and John Smith leave. It's probably best you don't know how.'

'Does anyone have any problems with this?'

Everybody laughed. Circus folk obey the laws of common sense and the law of the road, and are not generally impressed by jobsworths, whatever form they come in. We all started packing as if our lives depended on it, which they probably did.

That night we slipped out of the grounds and wended our way to the harbour. It was only a short distance but I couldn't believe a

A Brush with the Orient

whole circus could move out without being spotted. They boarded the boat smoothly, the elephants walked up the gangplank holding on to each other's tails. The customs official was unbelievably friendly and stood beside me watching the spectacle. He even asked me for my autograph. I watched in satisfaction, puffing on a cigar as the ship cast off and sailed out to the open sea.

Now they were safely away I couldn't avoid my own escape. I was nervous, probably the most nervous I've been in my life. I had booked tickets for John and myself on a flight to Copenhagen that morning as a token effort to remain anonymous. As I walked through the airport I was expecting a tap on the shoulder and a uniformed man to say, 'Hang on,' at any moment. We had arrived with plenty of time to spare, so the wait was interminable. I felt like a cross between an international man of mystery and a crook, even though I knew I had done nothing wrong. As we passed through each barrier – check in, customs, boarding the flight, and then waiting for take off – I got a bit more excited. I felt like I was starring in my own movie. In a role I would rather not have. When the plane was finally in the air John and I shook hands and ordered a bottle of champagne. Even I fancied a drink.

The next day the headlines of all the South-East Asian papers were full of our escape. The *South China Morning Post*'s headline was 'Circus Disappears Overnight'. I later learned that although the authorities were expecting us to try to escape they thought we would go back the way we came, so put guards at the train station and ignored the ports. Then I was incredibly fortunate that on the day John Smith and I flew out they were installing a new computer system at the airport, so nobody was doing any checks. Some people might call that the luck of the devil.

In September 1983 I arrived back on British soil in high spirits, money in my pockets and my reputation as one of Britain's greatest circus bosses restored.

Ten things you didn't know about
Clowns

1. Barnum said, 'A circus is not a circus without elephants and clowns.' Now the elephants have gone, clowns are the glue that holds the whole production together.

2. Study any show anywhere and the comedy element is at least 25 per cent of the whole production. A good clown has to be a talented all rounder, proficient at riding, the wire, stilts and acrobatics.

3. Joseph Grimaldi (1778–1837) is regarded as the father of modern clowns. In fact, Grimaldi never called himself a clown and never appeared in a circus ring – performing at the Sadler's Wells Theatre in Islington and the Drury Lane Theatre in Covent Garden.

4. The Holy Trinity church in Hackney is known as the clowns' church and every February the Clowns International holds a service on Grimaldi's birthday.

5. Queen Victoria's favourite clown was Whimsical Walker, known as Whimmie. His great grandson Philip Walker, also known as Whimmie, is still a very popular clown. Philip's mother is Louise Fossett.

6. Probably the most famous clown in Britain was Coco – the Latvian Nicolai Poliakoff. After being with the great German Circus Busch he joined Bertram Mills' Circus in 1930. He was very famous for his large check suits, very very large boots and fabulous wig.

7. The Russians specialise in training their clowns. They have a special clown school. Oleg Popov is my favourite. To me the Americans are the poorest in the world. More like a dressed-up chorus line.

8. Clowns in TV and film – where do you stop? Charlie Chaplin, Laurel and Hardy, the Marx Brothers and the Three Stooges. Benny Hill loved the circus and used many basic circus routines in his work.

9. There are many different types of circus clowning. The white face clown is the ringmaster clown, in smart spangled suit, who sets the story and tries to sensibly control the storyline. Carpet clowns are the group that run in and out while the props are changed.

10. Often part of the carpet clowns are the midgets or little people. They stick up for themselves and become part of the circus family, although they are rarely from a circus background.

Chapter Eight

A Dangerous Blonde was my Downfall
1983-86

I first caught sight of her standing on a street corner behind Marble Arch in the early hours of the morning. I was travelling back from a visit to the circus at Blackpool when on a whim I turned off the motorway and took the road into London. How different things would have been if I'd just carried on round the M25 back home like I was supposed to. It just felt too early for the night to end.

It was lust at first sight. Kerry was stunning – Amazonian with a mane of thick blonde hair and an inviting grin. She was a little bit the worse for wear. I wound down my window.

'Are you all right, love?' I asked.

In reply she took me back to her flat in Olympia. We spent an amazing night together, but as the light dawned she asked me whether I wanted a fix of cocaine.

'Oh no, I never touch it,' I replied. And I wasn't lying. I hated the stuff. I loathed alcohol and drunks. I had been teetotal for years. Dope was an anathema to me. I was trying to give up cigars. So drugs were beyond the pale.

I knew nothing about them. I could be wrong, but I get the impression that drugs like cocaine were less widespread and accept-able in society then than they are today. In the mid 80s they were just becoming fashionable for the new rich city types to play with, but of course I was certainly not part of that world. Drugs were unheard of in the circus. For a start, can you imagine trying to do the acts they do without a completely clear head? Strangely enough, and maybe this is a reflection of what was going on in Britain anyway, I had been offered drugs for the first time only in the previous six months. When I came back from Hong Kong I had to hire a new bunch of publicity boys to put up my posters for me. They were on dope then heroin. It was horrible, there were fights and money went missing. I did not like what I saw. I told my girls, 'Whatever you do, never ever take drugs.'

Kerry offered to inject me with cocaine. I refused. But she was very persuasive, 'Come on. I'll fix you. If you take it like this you won't get hooked, because you can only take it if I give it to you.'

Perverse logic but faced with a beautiful naked girl with long blonde hair, I wasn't in the most logical frame of mind. It was too sexy a proposition. I agreed and the rest is history.

Cocaine and I fell in love instantly. It was sensational, much much better than sex – and you know how much I like sex. It blew my mind away. We spent the next day taking fix after fix. By the evening I knew I had to get back to the circus at Southsea. It was Sarah's boyfriend Willie's birthday party. It was weird, I was walking around at the party feeling strangely detached from myself. I felt like this huge thing had happened to me and no one knew about it and I couldn't tell anyone. I felt like it must be written all over me, but everyone was treating me like normal. It was weird. The only thing I could think of was, When can I escape back to Kerry for my next hit? As soon as I could I slipped away from the party. I stayed with Kerry for the next three weeks. No one knew where I was. I didn't care. I only left when my money ran out. Cocaine had me hooked from that very first fix and became my problem for the next thirteen years.

I guess it would be easier if I could put all the blame on Kerry's shoulders, but of course it wasn't as simple as that. I was an addict waiting to happen. I was in the middle of a midlife crisis. A bit early I grant you, I know the male midlife crisis is supposed to happen to men in their fifties. All I can say is I do have to be first with every-thing, don't I? Or maybe it was a delayed adolescence. No university or gap year for me. I'd been working my socks off since I was fifteen.

A Dangerous Blonde was my Downfall

Whatever, I think it was no accident that I became an addict a couple of months after a disastrous fortieth birthday party.

A couple of years earlier, I had come back from the Far East a huge success with money in my pockets. But the Britain I returned to was depressing. The animal lobby had grown in power since we had been away. The GLC and certain other big city councils had banned animals performing at Blackheath and Clapham Common. After the enthusiasm of the people in the Far East, the thought of scrabbling for grounds on farmers' fields and battling with protestors made my heart sink. If the councils wouldn't have performing animals, then I would have to put together a circus without animals.

To own Britain's biggest and best circus was not my only ambition. Over the years I had also started to play with the idea of setting up Britain's first-ever circus school. America had them, Russia's were renowned, French circus wouldn't exist without them, but we had never had one. I decided to scour the country for young students from non-circus families and make a non-animal youth circus – a sort of travelling fame academy. We held open auditions in major cities. I guess you call it a forerunner of *The X Factor*. We got fantastic publicity and lots of kids came along. There was plenty of enthusiasm and a little less talent. But among the hundreds we found some real gems. Jackie Williams, a young minor civil servant working in the Dagenham tax office, desperately wanted to learn the trapeze. She teamed up with a boy called Andrew Watson and they became a top trapeze act and joined Cirque de Soleil straight after leaving me. Andrew is now a creative director at Soleil – he has just devised their new adult show in Vegas – and Jackie has set up her own circus school working with deprived kids in Bristol.

I asked the big circus fan, trapeze artist and historian Basil Schoultz, to come and train the kids, create the costumes and produce the show. After my disastrous experience with the Rainbow Circus I felt we should still use the name Gerry Cottle's Circus but bill it as 'featuring

Students of the First British Circus School'. It got a lot more publicity than the Rainbow Circus because of the auditions. Of course the old circus establishment hated it. It was a betrayal, a circus without animals. I was now the enemy more than ever. Insults were traded at the Circus Proprietors' meeting. Conversely I was suddenly being wined and dined by the liberal left wing. Not people I had much in common with, I can tell you.

The councils, especially the GLC, were very enthusiastic. I managed to book some top venues. I loved the show. It was full of energy and the kids were great fun, although the turnover was quite fast (it was the usual thing, some took to the life, and some didn't). The reviews were very good, but the public weren't sure. With a more affluent arty crowd we did very well, but the show bombed in other places. If only the whole country could have been Islington, we would have been fine. I didn't make a fuss about not having animals. I didn't want to get involved in that debate, I certainly didn't want to knock having animals in circus. But because it was still Gerry Cottle's Circus, people constantly asked us where the animals were. Many people knew our circus from years ago and wanted to see our beautiful elephants and lions. Mummies with toddlers would turn up in the mornings hoping to have a peep at the animals and we had to turn them away. At Acton I was accosted by a woman coming out of the show shouting, 'I want my f—ing money back, there are no f—ing animals,' in front of people queuing for the next performance. We ended this mixed season with Christmas on Clapham Common and a live BBC broadcast on Christmas Day. Not bad. I felt we were heading in the right direction, but what should we do for the next season? I decided to take Basil the producer out for a Chinese meal to see what he thought. I started by putting my cards on the table.

'I really like the show. It's got a lot of good comedy, but we are not quite hooking the audience in. I would love to create a cult following like Roncalli has managed in Germany. What do you think?' I asked.

I think Basil already had his speech prepared, 'Gerry, I really appreciate the support you have given us this year. You've been great. But I don't think we've gone far enough. I think we need to be more the-atrical, more serious, have a central unifying theme which would bind all the performances together.'

It turned out to be one of the longest meals ever as Basil, never quick to get to the point, slapped a series of sketches and scripts on the table. He had already prepared a show based on Pushkin's poems, a series of tableaux of gypsy life in Russia. Very arty – artists with faces painted white and acrobats in carts pulled by men (no horses, of course). I decided to give it a go. As usual I threw my all at it. I spent what was left from the Far East building a fleet of bow-topped old-fashioned wagons for the artists to live in at enormous expense. Betty was furious.

'What happened to the new ranch-style house you promised me then, Gerry?'

'This show will be so successful, darling, that next season I will be able to build you a stately home.'

'You may be right, Gerry. You may be right. But you know what I think? I think you are ten years ahead of yourself. I think eventually a non-animal circus may well be successful, but not this year or even next year. I think whatever the councils are doing, the public isn't ready for it. I think you may as well throw all the money we've earned straight down the drain.'

As a parting shot she added, 'And no one is going to take a second look at those new wagons of yours. They'll be far more interested in my brand-new American caravan. You'll see.'

I hated the show from day one. It looked beautiful but I felt there was no humour or spark to it. It was just pretentious. One of our first sites was Harrow – somewhere I thought would be good for us. It died. My instinct was to close the show down straight away, but I had a whole summer booked including six weeks in Eastbourne's Congress Theatre. When do you call it a day? With hindsight it's easy, but when you are actually there in the middle of it it's an incredibly difficult thing to do, especially when you've invested a lot of money, had a lot of publicity and are employing a lot of people. How do you say, I was wrong, it's a flop? It takes a brave man, and the difference between this and Rainbow and Glitter was that this time my name was at stake. I had so publicly put myself behind the show. I had announced to the world what a risk I was taking. My pride would not admit defeat – not yet anyway – especially as the circus establishment were so desperate to see me fail. So I decided to keep the show on the road and give it a chance. Of course Betty was right about the beautiful wagons. The public totally ignored them and crowded around her American caravan.

It was against this depressing background that I had my fortieth birthday. A cold grey dripping April day in Bournemouth. Usually we were in or around London for my birthday and we had a huge party. All the circus world would turn up and dance the night away. This year it was very quiet. The children performed a little circus of their own to surprise me, but I couldn't shake a terrible feeling of gloom. I knew that I was nearly back to where I was before the Hong Kong job – staring into the financial abyss – but I couldn't see any way out. I had put so much effort in and all my hard work seemed to come to nothing. My ambition to own Britain's biggest and best circus had slipped through my fingers and it looked like I would never get it back. Now the money had run out. I couldn't even unwind with a drink. I spent the night in earnest conversation with my brother-in-law. Afterwards he said to my sister, Jane, 'Gerry's very uneasy, very restless. He's looking for something.'

Two months later I found cocaine.

It was a pretty miserable squalid existence, although I didn't think so at the time. At the time you think you are being really clever. I thought, I'll just do it for the summer, and then I'll walk away. I thought I wasn't hooked because I didn't fix myself. I thought I was in love with Kerry. Even more stupidly I thought she was in love with me.

Girls like Kerry don't fall in love. They can't – they've already found the love of their life, it comes in a packet. They become your girlfriend because you buy their gear for them. You buy their groceries so they stop working – of course they do, very few of them actually want to have punters. They just want whatever substance they are addicted to. Most of the girls I met were very well educated, and they spent half their time talking about how they were going to sort their lives out. But they never did. They couldn't – there was no routine to their lives. They worked all night, slept all day if they slept at all, drifted from party to flat, their bills never got paid and before they knew it the bailiff was at the door. The drugs they took became more and more complicated. Kerry would inject cocaine and heroin – a snowball – and then inject Mogadon sleeping pills to try and get to sleep. Most of these girls were insecure, the drugs gave them confidence. Kerry was shy, but after cocaine she turned into this wild dangerous outrageous blonde. I only took her out to a restaurant once. She was very noisy and very impatient. Instead of catching the waiter's eye, she just turned round and shouted, 'Where's our bloody food?' That most wild of summers I was asked to judge the *Time Out* street performers' competition. I turned up in Covent Garden with Kerry at my side in the tiniest red mini skirt and the tightest red top and the highest red stiletto heels. Most of the time working girls do not dress like Julia Roberts in *Pretty Woman*. Forget the fantasies of ladies in thigh-high boots and postage-stamp miniskirts. They wear anoraks to keep warm and jeans, so if the fuzz come along they can pretend they're doing something perfectly innocent. On this day however Kerry had pulled out all the stops and looked what she was. I introduced her to Bob Wilson, the editor of *Time Out*, who was one of the judges. His face said it all.

But we didn't go out very often. There's a fine line between losing your inhibitions as you go up and feeling very vulnerable as you come down. That's the flip side. So I lost whole days of my life holed up in a miserable flat in West London listening to Bob Marley ('I Shot the Sheriff') over and over again. The first hit is brilliant. Time goes very quickly, but you keep trying to prolong that high by taking more drugs. Yet the next hit is never as good as the first and you start to feel very sweaty, then even getting up to go to the loo is an effort and you can't sleep. You toss and turn, and then because you are incapable of doing anything else, you take more cocaine. When I think back I'm amazed I'm still alive. Kerry and I used to egg each other on and take ridiculous amounts of drugs. We spent two weeks once doing nothing else, occasionally taking a break going to the Kentucky Fried Chicken looking like skeletons. And you get paranoid. I wasn't bad but I still remember spending an afternoon peering under the front door waiting to be raided and flushing the most enormous amount of charlie down the loo. Then you get ratty with each other because junkies are selfish.

'Please darling, could you give me a quick fix?'

'Yes, of course ... Actually I'll just do myself quickly first.'

'No, do me first.'

'Why? It'll only take a few seconds.'

'But you know you get wobbly. I'm covered in bruises.'

'I won't.'

And on it would go.

Actually it's incredible I did it at all. Before I met my nemesis, I couldn't stand having blood taken. I'd fainted at Bristol Infirmary once. They had to give me those biscuits to keep me from going under. But after a few weeks of relying on Kerry I got fed up and started fixing myself. And then I was so greedy I took stupid risks. I remember being as high as a kite, getting in cabs, meeting people in phone boxes and doing ridiculous things to get drugs. After a few months I got more organised. One day I was getting some spare parts for the circus at a motor dealer's run by a couple of brothers I'd known for quite a long time.

'God Gerry, you're looking a bit rough,' one said.

'I feel a bit rough. I was up late last night having some charlie with my girlfriend.'

'Oh. Do you need a supplier? We can always get hold of some of that for you.'

After that they were my sole supplier. It was much safer. There were certain times you could go to a certain pub and use a certain code word.

I still had a near escape one night after I rented a flat in Earl's Court. There was a huge party going on in the flat upstairs and Kerry insisted on joining in. It was full of people going absolutely wild. Right up Kerry's street, but it made me feel nervous, so I slipped out and decided to go and do my washing instead – I can't think why, but then junkies do strange things. But thank God I did. The laundry was tucked away in the basement. Just as I started filling up the drier, there was the wailing of sirens and a terrific racket as the front door was kicked in. We were being raided. I made a swift exit out of the back door, leapt over the garden fence, and started walking casually down the street. But Kerry, hanging over the balcony like some kind of X-rated Rapunzel, with her wild hair billowing, fag in hand, cool as a cucumber while behind her people were being dragged away in handcuffs, shouted at me, 'Gerry darling, don't forget your hat.'

She flung my trilby down into the street. I didn't stop to catch it but turned and fled. I never returned to the flat. My clothes may still be in the drier for all I know. I said to myself, let that be a lesson to you Gerry, never again'. But within a week, deranged as I was, I had tracked Kerry down.

Of course the real danger was what we were doing to our bodies. I saw Kerry overdose several times. It was frightening. Too nasty to think about. She always came round, thank goodness. Then there was the time I thought I was having an overdose. It was the middle of the night and I had just taken a huge hit.

'Kerry, Kerry, I can't breathe.'

My heart was racing at 2,000 miles an hour. I was writhing on the floor. She was out of it.

'Call an ambulance, for God's sake.'

'I can't call an ambulance. We'll get arrested.'

'I don't care. Call a f—ing ambulance. I tell you, I can't breathe. I'm dying,' I screamed.

The ambulance came and rushed me to Charing Cross Hospital. I was lying in A&E wild-eyed with pinpricks all over my arms. It must have been totally obvious what was wrong with me. After a while I started to feel a little better and a little more worried about the consequences. A doctor had seen me and had gone off to get a second opinion. He obviously didn't think I was about to leave this mortal world. I decided that now was the time to make my exit. As I got off the bed the matron blocked my way.

'I don't think you should be moving about. Not until Dr Brown has checked you're OK.'

'Look, Matron. I'm absolutely fine. Much much better. I just need to nip to the loo.'

I pushed her aside, ran out of the door and jumped in a cab.

'Are you all right, mate?' the driver asked.

'I've just had a night with a real wild blonde. I thought I was having a heart attack.'

'Oh well, as long as you're all right now, mate.'

We arrived at the flat to be greeted by the sight of Kerry leaning over her balcony smoking a fag, her ample cleavage barely contained by the skimpy negligee.

'I'm surprised she didn't f—ing kill you,' said the cabbie.

I was surrounded by cautionary tales of how drugs could screw up your life. One of Kerry's old punters was high up at the BBC. He worked just up the road at Shepherd's Bush. Every night he slept outside her flat in his car because his wife had kicked him out and he had nowhere else to go. He was totally addicted to cocaine and needed Kerry to fix him. He was a very intelligent man reduced to a pathetic state, although he still managed to hold down his job. I was appalled. But why did I think I was any different? You just do. There's so much self-delusion involved in addiction. I couldn't see what it was doing to me. I lost weight, never slept, never ate. I knew it was bad but . . . that summer I was Cock of the North. I thought I was still in control despite all the evidence to the contrary. The only reason I went back to the show was because my money had run out. I went back to literally empty the tills. I was robbing it. Not that there was anything to rob. The public seemed to agree with me about Pushkin's poems. We were heading for financial disaster.

Despite the desperate state of my finances, I still managed to buy one of the first mobile phones. It cost me £2,500 and was the size of a house. The lines were always engaged and you had to start any conversation with, 'Look, I'm on one of these new mobile phones. I might get cut off at any time, but don't worry, I'll ring you back.' A lot of time was wasted climbing hills and wandering around car parks trying to get a signal. I was embarrassed using it in public. Those were the days when people thought you were showing off, but Kerry had no such inhibitions – any excuse to whip it out. She was forever ringing her friends, offering to order their gear on it. I can still remember the number: 0836 222232. For all the teething trouble, the phone turned out to be a really good investment. I'd only had it for a week when I got a call from Paul Sanders.

Paul was one of those people who hung around the fringes of the circus world. He had worked for us a couple of times on *Seaside Special*. He had a lot of contacts in the theatre world. (He had married a showgirl called Wendy who was badly injured when she smoked a fag on the loo after the fire-eater had spat his meths down it. You can imagine what happened when she dropped her fag end down there . . .) The Moscow State Circus was over here for the first time in twenty years, performing in theatres around the country, but had nowhere to go for the end of the season – all the theatres in the seaside towns were already booked. Paul gave me a ring. Did I have any ideas? Could I help fix them up with a tent? Oh yes. One call and I had fixed a five-day stand in Bristol. A great town for circus. Another call and I'd hired an extra-large tent from my old partner, Brian Austen. (Brian, the wise man, had started diversifying from the circus business into the much more reliable tent hire business.) I sensed a great money-making opportunity.

I dashed down to the circus at Eastbourne to get ready. What I found was a very demoralised crew. Everybody had measles. Betty had been in the caravan for days with four sick children. Did I care? Did I heck. Such things don't register on a junkie's radar.

'Look, Betty. I want you to stay with the circus. I've got a great opportunity with the Moscow State Circus. So I'm taking the spare caravan and going off to Bristol for a while.'

'Do I have any choice?'

'Don't be like that. We need the money. I'm working hard, you know.'

'At what? You look dreadful. Where have you been?'

'Getting this gig.'

'Look, Gerry. I've had enough. You can go off whenever you want, wherever you want, do whatever you want with whoever. When you come back you know where I am. I'm in my caravan, in my own bed, on my own. Maybe I ought to do what you do. What would happen then?'

'If I came back here and found you with anyone else, you'd be off the show.'

'What, your girls as well?'

'You'd be off.'

Double standards, I know. I grabbed the caravan and drove off at high speed. No goodbyes. Somehow I managed to take Betty's dog food, which she had temporarily left balanced on the back of the caravan. She turned round and I'd gone. 'Where's Gerry?' She went round the circus asking. Everybody shrugged their shoulders. I was a man possessed.

I think this is the point where I lost the plot. Rather than stay on the circus, I moved into the Holiday Inn in Bristol with Kerry. Never has a show been so well publicised. Fuelled by copious amounts of cocaine, I managed to plaster Bristol with 45,000 posters. I was either taking drugs, having sex or putting up posters. Bombarded by the most intense poster campaign any city has ever seen, I made more money that week than I have ever done in my life. Thousands of people turned up to see the Moscow Circus. It was pretty spectacular. It starred the world's most famous clown, Popov, and seventy high-wire artists, jugglers, trick cyclists, acrobats, illusionists and musical eccentrics. Lord Snowdon came down and took beautiful photographs which ended up filling *The Sunday Times* magazine. We had to turn dozens of people away. I remember vividly the sight of the table piled high with bundles of money. But I was in a terrible state. The mayor came to the opening night. I managed to make it there to greet him but my dress shirt was all stained, I was all sweaty and wild-eyed. I still feel acutely embarrassed when I think about it now. People kept on asking me if I was all right. I told so many lies. One night Kerry and I thought we were going to run out of supplies so we drove all the way to London, picked up some gear, and drove back all in one night. We were mad but the money we made in Bristol saved the student show and kept me solvent.

But I was losing my head. I had to do something.

On an impulse I drove to see Betty. She knew something was up. But during the nearly twenty years we'd been married there had often been something up. Not like this though.

'I think we should split up,' I said.

'What? What do you mean?'

'I can't stay in this marriage any longer.'

'Why not? What's the matter?'

'Things are happening.'

'What are you talking about? What things?'

'I can't tell you. I just want a divorce.'

With that I walked out. Not surprisingly Betty was devastated. She went to see her big sister Julie.

'I just don't understand it. Where has this come from? What's got into him?'

By coincidence Julie was now married to Brian Austen's youngest brother Patrick and had been up to Bristol to see the Moscow, so she had the answer.

'You know he's taking drugs.'

Betty was dumbfounded.

'Don't be daft. I know Gerry's done some stupid things, but he's not that stupid. That's the one thing he's always told the girls, "Never take drugs." He hates them.'

'I'm sorry, Betty, but he is on drugs.'

'Well how do you know?'

'Because Brian Austen told me. He's got a girlfriend too. I've seen her. She's living with him in Bristol.'

It was a lot for Betty to take in. But after she'd had a drink or three and thought about it, it all made sense – I'd even asked her not to buy any more short-sleeved shirts. The drugs were particularly hard for Betty to take. They are not part of the circus world and are very much looked down on. She drove back to the circus the next day and was waiting to confront me when I walked in that evening.

'I know all about your drugs and all about your whore.'

'It's nothing, Betty. It's no big deal. I can handle it.'

'And what if you can't? After all the things you've done – this is the worst. We will lose everything. What about the circus, our house, the family? You will lose everything and most of all you will lose yourself.'

The argument went on long into the night. At the end of it I had agreed to go and see a doctor.

'Look at her, Gerry. Isn't she beautiful?' he said smiling beatifically at Betty.

At that moment Betty looked as if she wanted to swing her hand-bag at him. We were in the posh Harley Street offices of Dr Tom Stuttaford, distinguished doctor and *Sunday Times* columnist. He was a lovely man but I think his advice wasn't quite what Betty expected. While in no way condoning my behaviour, the doctor explained to Betty that a great percentage of men stray. Very successful, very ambitious men often have mistresses or girlfriends they visit from time to time. He gave the example of one of his clients who was even driven by his wife to visit his lady friend. His wife went off and played a hand of bridge and then picked him up on her way home. They had been happily married for forty years. (The image of Betty playing a hand of bridge dressed in spangly leotard with feathers on her head sur-rounded by blue rinse ladies of the WI flashed into my head. It was dismissed instantly.) He ended the appointment by saying that I was obviously a very ambitious, very obsessive person and had had a bit of disappointment in life. Everybody has their poison, he explained – one that uniquely suits them and their personality. With some people its alcohol, others its nicotine. It can be gambling, food or even vin-tage cars. Most people never find their poison. It seemed that I now unfortunately had found mine. Somehow I had to find the strength to walk away from it. I remember his words: 'This drug will ruin you. The answer of course is to stay away from the source. Stop seeing this woman right now.'

I took Dr Stuttaford's advice seriously. I walked out of his office and went straight round to Kerry's flat, handed her a handful of notes and said I could never see her again. I thought she would be upset but she was too delighted by the wad of cash in her hands. I heard later that within a week she had spent the lot on drugs, was back on the game and in a sorry state.

I stayed clean for about three weeks. Just long enough for me to take stock of my business. Pushkin's poems continued to be a financial disaster. I'd reached a point where I could either try and improve it or I could completely scrap the whole student non-animal circus idea and go back on the road with a traditional circus, especially as I had received another invitation to go back to Hong Kong. Despite all the work, all the publicity, all the young people whose hopes depended on me, I got myself a pack of tigers and went to Hong Kong.

With hindsight it might have been better to have stuck with the new circus – I had been brave enough to start a revolution from which I never reaped the benefits. Certainly other non-animal circuses came along in the following years and did very well – Zippo is a classic example. He started his non-animal circus in 1986 and within a few years had a monopoly on all the best London sites and did very nicely, thank you. (Although today he's put back budgies, dogs and horses into his show.) Not to mention the likes of Cirque du Soleil. More importantly, the young people I trained went on to travel throughout the world, and in this way the student circus influenced a whole new generation, laying the foundation for all the alternative circus that came after.

Perhaps I gave up on the student circus because it never got any credit from the circus establishment; the people I desperately wanted to impress hated it, and instead I got recognition from people I had no respect for. But I think the main reason I gave it up was that I was so addicted I just wanted a way to make money as quickly and as easily as possible. I was in no fit state to do anything innovative; I wanted a quick fix all ways round. Drugs ruin your ability to take decisions; you are always doing things for the wrong reason.

That summer I was too out of it to even make the easy option work. I held my head together long enough to assemble a pretty good programme. But by the time I was ready to fly out to meet the officials of the Royal Jockey Club to hammer out the deal, I was off the wagon big time. The night before my flight I went on a monster binge. When the taxi rolled up outside a girl's flat at six in the morning I was still high as a kite. I nearly missed the flight. It was slightly delayed so I went walkies and fell asleep for three hours, head slumped on a coffee shop table. My shipping agent, John Smith, searched the airport frantically but couldn't find me. In the end I woke up and rushed to the gate with a minute to spare. I then spent the whole flight asleep on the floor. As I tried to negotiate the finer details of the contract I was all over the place. I couldn't remember what day of the week it was. The respectable expat officials must have wondered what on earth was going on. Anyway I ended up with a deal that meant I could make a lot of money if we did well. If we did badly I was on my own and vulnerable.

Audiences are funny things. Sometimes I think too much success can kill a show. Look at safari parks – for the first couple of years the residents of Wiltshire were going mental because the roads were completely clogged every weekend with people trying to get to Longleat. Then suddenly everybody who was going to go had been, and they were old news. Riverdance is another great example. Where are all those tap dancing girls now? Playing at the end of the pier, I shouldn't wonder. I think our circus was the Riverdance of Hong Kong. In two seasons everybody had seen it and the ones who couldn't get tickets had got cheesed off and gone somewhere else. Hong Kong in particular had also changed. The stock market had crashed, there was massive uncertainty about what was going to happen when the Chinese took over. I don't think anyone was in the mood for circus. Although the show was completely different, and I think it was a very good show, we really struggled to fill the seats.

I handled it badly and just took more drugs. I got to the stage where I was having a quick fix between dismantling the lions' cage at the beginning of the second half and coming back for the finale all sweaty. It was a truly terrible time. In the end I made my excuses and flew back to England on the pretext of sorting out our Christmas circus, which was playing at Camden. Back in London I got totally overexcited. I found two wild lesbian working girls and became their sugar daddy.

Now the main thing on my 'to do' list was to find a pair of Siberian tiger cubs. As we had donated the two lion cubs to Canton Zoo last time we were in the Far East, it was suggested that this time the polite thing to do was give a couple of tiger cubs. No problem I thought, and duly offered up a couple of Bengal tiger cubs. They were graciously declined and it was suggested that I might like to find a couple of Siberian tigers. Easier said than done. They are very very rare. In fact when I made some enquiries I found the only place in the whole world I could get them was from a safari park in Amsterdam.

You can imagine my reaction when I heard I had to spend a week in Amsterdam. I practically ran to the airport with my two new lady friends in tow. We spent two weeks above a pub in the middle of the red light district. No one had the slightest idea where I was. When I finally sobered up, I gave back my Avis hire car and managed to leave a plastic bag full of charlie in the boot. Somehow these two lunatic lesbians managed to persuade me to go back to the hire car desk and ask for my lost property.

Without blinking the guy at the desk asked, 'Could this be the bag you are looking for?' He held up a little bag full of white powder.

'Ah yes, that's mine,' I spluttered. I hardly dared take it out of his hands in case the alarms went off and I found myself surrounded by a load of police with a gun to my head. (I was getting a bit paranoid.) But nothing happened except, 'Have a nice day, Sir.' It's a different culture out there. I compounded this act of folly by then stepping on a plane straight back to Hong Kong still in possession of the charlie (I won't tell you where), looking every bit the junkie, again spending most of the flight asleep on the floor. How I managed to avoid getting myself arrested, I will never know.

Back in Hong Kong things were no better. Business was abysmal. I couldn't bear it. I went walkies again. The effect on Betty, who had come out with me, was devastating. Struggling to cope with four children, she had begun to have a brandy first thing in the morning just to face the day. She went through the motions of looking after the children – they were fed and clothed and bathed and put to bed, but she wasn't doing anything else. She had started to drink heavily and couldn't sleep at night. Days just passed in a haze of misery. She knew she was going down with me and something had to be done if the family was to survive. She went to the doctor and told him the whole story.

'Mrs Cottle, I cannot count how many European ladies I have had sat in that chair, crying like you, telling me a story just like yours. Some men just lose their heads when they come out here and do silly things. I wish there was a pill that I could give you that would make it all better, but there isn't. There's only one thing you can do and it's the advice I give to all you ladies. Gather up your children, catch the next plane home and when you get home change the lock on your door and never let him in again.'

The doctor did give Betty some anti-depressant pills anyway, but when she got back to the circus she opened the bottle and tipped them straight down the drain. She marched into the caravan, packed all my belongings into plastic bags and threw them into my office. John Smith was sat in there on his own.

'Tell Gerry he can go and book himself into a hotel. Whatever. I have had enough. He can go to hell.' Poor John didn't know what had hit him.

That night I sought out Betty and begged her to stay, 'Don't leave me. I love you. Let's have another baby. I'm sorry.'

I said anything I could think of to stop her from going. I was very frightened of being left on my own. Betty and the children were the one solid thing I had. A place of sanity to return to. If they went, where would I go? I felt I would go completely off the rails, although looking back I was completely off the rails anyway. I was just very very frightened of what I would do if Betty wasn't there.

Betty had heard me say these things all before and wasn't having any of it. The next day she took herself and the children back to England. Business was so bad I could see no reason to stay, but I had so little money left I didn't have the money to ship the circus home. I was stuck and beginning to panic.

A Dangerous Blonde was my Downfall

Brian Austen had decided to take a holiday and see what business was like in Hong Kong. Having him around was one of the few positive things about the trip. Every lunchtime we went hunting the streets for some unusual food to try. When we came back we would both go to sleep balanced precariously on any old bit of plywood we could find, to the great amusement of the Chinese who gathered around giggling at the sight of us *gweilos* flat on our backs snoring away. Brian knew exactly the predicament the circus was in and offered to cash in some insurance policies to get me home. I don't quite know what would have happened if he hadn't been there.

Of course my problems didn't end the moment I set foot on British soil.

For a start Betty wouldn't let me back into the house. She pleaded for me to go and get a flat of my own. 'I can't bear it any more, Gerry. I never know when you are coming home, if at all, and what state you are going to be in. Just find yourself somewhere else to go. I don't care where it is or who it's with, just leave us to get on with our lives.'

'No. I'm not moving out.'

'Well if you won't go, I will. I don't know where, but I will take the children and disappear.'

'If you leave me, I will kill myself.'

Betty was desperate but she wasn't tough enough to take that risk.

When she told my sister, Jane said, 'Go Betty, if that's what you need to do. He is not your responsibility and if he tops himself, he tops himself.' But Betty couldn't do it. She lived in fear of the telephone ringing or the police knocking at the door. The only end to this nightmare she could see was my death. She thought that was the only way I would ever stop taking drugs. One night I wouldn't come home and they'd find me dead in a ditch, or worse in some seedy hovel with a woman. Betty spent many sleepless nights wondering how she would cope with what she thought was inevitable.

Meanwhile I was worrying about money. I arrived back from Hong Kong even more in debt than when I had left. For the first time ever I had absolutely no idea what we were going to do for the next season. Most of all I was feeling very lonely. I had lost my partner in crime, the wild Kerry. She had attacked her neighbour with an umbrella and was languishing in Holloway prison. I really missed her. I thought I was in love with her, so I went to visit her inside. It was horrible. I had never been in a woman's prison before and I was shocked. Just the way they treated the visitors standing in the queue was demeaning – shouting at us, making us wait forever, tough body searches. I was trapped in an episode of *Prisoner: Cell Block H*. The other visitors were mainly mums going to visit their daughters, so I stood out like a sore thumb. I sat opposite Kerry, with a table separating us, in a huge hall with dozens of hard inmates and their relations. Stupid, gullible me, I thought Kerry would be pleased to see me. Well she was pleased to see me but for one reason only.

'Gerry. I'm so glad you've come. Now it's really important you come back next week and bring me some gear.'

'You must be joking.'

'No I'm not. It's easy, lover boy. Just put it into your mouth and give me a little kiss and I'll take it from you like this.'

She lunged over at me, mouth open. I backed away. I could no longer ignore the fact that the only thing she cared about was cocaine. I was very low on her list of priorities. I did not go back to see her again.

My friend Tony Shuker, who travelled with us for years doing our posters and publicity, always displayed a sticker very prominently in his office, 'Cocaine is a sign you are making too much money.' I never asked him about it, but I always felt it was there for my benefit. Well I wasn't making too much money. I was struggling to find the money to buy the gear. But it was a vicious circle because the more money trouble I was in, the more desperate I was to lose myself in a fix.

Christmas 1985. I reached my lowest point. Let me tell you a couple of stories which say it all.

We were supposed to be having a festive family meal with my sister Jane and her four daughters. I had been out living it up all night but I did manage to make it home in the morning to drive the family down to my sister's house in Sussex. How I drove I don't know, but as soon as we got there I went straight upstairs and fell asleep on my sister's bed at eleven in the morning.

Betty suspected I had more cocaine with me. She quietly rifled through my trouser pockets and found my car keys and gave them to Jane. Let me say now, my sister is pretty unshockable, years as a hospital matron had made sure of that, but what she found took her a few seconds to take in. My car boot contained a plastic bag full of what looked like washing powder. Jane picked it up, had a sniff and a taste and came to the conclusion she was probably holding a substantial stash of cocaine. This posed particular difficulties for Jane. Her first instinct as a tough law-abiding citizen was to call the police. She felt I deserved everything I got. But then she remembered that she was the school matron of a boarding school for young girls from good Quaker families. At that moment she was standing holding a huge amount of cocaine in the middle of the school grounds outside her grace and favour house. An image of a front page in the local newspaper, worse, the tabloids came into her head. She would probably lose her job and her house. Not a risk worth taking with four young daughters to support (she was going through an acrimonious divorce at the time). So instead Jane marched straight inside the house and ignoring Betty's questions strode into the bathroom and flushed all the charlie straight down the loo.

When I came downstairs instead of being greeted by a happy family gathered round a festive table, the children were nowhere to be seen and two accusing faces glared at me.

'How could you do it, Gerry? How could you do it? Look at what you are doing to your family, Betty, your four children. Never mind that you could have lost me my job and my house.' Jane was seething. I was confused.

'Hang on. What are you talking about?'

'That filthy stuff in the boot of your car. That's what I'm talking about. You disgust me. I can't believe you are my brother.'

'What are you doing looking in the boot of my car?'

'What are you doing with all that cocaine?'

'That's none of your business.'

'It is my business when you bring it to my home. Well before you go looking, I've flushed it all down the loo.'

'You've done what?'

I rushed to the bathroom. There was no trace. Now I was absolutely seething.

'You fool. Do you realise you may as well have thrown hundreds of pounds straight down the drain.'

'I can't believe I'm hearing this. It's time you left.'

It was a measure of how low I'd sunk that I didn't speak to my sister for a long time after that.

A couple of weeks later I was driving home from Manchester. I was that desperate, I pulled off the motorway and fixed myself. Cocaine makes you lose all your inhibitions, so I used to take my clothes off – one thing when you are holed up in a flat, not so good in a lay-by. Off my head I went walkabout and ended up on private land, walking into the middle of a field stark naked. Suddenly I was surrounded by barking dogs. Lying in the distance was a row of men pointing guns at me. I think I was in the middle of a grouse shoot. The gamekeeper came running over and shouted, 'What the hell do you think you are you doing?'

'Sorry, mate. I've been taking drugs. I don't know where I am.'

'If I were you I'd get dressed and get off our land as quickly as you can, before I call the police.'

I sobered up pretty hastily and ran off.

That night Betty spent hours with a pair of tweezers picking thorns out of my legs and feet.

So you see I couldn't go on like this.

It was Betty who finally put an end to the madness. Not long after my naked wandering I walked into the house to find Betty sat at the kitchen table, looking grim, tissues in hand. 'She's been crying,' I said to myself. A policeman neighbour of ours was with her. Oh God, what's she been saying? There were four empty coffee mugs. He'd obviously been here a long time. Alarm bells started going off in my head.

A Dangerous Blonde was my Downfall

'Hi, John. How are you? If you don't mind I've been up all night making arrangements for the circus and I've just got to get some kip.'

'It's no use, Gerry. I've told John everything,' Betty said.

'What everything, Betty? What do you mean?' I suddenly couldn't breathe.

'About your addiction to cocaine,' John replied. 'Gerry, you can't go on like this. I'm not going to let you. Now you have a choice – either I arrest you here and now or you can let me take you to a place where they can help you.'

It was at that moment that I knew I didn't want to carry on living this way any more. A huge burden was lifted from my shoulders. The game was up and it was a huge release. I sank into a chair. 'OK, take me. I want to go,' I said. Then I put my head in my hands and wept.

John Bridger was an old friend of our family. He lived down the road from us in Addlestone, our daughters were friends at school and his wife had done a bit of secretarial work for me. With the nose of a policeman, he'd seen my behaviour change and knew exactly what was going on. He also may have heard talk on the police grapevine, I don't know. But for whatever reason, he decided to confront Betty and when asked outright whether I was on drugs, Betty couldn't lie. John was a true friend to us. He phoned up one of the best rehabilitation clinics in the country and booked me in. He then drove Betty and I there straight away (before I could change my mind, I think). The clinic was a beautiful big Georgian house in the middle of the Surrey countryside, run by a pair of Americans, Jim and Joyce. John had booked me in anonymously. As I arrived a kind lady took my details and searched me for any substances. All my personal belongings were taken away.

'Name?' she asked

'Gerry Cottle.'

'I see now why you wanted to remain anonymous, that's fine. You will be completely safe here,' she said. They were used to dealing with celebrities far more infamous than myself.

Within a month I had been diagnosed as one of Britain's first sex addicts. The staff decided cocaine was not my problem – it was just part of my greater addiction to sex. In those days it was so rare, they had to send off to Minnesota for a manual to treat me. (This was before Michael Douglas and the rest. It's a recognised illness now.) Basically I was addicted to cocaine because it enabled me to lose all my inhibitions and try out all my sexual fantasies. Usually people stayed in the clinic for six weeks. In my usual egotistical way I thought I'd be out in a couple. In the end it took twelve weeks before they were happy to release me into the outside world, I was that complex a case.

People were in there for all sorts of reasons, and were all ages. There were lots of alcoholic ladies of a certain age, often ladies who had been dedicated housewives, whose children had left home and husbands either died or run off with young girlfriends. These alcoholic ladies tended to despise the junkies and vice versa. As you know I've always had an aversion to drinkers myself. Then there were the pretty posh young girls who had eating disorders and drug habits. They were a much jollier crowd, some of them absolutely lovely. Then there was a clique of noble lords who you may have heard of.

I shared a room with the most infamous – let's just call him Angus. He was a powerful character and pretty much ran the place. He was so vain he loved reading about himself in the society columns. Every morning he would rush downstairs to get his hands on the newspapers. Angus and I had the most terrific rows. I felt everybody was a little scared of him, so I had to stand up to him. He called me 'wide boy'. 'You are like a market trader, Cottle. You have an answer for everything.' He was totally obsessed with his sweet tin (typical junkie behaviour really). He hid it but we all knew where it was kept. 'Keep your bloody hands off my sweets, wide boy. I know you've been at them. I'm warning you.'

He always monopolised the TV, so when he was being obnoxious, I would start loudly fiddling with a sweet wrapper in my pocket. All hell would break loose. He'd jump up and start shouting at me and everybody would pile in. Angus had a young honourable sidekick, the nice but dim Giles. Only seventeen, he was a total nutter who spent his whole time trying to sniff furniture polish, deodorant, anything he could lay his hands on. One day a brand-new Mercedes sports car tied up with a big red ribbon appeared on the drive. It was Giles' eighteenth birthday present, even though he couldn't drive! (I came to the conclusion spoiling your children was unproductive.) He abused himself for many years but I now believe he has sobered up and knuckled down to looking after the family estate.

One day the three of us had the most terrible row over the lawnmower. Jim came out and broke up the fight. Furious, he showed us all into his study and launched into a stern lecture.

'Although you don't realise it, you three boys are very similar. Now I'm going to make a predication – within four years one of you is going to be dead whatever happens, and if you carry on like this the other two of you will be dead as well. You think it's just about taking drugs. Well let me tell you it's not. It's about a whole pattern of behaviour, an attitude to people, a complete selfishness.'

I took Jim's words to heart. The three of us got on a lot better after that.

Some of the guests didn't fall into any category. There was a lovely GP in his early thirties with a beautiful wife and family. He'd never taken any drugs in his life, then one night after everyone had left the surgery he injected himself with morphine, out of curiosity, just to know what it felt like. He was instantly addicted. He started doing weird things. He was at a dinner party with his wife when, desperate for a fix, he said he had to go home for a shave and walked out. He responded very well to treatment and never touched drugs again. We had come from a similar background – he had pushy parents, and all his life up to that point he'd been working hard to become a doctor. There was a bit of rebellion or a delayed adolescence going on.

The treatment at the clinic was based around a strict routine. The day always kicked off with the prayer which I have always remembered, 'God, grant me the Serenity to accept the things I cannot change, the Courage to change the things I can, And the Wisdom to know the difference.' We all had jobs to do. There was a rota – one week you would be clearing the kitchen, the next chopping logs or doing the hoovering. It was all done at a leisurely pace and I was happy keeping busy. We also had two sessions of group therapy every day. They were highly structured. We'd sit in a circle and have different topics to debate. There was terrible competition between the junkies and alcoholics and the arguments got quite fraught. We would take turns to stand up and tell our story. The others could ask any question or pass any comment. We were supposed to gee each other along and give each other positive encouragement, but often it turned into character assassination. After two weeks it was my turn to speak. I was shocked at the reaction of some of my fellow residents. My addiction to naughty ladies was beyond the pale for the slushy ladies. I'd say, 'I met this girl on the street.'

And the old dears would pipe up, 'What do you mean, you met a girl on the street?'

'I mean a hooker.'

Gasps of dismay, 'Disgusting,' and, 'Tut tut,' would reverberate around the room.

Afterwards everybody wrote you a letter saying what they thought. I still have these letters. People remarked on two things – my selfishness and my total obsession with the circus. The slushy ladies in particular condemned me for cheating on my wife and my family. After reading the letters I looked at myself in a different way in the mirror in the mornings. It was the first time I could really see how self-centred I had been. On Sundays we were allowed visitors and they were encouraged to join in a group therapy session. Betty got up at one point and said, 'It's such a relief to have Gerry in here. It's the first time in years I actually know where he is.'

There was laughter all around, but it was the first time I felt a tiny bit of the sheer misery I had been causing her.

I also learned some positive things, which have stayed with me – to take one day at a time, have confidence in myself (all this need to be seen to be the biggest and the best was all part of deep insecurity) and I realised that other people have problems too. I came out much more laid-back and a better negotiator because for the first time I was forced to listen to people and see things from their point of view. I probably came out a nicer person.

On an individual level, treatment centred around the 'Minnesota

A Dangerous Blonde was my Downfall

Method' – Alcoholics Anonymous' Twelve Steps – which can be applied to any addiction. Basically you have to admit you are addicted, make a full confession of all the dreadful things you have done, learn some humility and start to pray to a higher power. There was a lot of God going on. I found that bit easy. Although I rarely went to church because it smacked too much of my mother and 1950s suburbia, it may surprise you that I actually do believe in God. The only disappointment was my one-to-one counselling. My counsellor was a young woman who was very harsh. I think a man might have been a bit more understanding about my terrible obsession with the opposite sex. I was forced to confront why I chose to spend time with working girls in particular. I hadn't always done it. Over the years I had had a succession of intense love affairs, but inevitably the affairs always ended with one of us, and often both, getting hurt because I never wanted to walk out of my marriage. I may not have acted like it, but I loved Betty and I loved my children. So I had reached the stage where I didn't want a proper relationship with anyone else. I didn't want commitment. The working girls gave me physical intimacy, no strings attached.

After the shock of the first couple of days, I settled into rehab. It's amazing how quickly you become institutionalised. I was happier than I had been for a long long time. My sister Jane says I'm like a baby, I need regular meals and naps otherwise I'm liable to throw my toys out of the pram. We were not in prison – the gates were always open. But it was clear that as soon as we left we could never come back, and if we managed to get hold of any substances while inside we would be asked to leave. But while I was in there I had no desire for drugs or sex. I walked to the end of the driveway a few times and stared out at the outside world but I was never tempted to step outside. I had found a haven of peace and order. And when the time came to leave, I was in tears. I didn't want to go. In rehab there had been no circus to worry about, no debts, no animal protestors, no councils and, most of all, I was safe from myself. I didn't have the confidence that I could survive outside. I was really scared. Somehow Betty persuaded me to get into the taxi but it wasn't easy.

My final view of rehab was of Angus and Giles trapped on the roof. They'd gone up to fly their model aeroplane but the door had shut and locked behind them. They shouted as we loaded my case into the taxi, 'Gerry, help us. We're locked out. Get Jim. Help us, you bastard.'

I ignored them. I was in no state to do anything proactive. I also thought it would do them good to have a few hours to reflect on their situation. As the taxi started along the long drive I turned and looked out of the back window. The two noble lords were jumping up and down like cats on a hot tin roof. However depressed I felt, I couldn't help but smile.

Ten things you didn't know about
Horses in the Circus

1. Up until the 1950s horse acts were the absolute backbone of the circus. I have circus programmes from the early 1950s, where out of 20 acts 12 used horses. Fashions have since changed.

2. You can train all kinds of horse. You can see mules, donkeys, a big shire horse with a Shetland pony who runs under the horse's belly (known as a Big and Little), and of course the stubborn zebra.

3. Liberty acts were where 2, 4, 6, 8, 12 or even 24 horses would pirouette, change and cross over in various formations. They were always beautifully harnessed with feathered plumes on their heads.

4. Traditionally Liberty horses are Arabs (grey and chestnuts) while, especially in the old days, many of the circus acts used coloured horses. Using a spotted horse is real circus.

5. You can have any number of individual horse acts. The intelligent pony is great for audience participation. My favourite is when the pony wanders round the ring and picks out the little girl who kissed her boyfriend last night without her mother knowing.

6. A great act is the riding troupes with 10 people in pyramids on 2 horses, or 5 on one horse, always with one good comedy rider. It's not an easy act and you can only use a safety lunge when first learning.

7. The Cossack Riders from the Moscow State Circus are wonderful. Traditionally from Georgia and Southern Russia they gallop around the ring at breakneck speed, climb under the horse's belly and back again.

8. The ballerina is the pretty girl on the back of a beautiful big horse who dances on its back and then jumps through a paper hoop as her last trick – difficult because you can't see where you are going to land.

9. You won't have seen Courier of St Petersburg for years. One tall man stands astride two horses, and gradually extra horses come under his legs, one-by-one, until he is controlling nine horses.

10. Health and safety means you will never see the unrideable mule or the riding machine today. A member of the audience is belted into the lunge and has a go. The last person to take a turn is usually a stooge who loses their skirt or trousers. It sounds corny but it was the act the great Bertram Mills' Circus at Olympia often finished on.

Chapter Nine

The Oldest Trick in the Book
1986-92

'How do you like Ireland?' asked the old man in the cloth cap.

'The people are great. It just won't stop raining,' I answered.

'Ah well. They'll build a roof over it one day,' he said.

I wish they had.

When I came out of my sanctuary in rehab, I flew straight to Ireland and into the worst spring weather on record. Can you imagine a bad spring in Ireland? The grey skies, the rain, the mud. Of course the audience chose to stay warm and dry in their houses rather than venture out to come and sit in a windy tent. With no audience and in deep mud the circus was completely demoralised. It was the last thing I needed straight from rehab. Mentally, I wasn't in a fit state to deal with it. It was so depressing. The only silver lining in the endless grey clouds was that stuck in rural Ireland, there was no one and nowhere to lead me astray.

Why, you may well ask, had we gone to Ireland?

When I got back from Hong Kong I hadn't a clue what I was going to do next season. It was totally unheard for me not to have a plan, but this was probably my lowest point. To try and find sites for a traditional animal circus in Britain would have taken too much effort and ingenuity for a man in my state. In a moment of sanity I sent my manager, Chris Barltrop, over to Ireland to see if he could find some sites – the Irish didn't have the same issues with performing animals (they still have twelve performing elephants to our one) and business was usually pretty good (circuses always do well in Catholic countries). It seemed like a sensible option.

But when Chris arrived back from Northern Ireland with eight sites for the circus in his back pocket, I had already left for rehab. So he went to see Betty.

'You have a choice, Betty. I can either go out into the yard and tell everybody they've lost their jobs, or I can tell them to pack for Ireland. You are the boss now, which is it to be?'

It was a decision Betty could do without. She had absolutely no desire to run the circus, but there were bills to pay and staff already hired, and no one had any idea if and when I'd be back.

'Well if we've already paid for the ferry tickets and we have four weeks of guaranteed work we'd be mad not to go, wouldn't we?' she said.

Chris grinned from ear to ear. 'I'm glad you said that. I'll go and tell everyone the good news.'

If only it had been that simple.

Yes, Chris had taken care of the sites for the first few weeks, but when I joined the circus a couple of months later we needed to find some more sites quickly. I set off for the Republic of Ireland. First of all I had to come to an arrangement with the two reigning Irish circus families – the Duffys and the Fossetts.

The Duffys were a mother and her seven sons, all tremendously good-looking and great showmen. Mother looked after the money, the boys looked after the show. Every one of the Duffys' posters said, 'One Day and One Day Only'. They opened at Easter and travelled until 1 October, moving every single night. An incredible feat. They were great singers (I think some of them ended up in the Eurovision song contest) and about twelve of the extended family played in the band at the beginning of the show, but by the end there would be just one son or niece left on the organ as the rest of them pulled down the tent around the ears of the audience. They never had any winter quarters and just pitched up on the nearest field at the end of the season. They were so laid-back one year they didn't bother moving the lions' cage in and out of the ring, but instead the whole performance took place inside it – a bit of a challenge for the stilt walker. They were lovely people and very relaxed about us coming over.

I was expecting a different story with the Fossetts. Of course they were Betty's cousins but when it came to business we may as well have been a tribe of Martians. Indeed when I had last tried to take a circus over to Ireland, in 1977, they raised it in the Dublin Parliament, objecting to a foreign circus being allowed in to take business away from native circuses and our visas were rejected. Which was ironic because the Fossetts were English through and through and had only gone over to Ireland in the lean years after the Depression. In fact they had originally called themselves the Heckenbergs (a German name) to sound more exotic. I drove down to Cookstown to meet with Teddy Fossett. They made me wait a long time. At one point a clown ran over and said, 'He's coming now, shortly.' Only an Irishman could say that. I waited another hour. Eventually Teddy came over. I agreed to stay well away from his route and we parted on relatively good terms.

However the difficult bit was still to come.

It's hard to imagine now, but Ireland in 1985 was still stuck in a pre-war time warp. It was a land of priests, formidable gossiping matrons and ploughs. Forget mobiles and fax machines, the telephone had yet to arrive. The only way they did business was face to face, but no one was ever where they were supposed to be. You'd arrive in the town clerk's office to find it empty, no sign of the man himself and his secretary would never be at her desk. If you were lucky you'd bump into someone in the corridor to be told in a tone of shock, 'Oh no, he would never be here at this time of the morning. He'll be having coffee with Farmer O'Hara at the second farm on the left after the hill.'

I remember calling in at a police station in Tipperary. It was completely empty – the only thing behind the desk was a rack of guns for any old Tom, Dick or Paddy to help themselves to at their leisure. So as you can imagine booking sites was a long drawn-out frustrating process.

Worse was to come. The Hazzard brothers were our clowns for the season and very good they were too, in fact I'm not sure they're not the best pair of clowns I've ever had. Perry was the son of the famous actor Michael Balfour and the grandson of Lady Balfour. Michael was a GP's son from Kingston. From an early age Perry had been taken by his dad round hospitals to entertain the patients. He developed a little clowning routine with his mate Michael. They went off to public school and had an educated sophistication that is very rare in a clown. They were very very funny. Perry's facial expressions were side splitting, Michael was the perfect stooge. After school they'd fallen into this hippy clowning set, performed at the first Glastonbury, and spent a lot of time following the sun around small villages in northern Spain in a rainbow-coloured van. They were great fun – Perry was forever having impromptu late-night parties. Chris Barltrop found him one morning still drunk from the night before dancing naked to the Gypsy Kings. They really helped cheer me up those horrible first few weeks in Ireland. The grand finale of their routine was hypnotising a chicken. It never went quite right. The chicken either wouldn't wake up properly and career wildly round the ring totally disorientated or do a runner and escape into the audience. Our horse act was next and they used to get distracted by this squawking chicken and try to find it, nosing under the audience's seats and hitting people with their feather headdresses. Sometimes it was hilarious and sometimes it was plain embarrassing. One day Michael came to see me.

'Gerry. We've got to leave. It's the weather, it's so depressing. I can't stand it any more. My wife's French, she's going to leave me if we don't get her out of the rain.'

'Please don't go. We really need you here. Just stick it out for another few weeks. I'm sure the weather will cheer up.'

But a week later the Hazards just upped and left.

Then tragedy struck.

Our star act in Ireland was Yasmine Smart and her beautiful Arabian horses. Yasmine was the granddaughter of the late Billy Smart who had made a fortune with funfairs. Old Billy had always had a passion for circuses and started his own in 1946. Betty's aunt remembers the day he turned up at the Fossetts and bought their three elephants. A charismatic man never without his Stetson and cigar, he paid for the whole lot in cash. The Fossetts were impressed. His circus went on to be massively successful – very cleverly Billy Smart saw the potential of television and while Bertram Mills' refused to get involved with the new medium and ended up closing, television made Smart's. Although Billy had a huge family – sixteen grandchildren I think – only two of them, Billy Wilson and Yasmine, stayed in the circus. Yasmine is a lovely lady dedicated to her beautiful horses. Later on she toured with the best circus in Europe, Roncalli, and is now with the Big Apple Circus in New York. Yasmine and her eight horses were definitely our star act. But one night as we crossed the border into the Republic of Ireland, one of the horses got colic. By the side of the road, working by torchlight in the rain, the vet gave the horse an overdose. The beautiful animal became very ill very quickly and by the end of the night had died. It was very shocking to watch such a beautiful healthy animal die in such a horrible way. Yasmine was inconsolable and left us soon after. I began to feel we were cursed. But Tommy Duffy very kindly lent me some of his horses, which Sarah presented and we struggled on.

Then a week later Chris Barltrop came to see me.

'I want to hand in my resignation.'

'Oh no, Chris. Are you serious?'

'Yes, Gerry, I need to go.'

'I can understand why you want to leave, but are you sure?'

'Yes. I'm sorry, Gerry. I don't want to let you down, but I really need a change.'

I was shocked, but I couldn't blame him. Chris and his wife Barbara had always been very loyal and held everything together while I'd been behaving badly. Sometimes I ask people why they are leaving, sometimes I don't. I didn't ask Chris – in view of my recent behaviour I was afraid what the answer might be. Years later Chris told me he simply wanted more money. I was astounded, 'Chris, why didn't you just ask me? If you had asked I would have given it to you.' Which shows perhaps you should always try to find out why people are leaving.

Very down and unsure what to do next I flew back to Britain for the weekend. Joe Gandey's Circus, now run by his younger son Phillip, was just down the road. I decided to pop in and be sociable. But it was a bit early in the morning – seven to be precise. There was one person up and working hard, that was Martin Lacey, their manager. Being an early riser myself, I thought, this is the man for me. Right there and then I offered him Chris' job. He accepted and handed Gandey his notice that night. Phillip was absolutely furious and instead of making him work out his notice told him he could sling his hook straight away. This made up my mind. With Martin and his marvellous pride of performing lions with nothing to do on the other side of the Irish Sea, I packed up what remained of my circus and came back to England. We managed to book good sites in the Wirral, Manchester and Sheffield through late September, and made a fortune. I was astonished and quickly got on my enormous mobile phone to book some more sites. We toured all over the north-west of England that autumn and had a fantastic run. Within three months I had paid off all my debts and was back on even keel.

Hearing I was back in business and doing well, Brian Austen came to see me. He'd booked Battersea Park for a four-week Christmas run, but his brothers were refusing to do it. 'They think it's too risky.'

'Well, I can see their point, Brian. I've had some disastrous Christmases. The tradition of the Christmas circus is dead. So many people leave London for Christmas and the ones that are left, well, they're too busy shopping or going to see *Babes in the Wood*.'

'So you don't fancy getting together and doing a joint Cottle and Austen's Circus?'

'No.'

'Do you know how long it is since there's been a circus in Battersea Park? I think there would be a lot of people who would jump at the chance to do something different for Christmas. As long as we keep it cheap and cheerful we could make a nice little profit. Think, Gerry, we can have the Austen Brothers' elephants, your children performing, Martin Lacey's lions, the Fossett Sisters reformed, and my manager Larry de Wit on the trapeze. We're practically there. What could go wrong?'

I was not convinced, but I had great faith in Brian's judgement. I agreed to give it a go. From the 1 December I had a team of sixteen boys putting up posters all over London, and just as Brian predicted we did really well.

For the next couple of years I spent the summers touring as Gerry Cottle's Circus and then got together with Brian to do Christmas at Battersea as a joint Cottle and Austen's show. Then in 1988, as well as doing Battersea, we also put on a show at Wembley. It was a terrific success. The next year Brian sold me the Austen Brothers Circus to concentrate on his tent business. (It is at this point that I would like to highlight a major difference between Brian and I. While I always ploughed any profit back into circuses, Brian very cleverly used his profits to develop more stable businesses, so when circus went wrong he still had other enterprises to fall back on. He started off in tent and seat hire and became Britain's largest business in that area, supplying nearly all major national events, like the Royal Tournament. Now he has the most amazing portfolio, which includes a second-hand helicopter company, an airfield and a fully-fledged industrial estate developed from our original headquarters at Cricklade. Brian is now a rich man. I am not. Enough said.)

Included in the package Brian sold me were Sarah, Jane and Suzy, the first-ever elephants I had bought for Cottle and Austen's Circus. We were chuffed to have them back. Once again I had two Gerry Cottle's circuses touring Britain, with Martin Lacey managing one and Chris Barltrop back with me managing the other. We divided them into Gerry Cottle's lion unit and the Gerry Cottle's tiger unit, but we found people thought they were one and the same show so the tiger unit became Circus Berlin. Those were good years, like the 70s all over again. With my two circuses I was Britain's biggest and best again. This time my success lasted longer. I was much more commercially aware this time and took fewer risks. At the same time it was less exciting, less satisfying than the glory years of the mid 70s, I think because my public success was clouded by the mess my private life was in – but more of that later.

Just writing this I can see you must be wondering how we suddenly started to make money again with a traditional circus. The answer is I turned to the oldest trick in the book – publicity. Now PR was one thing I always thought I was pretty good at, but it turned out there was still room to go up a few gears. I made three discoveries and, at the risk of giving away a few trade secrets, I'm going to share them with you:

1. It helps to employ a manager who has a nose for publicity
I think publicity is a thing you either 'get' or you don't. Martin Lacey did get it. It was a bit of a surprise really because more than anything else Martin was obsessed with his animals. He had a most beautiful set of lions which he spent a lot of time breeding. There were lion cubs everywhere which he lent to people who never gave them back, or sold to people who didn't pay. Sometimes he even gave them away. Likewise he was always having children. At the last count he'd had four wives and eight children. A lot of his time was spent fighting the animal protestors. He'd be on to the police about not arresting them, writing letters to newspapers and sticking up posters putting the case for animals. I'm not sure that it wouldn't have been better to keep a lower profile but that was his way.

Despite these distractions, Martin understood and put a lot of effort into getting us into the papers for the right reasons. One day he rounded up the press after an elephant was suspected of having swallowed a metal padlock. He called in the Royal Engineers, got the elephant to lie down and then asked them to pass their mine-sweeping equipment over him. It was such good publicity that we did it in four different regions in one year.

Likewise it helps if your manager's wife understands publicity too. Martin's then wife Sue was gorgeous. Pretty with so much personality it was fairly bursting out of her tiny frame. She was bringing up three sons but still found time to be trained with Martin's tigers. A man in a cage with tigers, well that's old news. A woman with a pride of tigers, a tiny beautiful woman, well that's something else. As far as we knew there was no other woman tiger trainer in the world, and we used that fact liberally. Despite the fact she had almost no experience with the tigers, Sue launched Cottle and Austen's Christmas Circus at Battersea as our headline act. She was an overnight sensation. Not only did every woman's page and magazine want to meet her, but she made the front page of *The Sunday Times* with the most spectacular photograph of two enormous tigers jumping over her head. (Unfortunately Sue and Martin split up a few years later, but Sue has gone on to travel the world with her sensational lion and tiger act.)

2. Get yourself a super-hot PR man

I was Mark Borkowski's second client. His first was an old man called Marcus who was famous for running 'The Smallest Theatre in the World' – it was the sidecar on his motorbike, but, as he's now dead, I have the honour of being Mark's oldest client. He was only twenty-five when I was introduced to him by Robbie Barnett, the clown and stilt walker. There was instant chemistry between us. If he had been a woman it would have been love at first sight, but let's just say I liked the cut of his jib. For a start he managed to look both smart and flamboyant at the same time, floppy hair, bow ties, trendy suits, you get the picture. Then as soon as he began to talk, lots of wacky different ideas just came pouring out. Mark loved showbiz. He loved taking risks, he had lots of ambition. He said that after God made me he trashed the mould. The feeling was mutual. It was a match made in heaven.

The first thing he did was raise my profile. Within months of meeting Mark, I had appeared on *Desert Island Discs*, *Wogan* and *Jim'll Fix It*. He organised a constant stream of articles in the broadsheet newspapers and Sunday magazines. I penned treatises on the animal question, the future of circus or even my favourite, the crippling effect of VAT on the entertainment business.

Secondly he introduced me to the idea of securing advance publicity for a new show by organising a press outing. The first time I tried this I took ten journalists, including Val Hennessy from the *Daily Mail*, Peter Gruner from the *Evening Standard* and Steve Grant from *Time Out* to la Foire Extraordinaire in the Pyrenees, supposedly the biggest gathering of alternative circus in the world, and hosted by the Hazzard brothers (they had agreed to take a chance with the London climate and come back for the next season). In reality the trip was a complete farce from start to finish. When we arrived at Toulouse airport there were two battered old Peugeots waiting for us. Unfortunately no one knew where we were going. I had to hold the door of the car shut otherwise it would have fallen off and was laughing so much that I blew my nose on the map, which was written on a Kleenex tissue. We followed signs to a circus and ended up at a completely unconnected small family circus. We were offered a drink in an old gypsy caravan where poor Peter Gruner was wrestled to the floor and kissed by an exceptionally drunk gay strongman. When we finally extracted ourselves and found the festival it was a bit like a little Glastonbury without the pop music. Steve Grant described it in *Time Out* as 'Crufts on Acid'. It was all a bit of a strange hippy shambles – the Hazzard brothers had even forgotten to book us any accommodation, so we ended up like Mary and Joseph banging on inn doors only to be given a stable at the back. Poor Peter had to sleep on a haystack in a barn. He woke up in the morning to find a man in a gorilla costume snuggled up to him. But everyone seemed to have a great time and we had great write-ups. I came to the conclusion that as long as you keep journalists well fed and watered, and don't take yourself too seriously, they have a good time and write helpful things about you.

Sometimes you can try to be too clever.

We took a group out to Belgium to meet two Argentinian brothers who rode motorbikes in the Globe of Death. It was a stunning act (think Elvis Presley in *Roustabout*). They rode their bikes at each other at perpendicular angles, criss-crossing at a speed of thirty-five miles an hour in a tiny cage. The noise was phenomenal and it was unbelievably dangerous. But the story had a delightful twist. The brothers had fallen out since they met two beautiful backpacking Swedes. One of them had made at a pass at the other one's Swede. Apparently they weren't speaking, but maybe it wasn't as bad as all that. We put them in separate restaurants on the opposite side of Brussels, because, as we explained to the journalists, they couldn't stand to be in the same room – incredible when every night their lives were in each others' hands in the same Globe of Death! It all went horribly wrong. The humourless pair couldn't speak English and the Swedish backpackers were translating. They just didn't get the gag and denied the whole story. It was very embarrassing, but Mark just shrugged it off as lost in translation so the story made it into the papers anyway.

We had more luck with the man in the bottle. Hugo Zamoratte was an enormously tall South American man who could do all manner of contortions, but the climax of his act was when he managed to squeeze himself into a tiny bottle. Mark had dreamed up the idea that while we had all heard of escapology (Houdini etc), Zamoratte was the first professional '*enterologist*' to come to Britain – ie someone who manages to get *into* things rather than *out* of them. Of course he was just a very good contortionist, but it was a good line. We managed to get a number of excellent journalists together and flew them out to the prestigious Royal Hanneford Circus in St Paul, Minneapolis, to see Zamoratte in action. Unfortunately someone had neglected to tell the owner, Tommy Hanneford, that Zamoratte was leaving, so when we turned up with twelve journalists he wasn't too happy. While Mark distracted the media posse with Hanneford's star attraction, I managed to placate Hanneford himself. At the last moment we also realised that Zamoratte had no idea that he was supposed to pretend he was the world's leading enterologist. I'd dashed off to Zamoratte's caravan only to find he spoke virtually no English except what he had manage to teach himself from a second-hand correspondence course he'd picked up in a junk shop in Buenos Aires. (It was noted during his stay with us, the harder he worked on the course the worse his English got). Anyway I don't think he really ever got the concept of enterology but Zamoratte was such a pro, a real camp showman who loved an audience, we somehow pulled it off. There was a great moment when

Mark told the journalists that Zamoratte had escaped into the US from Mexico by squeezing through a drainpipie. 'Si, Si,' he nodded gravely, and sucked in his cheeks.

The third area in which Mark excelled was the publicity stunt. Of course there are plenty of straightforward spectacular publicity stunts you can do with a circus – our first year at Wembley we organised a wire walk between the twin towers. Boy, was it frightening. Our wire walker was a French boy, Didier Pasquette, who had grown up in an ordinary suburban middle-class family on the outskirts of Paris. He'd gone off to circus school and come out the most amazing tight-rope walker, afraid of nothing. He was dead keen to have a go at Wembley. The rigging was very complicated – it was such a long distance between the towers we had to have extra stays secured by water skips. As he started walking the stays pulled and the wire wobbled horribly. He seemed to be losing his balance. No safety nets here. I couldn't watch, but I couldn't take my eyes off him either. It was a truly horrible moment. But suddenly he collected himself, regained his balance and walked the rest of the wire as if he was strolling down the street. Didier went on to walk across the Thames from the South Bank to the Embankment, he was a great showman.

That's the straightforward publicity stunt. Mark's talent was coming up with the more unusual gag. If you managed to tickle his imagination anything was possible. When Zamoratte arrived in London, Mark had the bright idea of taking him into the Savoy Hotel in the bottle. He was thrown out, not for being inside a bottle, but because he wasn't wearing a tie! We got a four-page spread in the *Mirror* out of that. Probably our most successful publicity stunt was the arrival of our black lady clown at Heathrow. I had heard on the grapevine about Danise Payne, a very successful clown in her native California. I thought she'd have great novelty value at least, but Mark spotted that we could do something a bit cleverer. Her arrival happened to coincide with a huge row over the States putting a trade embargo on European goods. It was also a time when a series of British actors had been picked to play lead roles in Hollywood blockbusters and American actors were going on strike in protest. Before I knew it

Mark had whipped up a mass protest from a group of our homegrown clowns. The morning Danise was flying in, I found myself on Radio 4's *Today* programme defending free trade. Meanwhile when I arrived at Heathrow there was a really charged atmosphere. I couldn't believe my luck. On the one hand there was the most amazing gathering of media – twenty-seven TV crews from across the world, at least ten newspapers, photographers everywhere, on the other were at least thirty clowns in all shapes and sizes with placards saying 'Yankee clown go home', 'What's wrong with English clowns?' 'It's not funny to take my job'. Among them I noticed a few clowns I'd never seen before.

'Who's the midget?' I asked an old clowning friend of mine.

'Oh, that's my mate, Dave. He's a gardener at Crystal Palace but he's got the day off.'

The midget looked fantastically realistic, complete with white face, red nose and orange wig. Of course he was the one all the TV reporters wanted to talk to. I was a bit nervous. 'How do you feel about this lady coming over and taking your job?' they asked him.

'Absolutely outraged. It's a disgrace. How can Gerry Cottle sleep at night?' the little man seethed perfectly on message.

Meanwhile I got a huge custard pie in the face mid-interview with the BBC. It was beyond my wildest dreams. At last the long-awaited passengers started to come through. One of the first was a huge jolly black lady wearing a hat and loud floral dress. Everybody lunged forwards and started sticking microphones in her face. The protestors hurled insults and threw custard pies. Of course we only realised when it was too late that this was not Danise, just an ordinary member of the public in the wrong place at the wrong time. But we got the most amazing amount of coverage. The chief press officer at Heathrow said we had got more press than when Madonna had gone through the week before.

3. Find yourself a friendly celebrity

Jeremy Beadle came and introduced himself during our Christmas run at Wembley. He had taken his two lively daughters, Bonnie and Cassie, to see the circus. I invited them back to my wagon where they played havoc with Betty's ornaments. It was the beginning of a long friend-ship. It turned out he was a great fan of circus, in fact of all forms of entertainment. I admired Jeremy's intelligence (a member of Mensa no less) and knowledge. We became great friends and I asked him whether he fancied having a go at being a Ringmaster. Despite being at the peak of his popularity (remember *You've Been Framed* and *Beadle's About?*) he joined us for a four-week run the next year at Wembley.

He was a natural. Great charisma and fun to work with, he was quite happy to get stuck in – running around with the clowns, being stepped over by the elephants and having knives thrown at him. I noticed how he made a point of finding out and remembering every-one's names. He would always say hello to the tent men. People liked him. He had a great nose for entertainment. It was his suggestion that we got a look-a-like of the Queen to sit in the audience. Every night during the interval Jeremy would lead her in followed by a couple of the tent men dressed as bodyguards. She would sit complete with tiara through the second half, but we used to let her go just before the end. She'd put on her head scarf and one of the men would give her a lift down to Wembley Park tube station so she wouldn't get caught by any of the audience leaving early. Unfortunately if her train was late she'd still be standing on the platform, in full royal regalia underneath her green Barbour and Hermes headscarf, when the punters poured on to the platform. We had a great laugh with her. People would ring and ask if the queen was going to be in again tonight because they wanted to see her. There was a hard core of patriots who would come every night just to get a glimpse of her majesty. Then there was a right royal pain of a health and safety inspector at Wembley who made a habit of deliberately trying to catch me out. Then he asked if he could have his photo taken with Her Majesty. We organised it, sent it to his office and never heard from him again!

Jeremy is incredibly gregarious. After this first Wembley gig we toured the country, Jeremy often agreeing to be ringmaster at his own expense for charity. (I used to do quite a lot of charity shows mainly for the Children with Leukaemia charity.) After the show, Jeremy always wanted to go out on the razz with the crew. Can you imagine being with Jeremy Beadle in the early 90s in Liverpool city centre late on a Saturday night? It was terrifying, everybody wanted to take a pop at him. Then I remember relaxing in the bar at a very posh hotel after a charity gig in Newcastle. We could hear a terrible row in reception.

'I have spent a fortune booking a room in your so-called top quality hotel and then my car gets stolen in the hotel car park. I mean, you are supposed to have security, aren't you? You have a man on the gate. What was he doing when someone drove off with my car? How can this have happened, tell me that?'

On and on the poor man ranted. The receptionist looked mortified. It was getting very nasty out there when suddenly the man caught sight of Jeremy.

'Beadle! Just tell me you've put the car on the roof or in the river or something.'

'I'm sorry, Sir. But I have had nothing to do with your car.'

'No really, it's OK. I don't mind. Just tell me where you put it. Great joke.'

It was excruciating – the poor man could not be persuaded that Jeremy had had nothing to do with his disappearing car.

So I was having great success with my traditional circus, but was I having a great time? I still felt unsatisfied. I wasn't content to have Britian's biggest and best circuses, I wanted to be a great all-round showman. I largely left the circuses in the hands of my very capable managers, Chris and Martin, and went off looking for the Next Big Thing. You wouldn't believe the number of things I tried. Let me tell you about just a few of them.

For thirteen years I part-owned a joke shop in Chiswick. The other partner was Max Butler. He was like the Graham Norton of his time. He was a gay, funny and quick-witted man, who had found early fame as a boy juggler on Irish TV and then joined the circus. He had a passion for Circus Ladies of Mature Years (purely platonic of course). Every so often he would go off to America for a few months to pay his respects to his favourite retired showgirls, who made a great fuss of him. It was a bit of a pain, but he did come back with some great ideas for the circus including Zamoratte and the black lady clown. He made a living touring the Masonic lodges, doing a bit of fire eating, a bit of juggling and a bit of cabaret, and hiring out small troupes of showgirl dancers. Max had supplied me with the showgirls for Oman and Hong Kong and we became great pals. He came to me with the idea of a costume shop selling jokes. It rather appealed so I put up the money and we found great little premises right on Chiswick High Road. When young Billy Smart sold us his old costumes he seemed uncomfortable with gay men, so Max would put on a wig and camp it up for him, 'Come on, Gerry, come over here and give me a kiss.' We called the shop 'Joker' and it immediately had a great atmosphere. All the locals used to call in for a chat; we used to send in acts from the circus for special promotions, Barry Walls doing card tricks or Sonny Fossett clowning to entertain the children. One Christmas we dressed twenty of the circus men in Santa suits and had them crossing and recrossing Chiswick High Road outside the shop. It had a flat upstairs which I used to retreat to when home got too much, and a local police chief borrowed to woo his girlfriend.

The shop gave me a bit of pocket money during the lean years, but we were never going to make a fortune. Max was too much of a character. He could be horribly rude to the customers. He wore a T-shirt with 'Gerry Who?' written on it, because he got so sick of friends of mine coming in and asking for favours. At one point he hired another gay manager called Fred with whom he bickered incessantly. Fred finally stormed off in a huff and opened his own joke shop in Camden, which made a fortune. Our finances weren't helped by the fact that Max had a little dog called Toddles which he insisted on taking for a walk four times a day, shutting the shop every time.

And then in 1989 I bought myself a swimming pool.

Don Robinson had been a wrestler and then went on to be a highly successful businessman. One of his sidelines was outdoor lidos. He ran thirty across the country but he just couldn't get the Wandsworth Lido in London to work. He rang me up and offered to sell me the lease from the council for a song. It seemed too good an opportunity to pass up. The summer of 1989 I worked very hard making the Big Splash. I put in high diving boards, crazy mirrors outside the changing rooms and a brand-new restaurant serving posh quiche. I got old Uncle Sonny Fossett clowning around the pool until he admitted he couldn't swim. I organised an underwater concert with Danny Baker. But it soon became clear that no matter what you did, the only thing that made any difference was the weather. The lido was empty until the sun shone and then everyone came mob handed. We had to employ security guards on hot days. One hot day Bob Geldof turned up with Paula Yates and two of his girls. I sent a message, 'Would he like a bit of security?' he politely declined and within ten minutes was thrown in by the locals.

After a couple of months there I knew the business didn't work as it was, but I thought if I could build a gym on to the changing rooms there might be a way of making money even when the sun wasn't shining. I applied to the council but they turned me down. Then towards the end of the season the council tested the water and found it below standard and gave me a fine. I was surprised, our own tests showed it to be clear. So I sent a sample off to a private laboratory – the results came back completely clear. I was totally cheesed off with the way the council had been so obstructive, so I gave the lido back to the council. They didn't want it but I'd had enough.

You know how I like to have the biggest of everything? Well in 1990 I bought myself the world's longest limo. It was a seventy-one-foot Cadillac made in California with eighteen wheels, weighing more than seven tons, and came equipped with a Jacuzzi bar with space for twenty people, three telephones, a television, video and sun deck. The only problem was you couldn't drive it.

It had been built by a Finnish pickled-herring baron called Henry for half a million dollars after he'd been released from a mental asylum. I had heard it was languishing in a lock-up in a bonded warehouse in Hamburg so I hired it to sit outside the circus at Wembley in 1990. It was quite an attraction and the Ideal Home exhibition contacted me about hiring it for £6,000 for the week. I asked the owner if he was willing to sell. Henry wasn't. But he was a big drinker, so I took him out for a long lunch and asked him again. This time he agreed to sell it to me for £60,000.

The day came for the launch. I called a press conference and took interviews sat in the Jacuzzi with a beautiful model on one arm and a glass of champagne in the other. One of the photographers shouted out ''Ere Gerry, have you seen who's on the front page of Penthouse magazine?' Mark dashed across to the newsagent. Of course I had my arm around a famous topless page three girl. Fun for me, but not quite the 'top family entertainment', 'hire us for your church fête' message we were trying to convey ...

The limo just about earned its keep being hired out at weekends. Patrick Austen was in charge. He built a special trailer and went off round the country to galas and fairs, although it once brought the whole of the South Circular to a halt for four hours on a Sunday evening when it couldn't get past roadworks.

I even took a big aquarium around the fairs of Ireland. Imagine driving round with a trailer filled with fifty tons of water and full of sharks. Not an overwhelming success.

As you can see, although I had two big successful circuses, I was restless and bored. And my attempts to find the Next Big Thing didn't seem to be getting anywhere. I was frustrated – a dangerous state for me.

So despite all my best intentions, I had relapsed. I was back taking cocaine. Quite quickly in fact. I had been fine in Ireland – let's face it, I didn't have much choice. But when I'd got back to England, once the circus was up and running, the temptation to go and visit my old friends was too much. Betty could tell I was up to my old tricks.

'What are you doing, Gerry? I thought you'd learnt your lesson. Please don't do this to me. I can't bear it.'

'It's just the once, Betty. I promise I will never do it again. Remember how they told us at the clinic that it was very likely I would have a couple of relapses but that wouldn't mean I was addicted again. And I'm not. I promise.'

And in some ways they were right. The crazy thing was I could go for long periods of time without cocaine. Three months, six months, once even a year. I was never addicted in the way I had been that first terrible year. Then I really had been a man possessed, crazy and dangerous. Now, my drug use developed a pattern which made me feel I was more in control and affected my business less. I confined my narcotic activities to school holidays. I was very organised and kept my diary clear. Come the end of the school term, Betty and the children would go and join the circus, and I would clear my desk, raid my safe and go into London for a couple of weeks. But please don't get the wrong impression, just because there was some method in my madness, doesn't mean it wasn't mad all the same.

For instance, one hot stuffy summer's night in 1990 I was at a big charity function at the Grosvenor Hotel with Jeremy Beadle. I find it difficult on occasions like that because I don't drink. I decided to go for a walk and grab some fresh air. Meandering along Park Lane, not really looking where I was going, I bumped into a lady – let's call her Faith – we got chatting as you do, or as I do anyway. Once you have been an addict you can spot another addict from a mile off. We swapped telephone numbers and I went back to the party.

A few days later, I gave her a ring. We instantly became partners in crime. She was a bad influence on me, well maybe we brought out the worst in each other. She was a naughty girl, addicted to everything that was bad for her (she had been to a strict convent girls' school, maybe that has something to do with it). I wasn't in love with her the way I had been with Kerry. She certainly wasn't beautiful (she had been addicted for twenty-six years and that takes a toll on your looks, believe me), but we just got on really well. We would talk for hours. I would do cosy domestic things I never allowed myself the time to do at home, like spend whole afternoons watching Wimbledon on the telly. But living with a junkie can never be that normal. Faith was very impulsive – she would insist on taking her Rottweiler for a walk at one in the morning, throwing sticks for him, shouting and waking the neighbours. Her father had been high up in the forces and she had wealthy relations. One day she was left £5,000 by a rich old aunt, which she decided to cash and spend all in one night with me. She marched into the Sheraton at Heathrow and loudly announced to the whole world, 'I'm taking my friend out. He's always been good to me but now I've got some money, I'm going to treat him.' I wanted the ground to swallow me up. We did manage to spend the whole lot in one night. Goodness knows how, my memory is a blank.

That was just it. I kidded myself my habit was under control, but it was classic junkie self-delusion. Just because I used less, didn't mean I wasn't still playing an incredibly dangerous and destructive game.

Bored and lonely one night that summer, I had a wake-up call. I was home alone at Addlestone, very unusual for me. Betty and the children were down with the circus in the West Country. I was stuck in the office trying to deal with tedious council problems. I couldn't sleep so I went for a walk along by the river at the bottom of our land and took some cocaine which I mixed with some water from the river. It must have been dirty water, I certainly didn't feel too good afterwards. The next day I drove down to see the family in Torquay, but I wasn't myself. I sat outside the caravan in a deckchair and drank loads and loads of orange juice. I just couldn't quench my thirst, I felt listless and sleepy, I hadn't been to the loo for a couple of days. Nothing was coming out the other end. Instead I seemed to be swelling up. My animal trainer Marcel drove Betty and I straight back to Addlestone and called the doctor. He took one look at me and called an ambulance. I was rushed to St Peters Hospital in Chertsey. They immediately stuck two tubes in my neck. One of my kidneys had failed. Waiting outside the room, Betty asked the doctor, 'He is going to be all right, isn't he?'

'If everything goes very well, but he is very ill. I'd say he's got a 50:50 chance.'

'A 50:50 chance of what?'

'Of pulling through.'

Betty went back into my room. I was lying in the bed, still conscious but with two tubes through my neck. I was in tears, 'I don't want to die.'

'Well you've got to stop taking those wretched drugs, haven't you? Maybe this time you will be all right. But if you carry on taking cocaine, one day you will die. Of that I am absolutely certain. Let this be a lesson to you.' Betty was terrified and livid in equal measure.

I struggled through the night slipping in and out of consciousness. In the morning they decided my condition was critical. I was put in an ambulance and driven at high speed to St Thomas' Hospital in London. Betty said she knew it was serious when she saw a nurse and a doctor getting into the ambulance.

'Surely it's not necessary to have all the sirens and flashing business?' I asked the nurse.

'We're not taking you to London for fun, you know,' she snapped at me.

After a couple of days my condition started to stabilise. Of course all the hospital staff knew exactly what my problem was. My nurse in St Thomas' made it quite clear what she thought, 'You are very lucky to be here at all. When you arrived it could have gone either way. I hope that makes you think more carefully about what you do in future, Mr Cottle.'

I certainly had plenty of time to think, stuck in bed with two tubes through my neck. After the fear of actually dying subsided I was left feeling acutely embarrassed. Everyone knew why I was there. I felt such a fool. I was stuck on dialysis in St Thomas' for a whole month, and just to push the lesson home the world's first ever Festival of Circus had opened on the South Bank right opposite. I was only able to gaze at it wistfully through the window. I vowed I would never do drugs again.

Well that didn't last for long. It will seem amazing to you, it seems amazing to me writing this now, but it didn't stop me for long. I just took more care. Certainly more care in how I took them. My next lesson took a different form.

In the summer of 1991, Faith had gone away and my usual supplier had also unexpectedly gone away. Of course I should have gone away too. Instead I hung around the pub in Shepherds Bush trying to organise a different supply. I was frightened of being left without access to any cocaine (you see how addicted I still was?). This pub has now been turned into a trendy gastro pub filled with BBC employees on their lunch break. In the early 1990s it was full of West London 'characters'. There was the posh burglar called 'Posh', the postman called 'Pat' and the Australian called 'Skippy'. They would spend a lot of time comparing notes on their experiences 'inside'. I was in the pub one night when one of the group was having a goodbye party – he was on bail and about to be sentenced the next day. He reckoned it was his last bash before he was off to the scrubs for a couple of years. 'Oh, I don't mind,' he kept saying, 'My mate Trevor is in there.' It scared me, but I didn't think I could end up in that position. I thought I was much cleverer than that. I was a successful middle–class business-man for a start.

It took me a surprisingly long time, but I managed to order four-teen grams of cocaine from a cousin of a cousin. I went along to the pub to pick it up at the allotted time, but I was a bit annoyed and a lit-tle concerned when they told me I would have to go to a house across the road to pick it up. I was ushered into the room full of heav-ies and given fourteen ounces. I was horrified.

'Oh no. There's been a mistake. I only wanted fourteen grams.'

The boys were not amused.

Let me put this in context. Most people would only ever use one or two grams a night, so if you are caught with over two ounces you will be taken for a dealer. Even fourteen grams and you look like a bit of a dealer. I had ordered enough to last me for the rest of the summer holidays while the family were away. I didn't want to keep risking get-ting supplies, but then again I didn't want fourteen ounces on me. Thankfully I had enough sense, despite huge pressure, not to take the fourteen ounces and left with my clutch of small packets – in total fourteen grams.

I drove straight home to the farm. All the way I felt uneasy. Something wasn't right about the whole incident. As I pulled off the M25 at Addlestone, I noticed a police car behind me. He signalled for me to stop.

'We have reason to suspect you are carrying drugs,' he said. I hadn't noticed but they'd followed me all the way from London. I had hid-den the cocaine in my usual place in the car, but I didn't see any point in trying to deny it. I gave the police the bag. I was immediately arrested and spent the night in Addlestone jail. It was only the second night I had ever spent inside. The first was when the police had taken pity on me when I was stuck without a bed for a night putting up posters for Joe Gandey's Circus. That night I didn't sleep a wink, it was cold, damp and noisy and the bed was hard, and this night was the same. I felt so stupid.

The next day I was let out on bail. I was on my own at the farm with only my assistant Anne for company. I telephoned Betty. 'It's your own stupid fault,' she said and wouldn't have anything to do with me. The press had been tipped off and were lurking round outside the farm but Anne managed to keep them at bay. Mark pulled a few favours and it stayed out of the papers until our circus was at Wembley for Christmas.

But in that funny way that stories do, they wait in journalists' files until suddenly they have their moment – maybe something happens that makes them more sexy, maybe it's just a quiet news day. Going to Wembley, and all the big publicity we generated, finally sparked a rash of stories about my upcoming trial. Capital Radio immediately cancelled their sponsorship of the circus. Funny really when you consider how many pop stars use drugs and yet it never stops them playing their records. Someone who did stick by me was Jeremy Beadle. He told me I'd been stupid, but he carried on as Ringmaster. I was grateful for his support.

Another friend who was a great help was Michael Hurll. As soon as it hit the papers he rang me, 'Gerry, you are an old friend. If you don't do what I tell you, I will never speak to you again. I know a man who can get you out of trouble.'

He gave me the number of a solicitor, Henri Brandman, who was renowned for working with the boxing and entertainment worlds. Henri was a charming, extremely courteous character, but what he said at that first meeting chilled me to the bone. 'I've been making some enquiries. It's looking quite serious for you. Even with fourteen grams you could be looking at between four and ten years. I think we should get George Carman on the case.'

I knew I was in deep trouble and I knew it was all I deserved – but four to ten years? I never imagined it was that bad. It was as if this was happening to someone else. I didn't really think I would get sent to jail. I wasn't like that. And George Carmen? He was the famous barrister – famous for taking on the most impossible cases and winning.

A few weeks later I went for my next visit with Henri. This time he was a bit more cheery. 'I've been making a few more enquiries and I think I've come up with a plan. For a start we shouldn't hire George Carmen. You would just look very guilty. Instead we should plead guilty and get the case heard in the local magistrates' court with a bench made up of the respectable ladies and gentlemen of Chertsey. Let's get a nice local barrister and put forwards the fact that you do a lot for the community and it's a first offence. Perhaps if you also helped them with some of their enquiries, I think there is a good chance you could avoid going to jail.'

It sounded like a good plan.

I remember the morning of my court appearance, 14 January 1992. As I got dressed I told Betty to pack a small a bag with my toothbrush in case I didn't come home. She packed my bag but refused point blank to come to court.

'No I bloody won't,' she snapped.

I was nervous. In fact I was shaking. The hearing took place as planned in the magistrates' court in a very unprepossessing 60s building. The corridor outside the courts was full of the usual eclectic mix of petty shoplifters, respectable middle-aged men up for speeding and the odd more hardened criminal, although you don't get many of those in Surrey. In fact I was just about as exciting as it gets down there. There was a little gaggle of press waiting for me.

'Hello, Gerry. All right?' the local press photographer asked.

Of course there were the counsels as well, having a last-minute word with their clients. I had Henri, my barrister and Mark Borkowski. Henri felt quietly confident. I felt like it wasn't really happening to me. The wait was interminable especially as I turned up early as I always do. Finally my case was called. I went in to face four magistrates – one man and three ladies who looked like my mother.

The atmosphere was electric. This was a big deal for this little court. The Crown Prosecution Service were in high spirits. They were looking forwards to the case being referred up to the Crown Court, a nice juicy public trial and celebrity conviction. They wanted to make an example of me, and who can blame them? This was a time when public anxiety and debate about the growing use of class A drugs was running high.

I tried not to look at the bench. I had been in court a couple of times before for speeding and I felt there was no point trying to catch their eye, it could backfire. Then it was my turn to say my piece.

'I've been through some tough times with the circus and I went the wrong way. I am very sorry for what I have done, especially the hurt I have caused to my family.'

The CPS put their case, they were a bit cocky. They made it clear they thought this was just a formality. My barrister got up to speak. This dashing forty-something looked the ladies straight in the eye and made a surprise opening gambit:

'It is difficult to comprehend how arrogant the Crown Prosecution Service can be, to think you don't have the ability to judge this case,' he began.

You could almost see their breasts swelling with righteous indignation and pride.

He went on in this vein, finishing his speech with a plea for mercy, saying that my behaviour was an aberration caused by the most terrible stress and I had learnt my lesson and I would never ever do it again.

His tactics were spot on. The noble magistrates of Surrey didn't like being patronised by the CPS and were determined to teach them, rather than me, a lesson. I stood up to hear the judgement.

'Mr Cottle, you have acted disgracefully especially for a man who runs a family entertainment business. You have caused great distress to your family. However we believe that in view of your previous good character you are unlikely to offend again. If you do, it will be taken very very seriously. In the meantime you will be fined £500.'

The only way to describe the CPS was gobsmacked. They could not believe I had got off the hook. For me the relief was immense, obviously. I think it was only at that moment that I really realised how much the case had been looming over me. It was a burden lifted from my shoulders. I skipped out of court a lighter man.

In answer to questions to the press, I said, 'That matter is now in the past. My thoughts are now for the future, particularly for the future happiness of my daughter Sarah who is to marry on February fourteenth.'

This upbeat statement reflected how I was feeling. Now I could get on with the rest of my life.

Ten things you didn't know about
The Madness of Local Councils

[1] We were once asked not to advertise our circus as a 'Christmas Circus' in case it offended anyone. Friends of mine weren't allowed to advertise a 'Traditional English Funfair'. You can have a Moscow State Circus or Chinese State Circus, but not an English Funfair.

[2] We needed direction signs off the North Circular for our Christmas Circus at Ally Pally, but the roads passed through 3 different local authorities. Each coucil insisted we put something different on the signs. The poor public were left totally confused.

[3] Another authority would not let Cottle Sisters use one of their sites unless the horses and dogs were taken out of the show. If they did, they could use the council's abattoir car park.

[4] We were asked, 'What precautions are taken for box office staff?' 'Oh, you mean in case they are threatened?' 'No. Not at all, to make sure they don't cut their fingers when they are counting £5 notes?'

[5] A certain council kept ringing up worried about the condition of the grass. 'Do you know what the weather's going to be like at the weekend?' Peter Norris said, 'I'll ring God and ask him.' 'Thank you. Please let us know what he says,' the young lady answered.

[6] One Health and Safety inspector said, 'This is the best circus I have ever inspected.' Beau Denning asked him, 'Which other circuses have you inspected?' 'Oh – none yet,' he replied.

[7] The same council suddenly demanded a large deposit for our next visit, 'In case you damage the grass.' We pointed out there was no grass on the site. 'Oh,' he said, 'I have just joined the council.'

[8] We were called 3 days in a row: our Russians were fishing in the river, had they got a permit? You just try telling the Russians not to do something because they haven't got the right piece of paper.

[9] One London council sent two officers with meters up to our show in Coventry to check the sound of the audience clapping. They said, 'Can you ask the audience to clap a bit softer when you visit?'

[10] Another council dragged me across London for two meetings. They couldn't offer us coffee as it could be taken as a bribe, although they had cups. It was 'not personal, just the rules'.

Chapter Ten

Saved by the Circus from Hell
1993-95

Two days after we opened at Haringey a council official walked into my office. 'We have reports of a live duck in your show. If you do not remove it immediately from the performance we will have no alternative but to remove your license.'

Those naughty Hazzard clowns.

Haringey council had let us on to their site on the specific condition we had no performing animals. Well, we had no performing animals, just a duck. At the end of the clowns' routine they lifted a dish to reveal a duck. OK, so it quacked in time to the trombone encouraged by a secret tickle to its bottom. But it was just a duck.

Mark got on the phone and, posing as a journalist writing an article for the Vegetarian Society magazine, asked each one of the thirty members of Haringey council whether they were a vegetarian. As it happened, only one of them was. Then we went out and counted the number of places you can eat a duck in the London Borough of Haringey (quite a lot actually, it's a great place if you want a Chinese takeaway). Well, we had great fun with this story. It was such a classic example of petty small-minded loony left bureaucracy. All the nationals carried it with headlines, 'You can eat a duck in Haringey but you can't watch it perform!' (We also found out that the council had convened a special meeting to debate the duck which we calculated cost the rate payers £800 in councillors' expenses. A fact we happily passed on to the papers as well.) I also took personal delight in pointing out that while the GLC insisted on a ban on performing animals in the circus, Ken Livingstone had been quite happy to not only hire but ride Rani our elephant to the opening of the Peace Pagoda in Battersea Park.

That same year I took it upon myself to rescue a turkey from being eaten for Christmas. We used the turkey to generate fun festive stories for several years afterwards: 'The turkey you can eat but can't watch perform. How Gerry saved a turkey from certain death!' The rest of the year it happily ran free range on site.

But I don't want to give you the wrong impression. Occasionally we were able to turn the animal question to our advantage, but they were the exceptions. Most of the time it was exhausting defending our position. With every story in the local press about the circus coming to town there would be at least a paragraph about the protestors. Just going through my files now it was relentless. Here are just a few:

Anger over Circus Act
A circus 'starring' a performing elephant is coming to Cheltenham despite a borough council ban on acts involving wild animals.

Big Top turns into 'Big Flop' as circus ban wins backing

Circus unpacks trunk
Circus Berlin, centre of a row when they visited Poole recently because they featured an elephant on their posters, are back in the area this month with the elephant.

Call to Close 'Cruel' Circus
A 5,000-strong petition and a specially produced report on alleged cruelty to performing animals have been handed in to City Hall in an effort to persuade councillors to ban circuses.

It was increasingly obvious that public opinion was swinging behind the animal protestors. We had gone from a country where even in the early 80s a circus wasn't a circus if it didn't have at least one elephant, to a country where a circus could be banned because it had a performing duck.

Martin Lacey grew very bitter and it started to take all of his time and attention. Meanwhile my old rival Zippo had started advertising himself as a non-animal circus and was travelling round getting the top London sites with great success. You can imagine how I felt about that.

So by the end of 1992 I had finally had enough of the circus. I hate to admit it but the animal protestors had finally won.

To be honest I miss the domestic animals in the circus – the dogs, horses and elephants. The relationship between a man and an elephant can be a very special thing. But on a practical level I'm quite happy not to have to take lions and tigers into the middle of London. There is so much hypocrisy about this issue – people are allowed to keep pets in completely unnatural conditions – the old lady in the flat with ten cats, sports such as horse racing where horses have a far greater risk of injury than in the ring. How about the training of police dogs or children's gymkhanas? I'm not condemning any of these things – my eldest grandchild has great fun with the Mendip Pony Club – what I'm saying is that if an animal is brought up in certain conditions then it generally thrives in those conditions and you know if an animal is unhappy. My animals were not unhappy. The ones who didn't like the ring were no good at performing, and were quickly found alternative homes. We were never cruel, I would never have kept a trainer who was cruel. All the trainers I had looked after and loved their animals. Nowhere else in Europe has a problem with animals in the circus.

I think it's all part of this country's peculiar snobbery against the circus. In the rest of Europe circus is seen as a precious art form, which is ironic when circus started in Britain. Here we are seen as barely better than gypsies, and we all know how they are treated. Instead of bending over backwards to help us, the government and councils throw every obstacle in our way. And this is a reflection of how a large proportion of the British public feel about the circus.

In the end I decided that if the majority of society did not wish to see animals in the circus, then I was not going to fight it. I was going to do something different.

Lurking at the bottom of my desk drawer there was a funfair file, now pretty full. It was something I'd been studying seriously for a while.

Back in Christmas 1984 we had shared Clapham Common with Carters Steam Fair. It was a happy coupling. I had shared sites with funfairs before and it could be mutually profitable as long as the funfair was big enough and beautiful enough. Carters was certainly that. John Carter was imposing both in body and mind. He was a well-built six foot four, with a long red beard, denim shirts and braces. He and his wife Anna were not travelling people. They met at art college and found a mutual intense passion for old funfair rides. They saved up their money, gave up their jobs, bought an old steam-powered carousel and spent a winter lovingly restoring it. The next year they toured the Home Counties, pitching up on village greens across the shires. Through sheer hard work they gradually acquired more rides (and children) until they had grown into a sizeable old-fashioned fair, all powered by steam and absolutely exquisite. Their attention to detail and reverence for authenticity was unique in the business. John and Anna were uncompromising perfectionists and the Carters really lived the life. They drove vintage cars and lived in old-fashioned showman's wagons, beautifully painted by Anna. Their rides included all the old favourites – old-fashioned swing rides and sideshows where you actually won prizes, the dodgems were all painted and named after 50s pop stars – Elvis Presley, the Everley Brothers, Little Richard. Unlike other fairs, the Carters publicised their fair like the circus, giving half-price tickets to shopkeepers in return for putting up a poster. This was great because it meant the fair was always full of people. I loved it.

That Christmas Betty and I spent a lot of time with John and Anna, the four of us got on really well. Betty used to tease John, 'When you go to bed at night do you sleep with your beard outside the covers or do you tuck it in?' Anna and I flirted a bit – she was my kind of dark-haired lady, with sexy wicked eyes and a great sense of humour. In fact John took me aside one day and said, 'You lay a finger on my wife and I'll flatten you.' John was a big man so I took this threat seriously. Instead I concentrated on learning about their business. And from the outside it seemed like they had a good life – once they had bought and restored the rides, all that was needed was a little maintenance now and then. There were no foreign acts to find permits for and they didn't travel great distances. Carters stayed within the M25 – perfect, I thought. They also seemed to have a great social life. Showmen had the best parties and the biggest weddings. Every one of those cold midwinter nights, when it got dark in the late afternoon, I walked to the other side of Clapham Common and gazed across. The fair and the circus together were very beautiful. The lights of the Big Top, the music of the old-fashioned funfair, the lights twinkling, people walking round with toffee apples and candyfloss, little children clutching over-large fluffy teddies. It gladdened my heart and got me thinking. When we got back to Addlestone three weeks later, I started a funfair file.

In one corner of my mind I had the beautiful but niche Carters Steam Fair. But also in there bubbling away were the huge travelling funfairs I had seen on my trips to the States. Sometimes called Midways, they are in a different league – huge travelling amusement parks where you pay one price to get in and everything is free. Over the winter of 1992 I drew up plans for Carnival USA, 'The UK's First Travelling Theme Park. Truckin' Good Fun!'. It would be full of old favourites – the dodgems, helter-skelter, an octopus, coconut shy and carousel, but with added extras, the world's longest limo, a wall of death and circus entertainers walking round juggling, a comedy bike and my nephew Beau on the dodgems as a comedy keystone cop with a blue flashing light on his head, hitting people over the head with a truncheon. I wanted to revive American wrestling, a boxing booth, fortune tellers, tin can alley, the Kentucky derby, swing the hammer hit the bell – 'the best of traditional and modern' principle. We would also stage forty-minute circus shows at regular intervals. All this just for a single admission fee. It was a radical idea at the time, but now there are several large travelling theme parks in this country, like Funderland and Europark, run by showman families which are very successful.

I needed some capital and conveniently Martin Lacey offered to buy Gerry Cottle's Circus. An animal man through and through, he still had plenty of fight left in him. He'd managed to find two partners – the husband of a famous author who had spent a year with the circus researching a book and Larry de Wit (whose father had been a manager of Smart's). I sold them the circus with the agreement that they could pay me in monthly instalments over the next three years.

I planned to use this money for publicity. As for the rides themselves, well I just presumed established showmen would come along with me, paying a fee to travel with my fair with their rides as was the norm on most funfairs. Indeed I'd managed to put on a Christmas funfair at Wembley alongside the circus by doing just that, and I was on very good terms with most of the showmen. I never in a million years thought I'd have to buy the whole thing myself. But as soon as word got around that I was giving up the circus and going into funfairs big time, the shutters came down. Men who had lent me equipment just the year before wouldn't return my calls. They might like me as a person but they weren't interested in helping any potential competition. I was stuck and scared.

Did you know that a big wheel can cost up to half a million pounds and even a little helter-skelter in need of renovation will knock you back £60,000? Of course these rides last forever. In Germany, where they do huge funfairs like nowhere else, I saw a big wheel that cost £500,000 make £3 million a year. Twenty Polish men were employed just to look after it. There were six separate booths selling tickets – it was a big business. Suddenly half a million doesn't seem so steep. But then you have to have the capital in the first place. I might have had enough to buy a big wheel but where was I going to find the money for the rest of it? Where indeed was I going to find any of it anyway? Nobody, but nobody was willing to sell me anything.

Saved by the Circus from Hell

I was beginning to despair when I saw an advert in the trade paper for four old fairground rides. It was rather a curious situation. Two brothers had inherited this funfair and had fallen out – one of them wanted to sell the funfair and the other wanted to carry on travelling. They hadn't talked for ten years (which was a bit of a problem when it came to negotiating) and the rides had been left to rust in a field outside Leighton Buzzard. In fact the field was on a prime development site. Tesco's and Sainsbury's were always trying to buy it off them but the brothers weren't interested. They also weren't interested in selling their rides to any other funfair families. I didn't rate my chances but for some reason they agreed to see me. I think it was probably because I wasn't one of their old rivals. I went down to have a look. What I found were six 1950s and 60s rides in perfect condition, except they had a few trees growing through them. It was a whole fair preserved in aspic, or in the undergrowth anyway. I was amazed. Suddenly I decided the fair would have to be retro affair, the beautiful fifty-year-old rides didn't really look very American. Before it had even hit the road the Carnival USA had turned into Xanadu – a stately retro pleasuredome.

I took the rides back to the farm and my team of loyal circus workers headed up by Patrick Austen spent the winter renovating them. I was stuck in the office trying to get sites. If I thought it was difficult trying to get rides, it was even worse trying to get sites. I had naïvely thought the role of The Showman's Guild was to host whopping riotous annual parties. Now it became clear its main purpose was to protect its members. The Showman's Guild had been formed over a hundred years ago and it was divided into powerful regions. It stopped any of its members pitching up within a certain radius of each other and more importantly it ensured that if, for example, a member had always been the fair at a certain festival he held that festival by right every year. When the father died this right would be passed on to his son, although it was possible to sell these rights to other members. It was very effective as ninety per cent of all funfairs belong to the guild, so the plum funfair sites were totally beyond my reach. Instead I had to make do with the odd council site and out-of-town farmers' fields I had been taking my circuses to since our animals had been banned.

We opened at Wandsworth in London at Easter 1994. For the first time the public were able to pay a one-off admission fee and all the rides inside were free. Straight away things weren't quite what I expected. The fair seemed to be attracting a different crowd to the circus. A rougher crowd. There were families with children, but there were also a lot of yobs. We had trouble. People didn't understand, or chose not to understand, the principle of not charging for individual rides – lads refused to get off the dodgems, 'I've paid to get in, I can stay here as long as I want.'

We would point out, 'You still have one turn and then get off and queue to have your next turn.' But the lads were angling for a fight. I noticed the difference between having a circus where you do the performance then the audience disappears, and a funfair which is still open late at night after the pubs have closed. The riff-raff just hang around and it's difficult to get rid of them.

I actually think we might have done better if our tickets had been more expensive. Our usual tactic of distributing cut-price tickets just attracted the wrong crowd. I am also convinced that one of the funfair families sent in spoilers to make trouble. For example one Saturday afternoon a group of lads started an argument demanding a prize they hadn't won. They emptied a shelf of teddy bears and ran off creating mayhem across the fair, throwing them at each other and anyone who caught their eye. Business was OK on high days and holidays, but during the week it was terrible. I changed the name. We went from Xanadu to the Rock and Roll Funfair to the Great British Funfair. A headless chicken springs to mind – I had been thinking about the funfair for far too long, had too many competing ideas and not enough money or time to execute any of them properly.

I was worried, but there was a great opportunity looming. We had been invited to the Channel Islands to be part of the Fourth of July celebrations (a quick switch back to some sort of American theme for us). It meant a month-long trip to Guernsey and Jersey. We had always done so well there as a circus, I jumped at it. We arrived on the ferry (it took a whole day just to pull the world's longest limo from the ferry to the fairground, me steering the back axle). We opened on Saturday 3 July. It was a baking hot day and the fair was full. But people were getting a bit overexcited. Two youths in particular were walking round causing trouble, jumping queues and being rude. Big Nigel had been my foreman for sixteen years. He was tremendously loyal and wasn't having any of this nonsense. He got hold of one of the lads just as they were getting into their car and pulled him out. His head was thrown back and it hit a support pole with a terrible force. The lad went out like a light and before we knew it a helicopter was taking him off to Southampton General for emergency surgery to relieve the pressure on his brain. Within forty minutes the police had surrounded the fair and arrested eight of my men. It looked incredibly serious. It looked like the lad was going to die and Nigel would be facing a charge of manslaughter. The police were pretty decent but they never told us what they knew – that these two lads were troublemakers, renowned drunks who'd been arrested a couple of weeks before for sniffing glue.

The atmosphere turned really nasty. Suddenly it was the islanders versus the mainland. Of course I couldn't carry on with the fair. We didn't reopen and I cancelled the trip to Jersey. The only problem was how to get out – we couldn't just jump into our trucks and head off, we had to wait for the next ferry which was over twenty-four hours away. We packed up the fair and waited on the quayside for a whole day. People were walking past shouting abuse at us. One of the tent men kept on trying to retaliate so Patrick and I locked him in his caravan. I was never so pleased to get on a boat. But we had to leave Nigel there in jail – to what fate we didn't know. It was a terrible feeling.

After ten days the boy came out of his coma and there was no lasting damage. Nigel spent four weeks inside and then I was able to bail him. I went over to Guernsey to collect him. In the end it was a year before the case was settled. Nigel had to pay a fine of £400 for causing an affray. But poor Nigel was never the same man after that. He gave up travelling forever and settled down.

I'd lost my nerve as well. The funfair wasn't for me. I didn't like it at all. Despite all the years of planning, all the money, all the effort. I cancelled all bookings and limped home to Addlestone, my tail between my legs.

It was bad for me but disastrous for my girls.

By this time they had all left school and gone into the circus. I was very proud of them but I would have been equally happy if they had gone into normal jobs. My girls made it quite clear this was never an option. From the very start Sarah loved animals. Like generations of Fossetts before her she was a natural trick rider. From an early age she spent all her time helping with the horses on the show. My old friend from Chessington, June, joined our circus and taught Sarah to train Liberty horses. Sarah's a very strong character, a determined hard worker, with beautiful long dark hair. By the time she was fourteen she had copied her great auntie Ellen Fossett's act, where dressed as a ballerina, she stood on the back of her horse, vaulted and skipped over it. As the finale of the act she stood on the back of the horse as it galloped around the ring, jumped through a hoop of flowers and landed back on the horse. It was a very traditional act and, as far as I know, Sarah was the last ballerina rider in England. She was as single-minded over men as she was about her act. The year she started riding in the ring she spotted Willie Ramsay. He was one of our new recruits from the student circus, a natural gymnast and hard worker, who had been taught circus skills and was using them to escape from a lack of jobs in Edinburgh. I took to Willie straight away. So did Sarah. Despite being only fourteen, within a week of meeting him she announced to Betty, 'I'm in love with Willie Ramsay and I'm going to marry him.'

Betty was a bit taken aback, 'But he's so short.'

'I don't care, Mum, he's kind.'

'Well if that's how you feel, Sarah, then you must follow your heart.'

And she did. Within months Sarah had devised an act with Willie. She bought a troupe of twelve Liberty horses and they moved in formation beautifully around the ring. They were soon travelling the world with their act and, as you know, I announced their engagement on the courtroom steps. We were delighted when they got married. Willie's like a son to me. Betty thought they were made for each other. We had an enormous wedding at Addlestone. Four hundred people came. It was a great day and a year later in January 1994 Sarah had her baby Ellen, after her great aunt.

April was still the rebel of the family. I'll never forget the day she walked into my office with a towel wrapped round her head. She can only have been about eleven.

'Dad, can you tell Mum?'

'Tell Mum what?'

She unwrapped the towel. She'd cut off all her lovely long dark hair and dyed it green.

I love April, despite all her naughtiness, maybe because of all her naughtiness. We have a very close relationship, she reminds me of myself. Of all the children she learns circus acts quickest and easiest. She was the best female juggler in the UK, although April can turn her hand to anything. Well she didn't even bother to go through the motions of sitting her school exams. She ran away at fifteen and moved in with Sarah and Willie, and joined their horse act. Sarah really took her in hand and settled her down. I'm not sure where April would have ended up without Sarah.

Polly followed the other Fossett tradition. Like her aunties Baba and Julie she was happiest in the air. We settled down at Addlestone when Polly was eleven and unlike Sarah and April she went to a good private school in Surrey where she did very well and became Head Girl. But all Polly wanted to do was perform. She was so precocious; even as a little five-year-old she'd sneak into every act, standing at the side of the stage, arms outstretched posing. She taught herself the trapeze one winter in the barn at Addlestone and created a beautiful aerial act using the silks.

Little Gerry was still at school but every holiday he'd join the circus throwing his diabolo and joining in with the clowns. Gerry was the only one out of my children who never wanted to join the circus full-time, but he loved being in the circus over the summer. He is incredibly charming and gregarious, he has a natural way with people – everyone loves Gerry Jr, especially women (some say he's a chip off the old block, I wouldn't like to comment).

When I started the funfair they all came to help with the small circus. They desperately wanted to work together and gave up their jobs on other circuses. I guess like Betty and her sisters, Sarah, April and Polly have always been really close. Of course they had their arguments. Circus girl spats are like no other – when April and Sarah got going we all ran for cover. But these arguments always blew over as quickly as they started. I remember one Christmas at Wembley when Beadle was managing the dress rehearsal for the show, April and Sarah started having the most terrible row. I ducked under the seats, I didn't want to get involved. Poor Beadle looked terrified, he looked wildly around and caught sight of me skulking in the shadows.

'Should I do something? Is this all right?' he asked.

'Yes, don't worry. It'll blow itself out. Just leave them to it.' And it did. The circus is a travelling community and there's no room to bear grudges – the person you aren't talking to one moment could have your life in their hands holding you upside down fifty feet in the air the next. No, you've got to get on.

The funfair reunited the girls and their boyfriends – by this time not only was Sarah married to Willie, but April was going out with my old mechanic's son, Ingo, and Polly was with another aerialist called Sellam. All of them gave up their jobs to come with us on the funfair. I used the circus I hadn't sold, Circus Berlin, its tent and equipment, to make a forty-five minute show – the Zincalli Gypsy Circus – which performed several times through the day. Sarah, April and Willie did their horse act, April did some juggling, Polly did whip cracking, we had Jeff Jay knife throwing, Barry Walls was fire eating, and Sarah and Willie got out my old illusionist box which Betty and I had performed with. I had also brought over a troupe of Kenyan acrobats. Lovely boys, they were always very enthusiastic, they'd muck in and help with whatever needed doing. You never had to ask. Once the school holidays started Gerry Jr joined them as well. They were all young and enthusiastic and really enjoying themselves. So when we had to pack up and come back to Addlestone they were devastated.

The lobbying started immediately. It was fierce, my girls can be quite frightening. Sarah took the lead.

'Dad, let us take the circus back on the road.'

'I don't want to do another circus. I'm finished with circus. I'm sick of the protestors.'

'We won't get protestors. We've sold all the animals. We'll just have the horses and the dogs. We've proved we can do a good little show without them. We'll get more grounds that way.'

One thing I wasn't prepared to do was struggle round the country with a circus. Just a year before I had been the boss of two big circuses. Now limping round the West Country with a medium-sized family circus didn't appeal. I guess it was a matter of pride. I also knew what crushing hard work it would be for relatively little financial reward.

'But you won't make any money. You'll have to pitch in farmer's fields.'

'We will be really cheap. We can do all the work ourselves.'

'What, no tent men?'

'No tent men, no box office. We've all grown up on the circus. We all know what to do. None of us is afraid of hard work. Let's face it, Dad, it's too late for us to get jobs doing anything else.'

Sarah and April did both have HGV driving licenses.

'Who's going to manage the circus? I'm not going to do it and I can't afford to employ anyone else. Do you know how bad our debts are?'

'Yes, and how is having the equipment just sitting around the yard going to help you pay off those debts? Anyway you don't need to employ a manager. I will do it.'

Sarah had called my bluff. Although all my instincts screamed against it, I had run out of arguments. I was also facing the united force of all my womenfolk, including Betty. I couldn't hold out. The Cottle Sisters Circus was born.

They pulled out of Addlestone a few days later, a motley caravan of brave young pioneers heading West in search of their fortune. Full of hope and enthusiasm, it reminded me of when Brian and I had set off with the first Cottle and Austen's Circus. I was really proud of them but depressed for myself. Where had all my enthusiasm gone? I felt disillusioned. Some of the mistakes were mine, but it seemed I couldn't make anything work and the harder I tried the worse I did. I had worked so hard for so many years, for what? Just to have a mountain of debts. What on earth was I going to do now?

The answer was to sit at my desk at Addlestone and get depressed. For a start I was very short of money. I tried to sell the funfair equipment, but of course everyone knew I was pretty desperate and I made a terrific loss on it. The helter-skelter, which I had paid £60,000 for and never got round to using, didn't sell at all but sat at the farm at Addlestone for a long time. The only way I kept my head above water was by selling my assets. First our precious elephants went, then the world's longest limo, then the joke shop. The costumes were put into an auction at Bonham's but the bidding was so desultory I called a halt to the proceedings and had a word with the auctioneer. 'Can't you do better than that? This is ridiculous.'

The poor man tried again but things just got worse. I had a small moment of triumph when Zippo bought a busybee costume but forgot to take the antenna hat. I ran after him, 'Here Hippo. You've forgot your hat.'

He turned round livid. 'Don't call me that. I hate it.' Zippo was the size of a small bungalow. (A few years later I bumped into him again. 'Hi, Hippo. Long time no see.' 'Oh hello, Gerry. How are you?' I blinked, he hadn't taken the bait. 'Don't you mind being called Hippo any more?' I leered. 'I did until someone told me you used to call me fat bastard.' We've been good friends ever since, but I digress ...)

I was in serious financial trouble. Martin Lacey wouldn't or couldn't pay me my next instalment on the circus I'd sold him. I'd only been paid half of the money he owed me and now I really needed it. I was late with a VAT payment. I wrote articles in the papers and letters to the secretary of state for culture and heritage, as it was then, and even to the prime minister, John Major, complaining about VAT. Here is an extract from the letter I sent:

It prevents us from improving our programme, and it makes it difficult to modernise or replace equipment – a particular problem, as we will soon be required to comply with new Health and Safety regulations. 'Adding' VAT to existing admission prices simply doesn't work. A circus seat has its market value like any other commodity and can't be sold for more.

We are not asking for subsidies for circus. We are a small business with a belief in free enterprise and in providing the public with what it wants. But we are nevertheless part of the artistic and cultural sector of society and as such we feel deserving of some special consideration. This view is shared by the rest of Europe. All other EEC countries have a lower rate of VAT (usually around 6%) or totally exempt cultural and entertainment activities.

In the light of this we think you will see why we feel unjustly treated in the UK, paying our crippling 17.5%. Ironic too when we consider that not only was circus invented in Britain (London 1768), but we even have a Prime Minister with a proud circus background!

We hope for a sympathetic response.

Yours faithfully,
Gerry Cottle.

Well, I was hoping in vain. The next thing I know I've got two VAT inspectors on my doorstep, poring over my accounts with a fine toothcomb. I have come to the conclusion over the years that there is absolutely no point in taking on the might of the authorities. They are just out to get you afterwards. Unfortunately the day before the inspectors turned up someone had told me a joke. I decided to repeat it as they closed the last of my books:

'The problem is I pay my bills in alphabetical order and V is a long way down the alphabet.'

They looked at me. There was an endless silence. No one laughed except for me . . . nervously.

'Right, let's take another look at these again, shall we?' they said.

They stayed another two hours. At the end of it I was presented with a huge bill which I couldn't pay and the company was declared bankrupt.

My lowest point came in the autumn of 1994. The funfair had closed and the Cottle Sisters were limping around the West Country, and Billy Smart's grandson, Gary, came out of retirement and decided to put on the ultimate circus. The Smarts have lots of money, they invested the profits of the boom years of circus very wisely. The Smarts spent over a million pounds putting together this superb circus – huge spanking new tent, brand-new equipment, top quality acts – and spent the winter on the best sites in London. Sarah and I went to see the show and although it sticks in my throat, I was really impressed (and jealous). The final straw was when Gary came over and said to me, 'The problem with you, Gerry, is that you just don't try hard enough.'

Sarah tackled me afterwards. 'Why didn't you say something, Dad?'

'Because there's nothing to say,' I replied.

This was the first and only time in my life I was properly depressed. I'm one of life's optimists – the glass is definitely half full for me. If I feel miserable I just go to sleep. You always feel better when you wake up. But no amount of sleep could help me this time. I even tried booking myself in for some therapy, to no avail. I'd never had so little money, or so few opportunities to make any. Even if I had an idea I couldn't raise the funds to do it. I didn't even have the money to lose myself in extra-curricular activities. I would go down to the circus to empty the tills so I could have a little light relief, but the tills were empty. I was stuck and I couldn't see a way out.

The answer came when I least expected it.

It was Boxing Day 1994. Betty and I were just about to leave the house to see the Cottle Sisters Circus at Alexandra Palace when the telephone rang. It was a very old family friend, Neville Campbell. He had the most shocking news. His son, Neville Jr, had fallen off the wheel of death at the Blackpool Tower circus and died. I collapsed into a chair. It was one of those pieces of news that shakes you to your very core. The Campbell family had been part of our lives for years. I first met them working with the infamous Count Lazard. Later, Neville and Pauline travelled with Gerry Cottle's Circus doing their stilt act and helping maintain the trucks. Their four sons were the same ages as our children and they were like brothers and sisters. They trained together and played together. In the winter our farm at Addlestone was their home. Neville Jr was particularly close to Gerry Jr – just a couple of months earlier he had been living at Addlestone, practising his new act and spending his free time painting the town red with young Gerry. Neville Jr was full of high spirits, just twenty-one and handsome.

This was the big Boxing Day performance. The wheel of death is dangerous because there are no harnesses or safety nets. I guess the best way to describe it is two hamster wheels at either end of a see-saw suspended high in the air, so the wheels move round and up and down. Two people do tricks inside them, culminating in one of them walking round the outside of the wheel blindfolded. It requires enormous skill, concentration and chemistry between the two performers. Neville was going too fast, he overran the top of the wheel, fell off, managed to stop his fall by catching the wheel coming up the other side, but he broke both his wrists. He pulled himself up but as he started running over the wheel again he fainted with the pain, went over the top and this time nothing broke his fall. He broke his neck and died instantly in front of a packed audience of 1,500 people. My heart broke for the Campbells, and at the same time whenever I hear stories of young people terribly injured or worse in the circus I think, 'There but for the grace of God'. I have had four children performing in the circus including Polly with her aerial act and two sons-in-law who do the wheel of death. You never know when it's your turn.

I felt a terrible need to do something to help the Campbells. But what could I do? In the absence of any bright ideas I got in the car and drove up to Blackpool. I arrived in the middle of a terrible scene. The whole Campbell family were gathered in Blackpool police station to identify Neville's body. The station had been built as if they expected trouble – a terrible concrete monstrosity of a fortress building that could only be entered by steep steps. Inside the Campbell family were in the middle of a terrible row. Pauline and Neville were blaming each other for Neville Jr's death, their sons were trying to keep them apart. A policewoman tried to calm Pauline down, but in the heat of the moment Pauline hit her (Pauline's the last person to hit anyone). Swarms of police then piled in, young Richard Campbell managed to headbutt another one and was promptly locked up. Unfortunately the police had no idea who they were or why they were there, they just took them for a group of gypsies. The situation was looking really dangerous when a voice of calm and reason spoke above the row. It came from a most unlikely source. There was a man with long peroxide-blond hair dressed in top hat and tails with leopard-skin trousers on. Dr Haze took control of the situation, stopped the Campbells rowing for long enough to explain to the police the terrible catastrophe that they were struggling to deal with. It was ironic that the only sane person looked like Alice Cooper. I took an instant liking to him and when it looked safe I suggested that he and I get the whole family a round of fish and chips. We stood waiting in the chippy and got talking. It turned out Haze had been on the circus with the Campbells for a few years, had become a firm friend and was Neville Jr's godfather.

'What are you doing now?' I asked.

'I take a small show round the universities called the Circus of Horrors. Have you ever considered doing a Circus of Horrors?' he asked me.

'What do you mean?'

'Well at the moment I'm making a pretty good living touring with this small cult show. We specialise in doing bizarre tricks to live rock music. It's really developed quite a following. I think we're on to something. Would you be interested in coming to see us?'

'I'm trying to break away from circus at the moment.'

'But this wouldn't be circus as you have ever seen it before. I think there's a real gap in the market for an adult X-rated alternative circus and I think you are the only person brave enough in the country to pull it off.'

I didn't understand what Haze was talking about, but I was intrigued by him. I found out that Haze had been the world's youngest fire-eater. He was the product of a whirlwind romance between a lion tamer on his winter break and an ordinary girl from London. The union was shortlived – Haze's dad ran off when he was still a baby, abandoning his mum in a van on a circus. Haze went to live with relations in Preston, until his mum finally caught up with his dad eleven years later and sued him for maintenance. The judge came to the unusual conclusion that Haze's mum and dad, after zero contact for eleven years, should have another go at their marriage, and his mum even more bizarrely agreed. Haze suddenly found himself out of school in Preston and into a circus in Ireland. Poor Haze had a lot of ground to catch up with the circus kids, but he rose to the challenge and within a week had learnt to fire eat. He loved the circus and stayed performing and then doing the publicity. Eventually he set up his own agency – Psycho Management and decided to pursue a rock career. That is until he was inspired by a whole new circus phenomenon that hit Britain in the early 90s.

Archaos came to the Edinburgh Festival in 1992 and was an overnight sensation. Like many alternative circuses, it came from France. The brainchild of Pierrot Bidon, the artists juggled with chainsaws and chased each other around on motorbikes. A car crashed into the stage every night. It was a circus for adults with a dark edge and was an instant hit. Mark Borkowski did the publicity. But every circus is vulnerable no matter how good it is. Pierrot overreached himself, was ripped off by a few promoters, and after four years of success the show went out of business. So Archaos had disappeared and Haze was right, no one else had appeared in its place. I went to see his show.

Afterwards Haze rang me up and asked me what I thought.

'Haze, I'm flattered you've asked me but I don't think it's for me. Why don't you ask Zippo?'

'Zippo's not the right man. I need someone who is prepared to take a real risk. Who understands publicity. I think you are the only man who has the nerve and experience to do it.'

'I don't think I am any more. Maybe a few years ago. I don't feel ready to take any big risks at the moment, especially not in the circus.'

'Look, at the moment I'm only asking you to give it a trial run at Glastonbury.'

Glastonbury. A week at the festival. We'd be given a guarantee so we couldn't lose money. The audience at Glastonbury was the target audience exactly. I could think of no reason why not. Especially as, without knowing it, Haze had caught me at a weak moment. In my heart of hearts I knew the Cottle Sisters was not the future, but I had the equipment and – most importantly – the whole family wanting to work together in the circus. I needed to keep some sort of circus going just for them and the Cottle Sisters was not it.

The Cottle Sisters had struggled from the very first.

After just a few weeks Sarah had to call together the artists in the ring and lay down the law. 'If anyone feels they need to keep ringing my father, there is the door. You can leave right now. You may not like it but I am the boss. It's not Gerry Cottle's Circus. It's the Cottle Sisters Circus and I am the manager. If you don't like it you can sling your hook.'

She was very brave. She reminded me so much of myself at that age. Hard working, tough. She was just twenty-three with a new husband and a baby barely a few months old and, I'm sure she won't mind me saying, it wasn't easy stepping into my shoes. She would ask someone to do something and they'd say, 'Oh, I'll just give Gerry a ring to check.' Or they'd refuse to pick up rubbish or wear their circus jackets front of house. No one would have dared argue with me. But Sarah had to work hard to assert her authority. It's all right for you, Dad,' she used to say. 'They do what they're told when they know you're coming.'

It was also difficult because it was the back end of the season, late July by the time they pulled out. Even though the only animals left in the show were horses and dogs they struggled to get grounds. The antipathy towards animals in the circus had reached the most lunatic proportions. One week before we were due to arrive in the sleepy retirement resort of Weymouth in Dorset, I received a letter from the council saying that unless we removed the picture of King Kong from our poster we could not use the ground – I kid you not. It was just a clown running around in a gorilla costume. Most of the time the girls took the rejection on the chin but occasionally it really got their hackles up and I pursued it for them. Epsom council in the Home Counties got all holier than thou about our horses – despite playing host to the most famous horse races in the world. I was shocked. You expect that from a loony inner city council, not from the Home Counties. The hypocrisy took my breath away. I fought it with letter after letter, and articles in the local newspapers. I invited the prime movers in the council to the show and to the farm to see the horses, how they were kept, see how they enjoyed performing. They flatly refused. I wrote back:

Dear Councillor Kington,

We were disappointed to learn through Mr Harris that you declined an invitation to visit our circus to see for yourself the standard of our show and the condition of our horses.

As you are in effect preventing us from pursuing our legitimate business we feel we are entitled to a proper explanation of the reasons for your objection. Presumably you would not accuse anyone of cruelty without proof. Have you any knowledge of the training of horses for Liberty routines or dressage whether within or outside the circus context? How much do you know about training horses and ponies for riding schools, show jumping, racing? Do you apply the same standards to these as you do to circus horses – after all Epsom is synonymous with horses . . . Kindly keep an open mind on this matter. We are very proud of our new young show; it is great family entertainment and as we are Surrey born and bred people we are very keen to come to Epsom.

I was wasting my time.

It was the same at Hove Park. The circus was pitched right next to a greyhound racing stadium but they wouldn't allow the Cottle

Sisters to have performing dogs. In the end the girls bowed to the inevitable. If they could get good grounds by taking the horses out, they did. In the end Sarah's horses were spending most of the time resting at the farm.

Some weeks the money was so bad Sarah literally had no money to pay the artists. When it came to Monday morning she would have to go round all the caravans and tell them she couldn't pay them that week, but would pay them later when she had the money, something I'd never had to do. It was really tough and she had to psych herself up beforehand. She used to say, 'If you want to go, then go. I understand, no hard feelings.' The camaraderie on the circus was so good, no one left. But Sarah would end up back in her caravan crying her eyes out.

There was a great spirit on the show. They were all young and enthusiastic. Everybody had great fun in the way you do when you are very young, working hard at something you want to do, with nothing to lose. The girls say it was the best time of their lives, even though they even had to put up the tent themselves. I was so proud of them. But taking the horses out of the show finally broke Sarah's spirit. The girls didn't want to carry on like this.

So when Haze suggested Glastonbury, it didn't seem such a daft idea. I got on the phone and within a day the site was booked and I had got us a guarantee, not very much for three days' work, but then we couldn't lose much money either. I introduced Haze to the girls. They loved the concept from the start – they all love rock music and have a touch of the dark side about them. I took the girls into Soho and got them kitted out in some sexy rubber costumes. I did get some strange looks, looking like an old perv buying sadomasochistic clothes for three pretty young girls – the girls made me leave the shop in the end. The whole troupe got the concept immediately. Haze's music seemed made for their acts. We kept the wheel of death, Polly and Sellam did their aerial act, Ingo did his dangerous swing act. It was pretty much the Cottle Sisters Circus without the clowns and the horses, but with a contortionist instead. Looking back now it was a relatively amateurish show with no unifying theme, but it felt new and exciting.

Saved by the Circus from Hell

The tent was full for the first performance at Glastonbury – there must have been over 700 people in there, but after the first half an hour 300 of them had walked out. The next day we were full again and this time only 200 people left, the third night we were packed and no one left and we had a thousand people outside clamouring to get in. We were on to something.

Next we decided to go to Brighton – we thought the young alternative vibe of the place would be perfect for the Horrors. All was going well with our negotiations with the man from Brighton council until we showed him our poster. 'Welcome to the Circus From Hell', it announced.

'What sort of music will you be playing?' he asked Haze.

'Oh, things like "The Only Sure Thing in Life is Death",' Haze grinned.

The man went a bit quiet and brought the meeting to an abrupt close. Next thing we know permission had been refused. When we made enquiries why we weren't allowed on to the excellent council site, he explained he was a fundamentalist Christian. 'I can't very well go to church on Sunday, after giving my blessing to the Circus from Hell the night before.' The thing is about the Circus of Horrors – you either get it or you don't.

We had to make do with a vastly inferior spot on Brighton racecourse, but we decided to make up for it by making a grand entrance into Brighton on a ghost ship. Haze managed to hire a real live galleon from somewhere. We called it *The Pride of Dracula*, and the cast in full costume emerged from a perfect autumn mist to sail into Brighton Harbour with a full media audience waiting. It was a great launch, but the audiences didn't match the hype. It was freezing on the racecourse and only in the last few nights did we start to make any money. Next the circus went to Crystal Palace for 'A Spooktacular Christmas'. Again no one turned up. (I think we were missing the Christmas spirit!)

We were booked for festivals in Bradford, Leeds and Stockton and then Edinburgh, so I decided to give it one last chance. Meanwhile we invited Pierrot Bidon, the brains behind Archaos, to come and direct the show. He was brilliant. He just added little touches – he put Polly's aerial act to the music of *The Exorcist*; he put the Kenyan acrobats in fluorescent skeleton costumes and they performed their routine in the dark; he got one of the tent men, Guy, to pretend to be a streaker and run round naked in the middle of the show. We added some acts – Kiss My Axe, a mad troupe of chainsaw and sword jugglers on motorbikes; a transvestite doing a tap dance routine to 'Singing in the Rain' holding an umbrella with silver foil strips taped on to it (the girls complained he took more room in the dressing room than anyone else). Ingo made a ticket office in the shape of a bat – the wings unfolded. We put up a big sign at the entrance saying 'Welcome to Transylvania'. We dressed two big Polish tent men with wonderful Lech Walesa handlebar moustaches in army great coats to take the tickets at the door. You get the picture.

I didn't have high hopes for Bradford and Stockton, they aren't normally great circus towns. But the first night in Bradford the tent was packed with young gothic rockers completely up for it and the atmosphere was electric. Where had they all come from? At the end of the show they went wild and started stamping their feet. A low rumble grew into a deafening roar. The tent shook, it felt like an earthquake. It was like an encore, but it wasn't an encore – it was more than that, it was a spontaneous expression of delight. Every night this happened, and when we went to Leeds and then Stockton the stamping carried on. I think we must already have had a dedicated fan base following us around. It was so exciting to be doing something that people really connected with.

We hit Edinburgh on a massive high. We were too late to enter the parade but we just crashed it anyway. Our reviews were tremendous. The nationals loved us and we had to turn hundreds of people away every night. I have to admit I was slightly non-plussed. I'd been trying to have a hit with something different for so long, and for ages the best I had done was break even and the worst, well you know about. I hadn't really thought it was going to work. It was the persistence of Haze and the enthusiasm of my girls that had kept me going with it.

The great thing about the Circus of Horrors was you could have such fun with it. We held auditions in every town – sometimes it was to find a girl to go inside the bottle (it's amazing how many ladies can actually do it, men aren't so bendy), sometimes it was auditions for a vampire. The most extraordinary range of eccentrics would turn up. Some came kitted out in full scary costume, some just turned up as they were. I remember one middle-aged chap who still lived with his mum turned up in a shirt, tie and pullover, clutching his packed lunch on his knee.

'Have you any previous experience in horror?' we asked him.

'No.'

'Why do you want to be a vampire?'

'I don't know.'

Haze got him crawling across the floor to *Hammer House of Horror* sound effects. It was cruel to watch.

Then in Stockton a young lad came in saying he could fire eat.

'Well we can all fire eat.'

'Ah ha. But I do it a bit differently. Let me show you.'

'Not in here, young man.'

We all trouped outside. The young man set his fingers alight. This is good, we think. Then he brings them up to his mouth and blows out a huge stream of fire which sets his goatee beard alight, which he tries to put out with his burning fingers at which point we all leap on him and roll him in the grass until he was put out. Thanks but no thanks, poor lad. We gave him some complimentary tickets and sent him to hospital. He came back the next day to see the show, hands all bandaged up, wearing a McDonald's uniform.

Among the hundreds of hopefuls we did discover some real stars. There was Captain Dan the midget who dragged a vacuum cleaner around with his willie. Then there was Gary Stretch. He's a household name now but he was completely unknown before the Horrors. He got the job after his wife sent us a home video. He's got a very rare skin condition (only ten people in the world have got it) which means his skin is like elastic. He can do amazing things with it like stretch his neck skin over his nose. But he does have to be careful – he bruises easily and it does snap. Once he was down the pub on his birthday and his mates decided to give him the bumps. The skin of his arm stretched, snapped at the top, and peeled all the way down to his wrist like a rubber glove. He went straight to hospital, where a group of junior nurses and doctors who had never seen anything like it in their lives sewed it all back together. But just because you have this rare condition doesn't mean you have a passport to fame – Gary is above all a great showman, and that's the reason since joining the Horrors he's appeared on *Richard and Judy*, *GMTV*, *Ant and Dec's Saturday Night Takeaway* and is an international star.

I can't believe some of the things we did. Looking back you think, 'But that's insane!' The human mobile definitely falls into that category. My idea – I saw a picture of a French trapeze troupe imitating a baby's mobile in a circus magazine. Suspended from a crane, high above the ground, was a wire contraption with about eight men dangling off it. I looked it up in the *Guinness Book of Records* – it was in there, and the record was twelve men. Easy. I picked a site on the bank of the Thames next to Battersea Bridge. We invited the national press to witness sixteen people hanging 150 feet in the air. Looking back it was incredibly dangerous – if one fell it was so delicately balanced that they would all come tumbling down. They were each standing on a metal bar, which ran up their backs and arched over their heads. They were strapped round their middle but they did need to keep their feet on the metal bar. Haze says the ten minutes he spent hanging over the Thames were the longest of his life. We broke the record and it became our favourite publicity stunt. That is until Argentina. The problem was some of the men had all been out on the razz the night before. I think they were still drunk. We got the mobile up with everyone on it, then suddenly our drummer slumped over. He'd fainted and his feet were slipping off the footrest. They started screaming at the crane driver to take the mobile down, but in typical Latin *mañana* fashion he'd wandered off. There was also a language problem. We had rock music blaring out of a tape recorder – the Argentinian helpers thought we just wanted the music to be turned up louder. The more everyone screamed the louder they turned up the music. Luckily, on the brink of catastrophe, the drummer came round.

Actually the whole tour to South America was a bit of a disaster. Feeling lucky after great trips to Amsterdam and Munich, I took the ambitious option and accepted an invitation to take the Horrors on a huge tour of South America. We spared no expense and booked huge national stadia, although the whole Horrors concept had never been tried on the Latin psyche. We lost money absolutely everywhere – you could blame the wrong venues, the more conservative Catholic culture, but I think in the end it was just plain rubbish promoting. It was always 'we'll do it tomorrow' but tomorrow never came. I would go to the promoter's office to see piles of posters stacked up in the corner that never saw the light of day. The final straw came when the tour ended, I left all the circus equipment packed up in containers ready to be shipped the next day. As soon as I got back to England I got a phone call, 'Unless you give us $100,000 you will never see your circus again.'

The equipment was being held to ransom. I managed to beat them down to $10,000 and we got our Horrors kit back, but I'd had my fill of South America.

So back in England with a whole cast and equipment and again debts, I was tempted to give the whole thing up. But we still had a couple of months left of the season – often the most lucrative months. I told Haze to give the Roundhouse in Camden a ring.

The Roundhouse is just the most perfect setting for a circus. An empty shell built by George Stephenson for turning trains around, it was turned into a gin warehouse and then in the 60s played host to lots of famous bands – The Doors played their last-ever gig there, Blondie her first. I just knew it was right for us. We booked a five-week stint to finish at Halloween. In the end we stayed there for sixteen weeks – the 1,500 tickets selling out nearly every night. The Circus from Hell had found its spiritual home in the alternative youth culture of Camden.

Our last publicity stunt came from another flick through the *Guinness Book of Records* – we decided to have the largest custard pie fight in the world ever. We had to stick to a strict recipe. A chef came in to make hundreds of flan bases, then we had two concrete mixers going flat out mixing the yellowy custard. Everyone spent the week-end slapping it on the bases. After the show we cleared the theatre and invited the audience to stay. According to Guinness' rules we had to have two teams of ten facing each other. Jeremy Beadle was planted in the middle acting as referee. Haze offered £10 to the first person to hit Jeremy. I walked around with a fake gun and top hat on my head, in charge of crowd control. He blew his whistle. For ten minutes the world went mad. Pies flew everywhere. Then there was the nervous moment as the Guinness official counted how many flans were left. For weeks afterwards custard was turning up in all sorts of unlikely places. It was a devil to get off. But we are now proud possessors of the world record for the Largest Custard Pie Fight Ever.

It had been a tough few years, and I certainly wasn't the biggest circus owner in Britain any more, but with the Horrors I felt I had a made a step towards finding the Next Big Thing. Basically I felt better than I had done for a long time.

Ten things you didn't know about
The Greatest Acts of All Time

1. **The Largest Lion Act Ever** Bertram Mills once had an act with 70 lions in it. Christmas 1925, London was covered with black posters stating 'Look Out – The 70 Are Coming'.

2. **Koringa and her Crocodiles** In the 1930s Koringa not only wrestled with alligators, but lay in broken glass, hung by her throat on a sharp sword blade and then lay buried in a coffin full of sand for 5 minutes.

3. **The Flying Trapeze** The flying trapeze was invented by the French man Jules Léotard, in 1850. As a child he practised over the swimming pool his father managed. The name leotard is still used for the one-piece costume that dancers and gymnasts wear.

4. **The High Wire** The French man Blondin found fame crossing Niagara Falls on 30 June 1852. He went over a 1,000-foot rope, blind-folded, pushing a man in a wheelbarrow and even carrying a cooking stove to cook an omelette which he then ate, 150 feet in the air.

5. **The Human Cannonball** The first known cannon act was a young woman called Zazel. In 1877 she was shot 20 feet (using a coiled spring) at the Royal Aquarium, London, and was a great sensation.

6. **Unusual human acts** The side show acts, or freak shows, who appeared especially at P T Barnum's. They were never a strong feature in Britain, excepting perhaps the elephant man and Tom Thumb.

7. **Illusion/Magic acts** When the Moscow State Circus first came to the UK in 1956, Kio was the featured attraction. He turned a cage of 6 lovely showgirls in the middle of the ring into a fully-grown lion.

8. **Jugglers** Italian Enrico Rastelli would have been a great asset to any football team, being able to balance 3 soccer balls on top of each other while balancing another on his head and yet another on his foot.

9. **Big troupe acts** Hungarians, Bulgarians and Russians specialise in springboard acts. The Czechs, Italians and French in trick cycling. The Chinese specialise in everything possible, from 16 on a bike to skipping.

10. **For an act worth seeing today** Try the Caesar Twins – 2 absolutely identical Polish twins who with supreme showmanship dive in and out of a 6-foot diameter goldfish bowl.

Chapter Eleven

Cleaning up my Act
1995-2005

When is a heart attack good news? When it's caused by a sexy Russian circus superstar (and of course no lasting damage is done).

For the first few weeks it looked like all my worst fears about the Moscow were about to be realised. The audiences for the grand (and expensive) Moscow State Circus were crushingly mediocre. That is until I made a flippant remark to Mark Borkowski. The next day page three of the *Mirror* ran as follows:

Two circus drummers had heart attacks watching Elena's big hoops
A Hula Hoop dancer was revealed yesterday as the big-top girl who makes drummers' hearts skip a beat. When an elderly circus drummer collapsed with a heart attack, the ringmaster put it down to old age. But when the 42-year-old replacement also keeled over with ticker trouble at the same point in the show an investigation was launched.

And the blame fell on sensationally sexy Elena Iniakina, 22, pride of the touring Moscow State Circus.

The hip swinging blonde sends pulses racing as she soars through her routine in thigh high boots and skimpy leotard.

'The band sit just behind where Elena dances,' said ringmaster Chris Barltrop, 'When she bends over they do get an eyeful. I admit I have to look away myself.'

Phil Langton was the first victim of Elena's charms.

'I've had problems with my heart before but I guess I got rather over-excited during the act. Elena's a very striking girl.'

Substitute Gordon Dunn started the next day. Within a week he was getting over a minor coronary.

'I felt dizzy early in the act. I suddenly realised I was hitting the saxophonist instead of the cymbals. I blacked out fell off my stool and woke up with a doctor standing over me.'

Elena denied that her act was too sexy.

'I like expressing myself. It's very free and natural – very provocative. The circus has something for everyone – children, mums and dads. My show is something for the dads.'

Ringmaster Chris said, 'If we have any more problems we will have to get a short sighted drummer.'

It was a silly story but it has to be said, Elena is astonishingly sexy. Our audiences doubled overnight. I guess a more lasting boost came from something one of Mark's young staff said to me. I was discussing the relative popularity of foreign circuses compared to home-grown ones.

'That's because people think that while the British circus will be around next year, this is their one and only chance to catch the Moscow.'

'A Once in a Lifetime opportunity – Don't miss' was slapped all over our next lot of posters. It seemed to strike a chord. The Moscow started to do phenomenally well, we were making tens of thousands of pounds profit a week.

It all started with my old partner, Brian Austen, having a bright idea.

October 1995 and I was having a bit of a problem with cash. Thanks to the Horrors, I was not as broke as I had been the year before (put it this way, I could pay my VAT bill), but I was still operating on the breadline. The instalments from my old manager, Martin Lacey, for the big beautiful Gerry Cottle's Circus were way overdue. I knew he was struggling, but I was not a charity and £60,000 is a lot of money. I was worried about my equipment being worn into the ground or worse, with all the animal fanatics prowling around, it being burnt to the ground. One day Brian popped in to see me for a chat. I was whingeing about Lacey.

'You've got to take it back,' Brian said. 'If you wait any longer the circus might not be worth anything anyway. If he goes bust, you'll lose everything.'

'I know, I know. Don't think I'm not aware of that.'

'Well just go up there and get it.'

'What do you mean "go up there and get it"?'

'Give him a final ultimatum. Say if he doesn't pay what he owes you in a couple of weeks, you are going to go up there and take back what's rightfully yours and if he stops you, you'll call in the bailiffs.'

'Blimey, Brian!'

'Do it. Look, there's a great circus which still rightfully belongs to you just up the motorway. Just think what you could do with it.'

'What could I do with it? Why should I do any better? I'm totally fed up with the circus.'

'You're not fed up with the circus. Look how much you're enjoying the Horrors. You're fed up with British circus. Why don't you put on a foreign circus? I'm trying to bring over the Moscow State at the moment. We could do it together using this tent. I'll put in the capital, you put in the equipment. How about it?'

I groaned. The Moscow State Circus and I had a bit of a history. OK, so I had made a small fortune when I first put it on in Bristol in the mad cocaine-infused summer of 1985, but that was a bit of an exception. As a sideline Brian and I in the late 80s had helped a theatrical promotions company called the Entertainment Corporation bring it over. It had made money but it had also been quite a bit of trouble. The artists were some of the worst prima donnas I had ever come across in my circus career. They wouldn't do any publicity unless there was a drink in it. They insisted on the best racehorse transport for their horses until we slipped them a few extra dollars. They liked going on strike. They wanted more money to load their own props, we refused, they went on strike. They wanted the best quality vegetables to feed the horses, we refused, they threatened to keep them out of the show – I found out they had been making stew for the stable lads with it. I said to the interpreter, translate this: 'Do you want cigarettes and whisky for the horses as well?' It was after a particularly stressful weekend with the Russians that I fixed myself at home and as you know I used river water and nearly died. So no, the idea did not appeal.

'Forget it. No way.'

'Go on. I think people will really go for it. It's got the class and snob value British circus just doesn't have. Not many people have seen it.'

'But it was doing so badly at Battersea Park a few years ago that they packed up and went home early. I've saved the press clipping.'

'Oh, the financing was all wrong. We'll book different acts and come to a different arrangement.'

'No way, Brian. Find someone else.'

And so the conversation went on and on, until of course I caved in, eventually, reluctantly, against my better judgement and everything else.

At the crack of dawn on a freezing cold December morning I counted my men. I had assembled fourteen of the strongest and most loyal, including Richard Campbell, my son-in-law Willie, April's boyfriend Ingo and Jeff Jay, who was now going out with Polly. We started on the long journey from Addlestone to Liverpool. I was nervous and sad. I didn't want to do this. Martin Lacey had been one of my best managers and on a personal level I had always really enjoyed his company. But I had met him four times since my conversation with Brian. Each time I had told him I needed my money and, despite promises that the cheque was in the post, it never arrived. I was worried there was going to be trouble when we got there but it was a bleak scene. The only sound was the squeal of tyres and hooting of horns as Martin shot off with his convoy without a backwards glance. In front of us was a cold grey deserted circus. Not a soul was left. A few jokers had put sugar in some of the diesel tanks and slashed some of the tyres but it didn't take long to fix those. We limped home in a rather sorry procession. Some of the trucks were in such a bad way they broke down – poor Jeff had a truck with no windscreen wipers and it rained cats and dogs all the way home from Liverpool, then he broke down three times just on the M25.

I guess it's not surprising that Martin Lacey has never spoken to me again. It's always rather awkward at circus get-togethers. While his ex-wife and two of his sons have become superstars in the world's best circuses working with animals, Martin has continued to stay in Britain fighting a losing battle. I saw him just the other day on television defending animals in the circus. I feel sorry about the way things have ended up for him.

So after a very mediocre start the Moscow State Circus really began to take off. And it wasn't just posters and sexy hula-hoop girls that were making the difference. The whole business of circus suddenly became a lot easier and more efficient. For a start mobile phones could have been invented for the travelling circus – I don't think we could have done it without them. Then the opening up of Eastern Europe meant for the first time we had a reliable source of hard-working tent men, often straight from working on their state circuses. Hungarians are the best, followed by the Poles. At the same time we hit the jackpot with the publicity men. We had always struggled to find and keep a group of men who could work a week or two ahead of the circus, putting up posters in the next town. It was hard, lonely work and required a good knowledge of the country. But in 1995 I was introduced to a fixer who supplied us with a bunch of men basically from a single housing estate in the North East. They were all related, or at least mates, and came with their own cars and caravans. If one was ill or wanted a break, they'd get their brother or uncle to cover. They had absolutely no interest in the circus but they knew the country like the back of their hand. It's the best system we'd ever come across. Travelling a really large show across the country was possible in a way that it never had been before.

There were of course all sorts of minor frustrations.

With all this success our competitors immediately tried to jump on the bandwagon. Martin Lacey hired a large tent and changed his circus into the 'traditional Russian Circus' – 'From Russia with Love' declared his posters. Yeah right. Peter Hoffman introduced the 'Real Russian Circus'. A 'Vladimir's Russian Circus' even appeared in Ireland with no real Russians in at all. It was interesting that while we prospered, none of these imitations lasted for long. I like to think that was because of the quality of our acts. As well as the super sexy Elena, I think our trump card was that we had the most fantastic high wire walker, Goussein (who is still travelling with the Moscow). He's the most wonderful performer, a dark swarthy Georgian. He has his wire on an incline that reaches to the roof of the Big Top. As he walks up he makes sure there are plenty of scary wobbles. There were plenty of the things the Russians are famous for – the big acrobatic troupe, the trapeze, the clowns. We also had lots of unusual acts – a magnificent hat-throwing act (it probably has to be seen to be appreciated), a floppy life-sized Russian doll which was chucked around between the troupe only to reveal at the end a real contortionist inside (always accompanied by a gasp from the audience), and a hot-air balloon comedy father and daughter act which consisted of the balloon whirling around at an impossible speed and them falling out and their clothes falling off.

In fact we never had any problem finding quality acts – there are 20,000 people working in circuses in Russia, most of them trained in their superb circus schools.

(Of course we didn't even try to have any animals in the circus – not even the Cossack riders – although the Russians are notorious for being able to train just about everything that walks, swims or flies on the earth. On one talent-spotting trip to Moscow I watched a woman swagger round the ring wearing the most amazing fur coat. She whistled and about 200 live mink ran off leaving her semi-naked.)

As I predicted, these artists, while magnificent in the ring, could be a real pain behind the scenes. There was something about the combination of the Russian melancholic vodka-soaked soul combined with their first experience of the West's consumer society. It created all sorts of – well, how can I put this politely – interesting situations.

The cars. They were obsessed. By the end of the first season every Russian on the circus had bought themselves a car – that meant thirty-two extra cars on the ground and because buying a car was such a big landmark in a Russian's life, they had a party to celebrate every single purchase. After the show the new vehicle would be driven into the ring, admired and christened, with copious amounts of vodka, singing, dancing and eventually weeping. And these cars were always terrible choices – old American imports which you could never find spare parts for, or couldn't get insurance for. And they'd only have obsolete communist driving licences.

I remember their conversations revolved round whether it was best to drive back home via Belgium and Germany or take the ferry to Finland and go down. And then there was the drinking. They could not understand the contradiction between drinking and driving. I remember one day driving home to Addlestone. As I came off the M25 at the roundabout one of my Russians' cars was in the ditch and the police were breathalysing him. Of course he'd had way too much vodka, and the next moment his mate turned up with one of the trucks to tow him, also completely plastered. The police were not impressed.

Then there was the catalogue shopping. Fresh from behind the Iron Curtain they'd never come across this phenomenon before – it was as if they'd died and gone to heaven. They started ordering stuff as if their lives depended on it. And it really was absolutely anything, they didn't care, it was just the principle of the thing. This would have been fine except because they were travelling they gave my office as the delivery address. I was totally inundated with tat, most of which they had no intention of paying for. (In fact I'm not convinced they ever grasped the fact that any of it would ever have to be paid for.) I couldn't get to my desk in the morning, and the phone wouldn't stop ringing with demands for payment. So I banned any more catalogue shopping and they immediately went on strike.

I could bear all of this 'eccentricity' because we were making money. Unlike any circus I had ever had before, we never ever had a week where we didn't make a profit of some kind. It was totally fantastic and made a huge difference to not have to worry about going bust every other week. It was good for my soul.

We made so much money that first year we decided to go even bigger and better the next. We bought a bigger tent and lots of equipment, but then what to do with the old circus? I was really impressed with the circus at Chessington Zoo. They'd got a proper director, Rob Goodwin, and put in some songs, dancing and a theme. We decided to start a new Cottle and Austen's Circus. My hunch was that the time had finally come for a British non-animal circus, if we made it big enough and more theatrical. 'Cottle and Austen's Electric Rock and Roll Circus' was born. We had our very best homegrown acts in it. It was young and fun and the family all joined when the Circus of Horrors was off the road – April ran the box office, Ingo was in charge of maintenance, Polly did aerial acts and her boyfriend Jeff was on the wheel of death. Baba's son, Beau, managed the circus and was head of a crazy crew of clowns, which had the most over-the-top custard pie fight. The Kenyans did their acrobatics, the old-fashioned ringmaster had disappeared and instead the show was presented by a bubbly blonde singer and her troupe of dancing girls. And it worked. It was the first time, for me anyway, that a non-animal British circus had made any sort of long-lasting sustainable success. It did not always deliver the audiences in the way that the Moscow did, we did sometimes make a loss, but not often. Here was a British, non-animal circus you could actually make a living out of. I think it was because it was a slick, happy, fun show. I loved it and was immensely proud of it, and while I take my hat off to the skill of our foreign circuses, this was the one I really loved going to see.

We thought the first year of the Moscow was good, but believe me the second year was fantastic, and with the additional income from Cottle and Austen's Circus we had money in our pockets and smiles on our faces. But it became clear as time progressed that we might be missing a trick. My team of Anne Owen, Peter Norris and Peter Featherstone had been booking sites from my little office for well over ten years. We knew the country like the backs of our hands, the towns that worked and the sites which were no hopers. We reckoned there were around ninety key grounds in the country where you were practically guaranteed to make money. A circus generally went to around thirty towns a year. If we had one more big circus, with three circuses we could visit every one of these ninety lucrative sites in a year. In fact we would be in a position to go to the councils and offer them a three-year deal – a different circus three years in a row. It would be easier for the councils and it would mean for the first time we could plan more than one season ahead. All sorts of deals could be done. It might even feel like a proper business. (Of course it also meant our competitors would be rather excluded. Could I make myself any more unpopular with them than I was already, I asked myself?)

There was one thing necessary to make this scheme work – the third circus would have to be sufficiently different from the other two and yet equally spectacular. It really couldn't be another British circus, and couldn't be from the Eastern block. The obvious choice was the Chinese State Circus. The problem was we had no contacts with the Chinese and over there it's all about who you know. The person who did was Phillip Gandey, son of Joe Gandey, whom I'd always been fiercely competitive with. But it's amazing how healing a really good business proposition can be. Phillip went over to China and started negotiating on our behalf. Eventually we were sent a video of a circus the government was willing to let us have (at a price). Brian and I watched the tape in my little office. It was a bit grainy, the music was horribly twangy in that cat-strangled oriental sort of way, and the costumes beggared belief. But apart from that, it was perfect. It looked completely different to anything else around in Britain – their acts centred around lots of people performing acts of great intricacy and skill rather than individual acts of great derring-do. I think it was the numbers plate spinning at once, or tossing the diabolo, or performing tricks on the bike. The sheer discipline of their formations. Of course there were individual acts – the Chinese are famous for their contortionists and this circus had a fantastically bendy young girl. But its pièce de résistance was the bike act. This troupe had the world record for the number of girls riding one bike.

Cleaning up my Act

'One, two . . .'

As they climbed on each other's backs, more and more piled on one tiny bike going round and round the edge of the ring.

'Thirteen, fourteen, fifteen . . . sixteen.'

Brian shook his head.

'Bloody hell. That's brilliant.'

He leant forwards and paused the video.

'Gerry, just count that again. How many do you make on that bike?'

It was like the number of people you can get in a mini. Totally unfeasible and looked horribly unsafe – the bike wobbled all over the place and the girls squealed most satisfactorily. Just think, they held a world record they could attempt night after night in the ring. I was already rubbing my hands in glee at the prospect of phoning Mark Borkowski to arrange the publicity stunt. He'd wet himself. So we forked out over a million pounds and bought from Gary Smart the exquisite tent and equipment that I'd been so jealous of a few years before (he'd decided to concentrate on his other businesses, 'revenge is a dish best eaten cold,' so they say).

I remember the day the Chinese arrived. Brian and I hung over the gate at Addlestone, shooting the breeze, intrigued to see what they looked like. As the coach swung into the yard and they started to get off we looked at each other perplexed.

'Gosh, they've got a lot of children. I thought they were only allowed one each.'

'I didn't think they were bringing their families.'

We waited for the grown-ups to get off and then suddenly the coach was empty and we realised *they* were the circus.

'I guess the Chinese do look young,' Brian said.

'Impossible to know how old they are,' I agreed.

For the next few days they rehearsed in the Big Top we'd put up in the yard. Every so often I'd stretch my legs and pop my head in to watch. What I saw made me apprehensive. The girls kept falling off the bike. Sixteen? More like six if they were lucky, and they were all so young. Meanwhile I was working hard with Mark on the launch. It was obvious we should try to break the world record for the number of girls on a bike.

'I know, let's stop at a service station on the M4 and maybe the coach could leave without them and they could all race after him on one bike down the motorway,' Mark suggested brightly.

'Mark, I've already had two nights in jail and I don't feel like repeating the experience,' I said.

In the end we decided to try it in Trafalgar Square. It was one of those cold grey April days, more winter than spring, and it had been drizzling all morning. I was nervous and I don't usually get nervous, let's face I had been around the block a few times. But absolutely everybody in the whole world had turned up. Every broadsheet, the *Sun*, the *Mirror*, the BBC, ITN. So far the girls had only managed fourteen on the bike. They needed at least seventeen if they were to break their own alleged record. There were always good excuses – 'Wai Lin has injured her foot', 'the stage isn't level', 'the bikes have the wrong tyres' – but Mr Tian, the interpreter, assured me that on the day they would do it.

'World record, it will be no problem, Mr Cottle.'

But when we arrived in Trafalgar Square the troupe gathered in an ominous huddle – all the girls, the trainer, the interpreter and Mr Pong, the cook. There was much pointing at the sky and pointing at the ground.

'So sorry, Mr Cottle,' Mr Tian approached me, with a grin on his face. 'Because it is raining we cannot do bike. Instead we will do plate spinning.'

'What do you mean, because it's raining?'

'In the Yuan province we do not have rain. We will do very good plate spinning.'

'Oh no you won't. You will do very good bike act, rain or no rain.'

'So sorry, Mr Cottle. It is too slippery for bike. Too dangerous. The girls will not do it.'

I could feel my temper about to erupt. 'Now look here, Mr Tian. I've been very patient with all of you. In this country we circus people are tough and we know when we have to perform. If we hadn't we wouldn't have survived. Today is the day when, whether you like it or not, it is your turn to perform. Otherwise (I gestured towards the line of camera crews) the name of the Chinese State Circus will never be respected. All these people have come to see the bike and see the bike they must.'

Mr Tian retreated, still smiling, and started having words with Mr Pong and the trainer, who in turn started shouting at the girls. Meanwhile I got Gerry Jr and a whole load of our circus helpers to start mopping up the pavement of Trafalgar Square with paper towels.

After ten minutes the big girl at the bottom started riding the bike.

'It would have been better on the M4. But with any luck one of them will fall off,' Mark whispered to me.

'Should be no problem there,' I growled.

The bike started to go round in wider faster circles, one by one the girls ran and jumped on the back and clambered to the top of the pyramid, six . . . ten . . . twelve up. Bloody hell, I thought. They're going to do it . . . thirteen . . . fourteen . . . suddenly there was a shriek as number fifteen tripped and fell flat on her face. The pyramid of little girls started to wobble, and then fourteen Chinese girls went arse over tit as the bike crashed in the midst of a chorus of high-pitched screams.

That night I invited Brian over to supper. A horrible thought had entered my head which wouldn't go away.

'I want you to take a look at a video,' I said. We went over to my office and I started to play the original video from the agency in China on the basis of which we had bought the circus.

'Bloody hell, it's not the same circus,' Brian said.

'We've been conned,' I said.

'They're completely different!'

'Well, they're grown up for a start.'

Forty years in the business and I could still be tricked. They were a completely different set of artists to the ones on the tape. I was fuming.

But the next day the Chinese were in all the papers, including a wonderful front page in the *Independent* with a picture of the girls falling off their bikes. We opened at Alexandra Palace to sell-out audiences, and when the girls fell off the bike or couldn't do their tricks they tried again and the audience loved them – the fact they were practically children made the audience root for them. They were young, cute and trying desperately hard. That season the Chinese State Circus was our most profitable circus. Under the circumstances it would have been churlish to complain ...

I had heard stories about Chinese circuses making pot noodles in complimentary kettles in hotels, so when the only condition of the deal was they brought their own cook, the aptly named Mr Pong, I happily agreed and built a kitchen wagon for him to work in. What confused me was the fact he was treated with the most extraordinary deference by everyone. All decisions had to go to Pong first. The next time I saw Phillip Gandey I asked him, 'What's the deal with Mr Pong?'

'Oh, I should have warned you. He's the deputy Chinese minister for culture for the Yuan Province, so try not to annoy him.'

Over the next few weeks I came to the conclusion that coming over here was quite a big deal to the Chinese, and Mr Pong was both keeping a very strict eye on all the artists and taking in everything that was going on around in the country in the wider sense, if you know what I mean.

Mr Pong needn't have worried. We had none of the problems that we had with the Russians. They worked terribly hard, took their performance extremely seriously and were incredibly disciplined. There was no inter-cast hanky-panky that we were aware of. Brian and I were impressed. I never saw any of them take so much as a sniff of alcohol, although they did develop a taste for fast food (maybe Mr Pong should have stuck to the day job), which meant they all put on weight and the tyres on the bikes kept bursting.

So I was really surprised when halfway through the tour I was woken up by one of those early morning telephone calls that you dread. It was our manager Larry de Wit calling from the circus, currently just off the M4 just outside Swindon.

'I think you need to come down. We had a bit of an incident last night.'

'What do you mean? It better be good waking me up at this time of the morning.'

'Oh yes, it's worth it. There was a huge row last night. I was woken up by the most awful screaming. I was surprised because as you know they're all normally tucked up in bed by midnight. The whole circus seemed to be packed into the trainer's wagon. I think the trainer had an argument with one of the girls. He thinks she's lazy. All the girls went bananas and started shouting at him.'

'Bit harsh, but not worth waking me up for.'

'No, there's more. I split them all up and packed them off to bed and told the trainer we'd discuss it in the morning. Next thing I know, I'm woken up by a policeman knocking on the door at 4 am. He'd only picked up twelve of the Chinese girls on their bikes heading the wrong way up the M4. As far as I can make out the girl had run away and all the rest of them had jumped on their bikes to go and look for her. Luckily the patrol car came along before they had an accident.'

'Yep. Well done. Worth waking me up.'

Brian and I went along later that day to talk to the grown-ups. In true Chinese style, with polite smiles on their faces, they avoided the issue: 'A family matter, all sorted now.' We let it be known that cycling along the motorway was not to be encouraged, and that was the last we heard of it. It has to be said, Mr Tian has become a very good friend and of all the nationalities I have dealt with over the years the Chinese have been the best.

So we had three beautiful big circuses touring the best sites in the country. Brian Austen and I had become the biggest and best circus owners Britain, and maybe even Europe, had ever had. In a very short space of time we had made more money than we had ever dreamt of. But I decided that I had to make some big changes, and this decision came about because I had finally stopped taking drugs.

It was Freddy Mercury's singing that did it.

June 1998. A cold wet Saturday evening. I was stuck in a dingy hotel room somewhere round the back of Hammersmith with my 'girlfriend' of the time. We were both high. She had a fixation on Freddie Mercury, and the Queen song 'The Show Must Go On' in particular. She played it over and over and over again, and something in me snapped. I was filled with the most intense self-loathing and disgust. On the television I was trying to watch the BBC's coverage of Glastonbury. It looked utterly miserable, endless rain pouring down. My children were there with the Circus of Horrors, drowning in mud. I should have been there helping them. Instead here I was wasting my life listening to Queen. I didn't want to do it any more. I got my stuff together, threw some money on the bed, walked out of the hotel and never touched drugs again. (I also never played Queen again.)

It had taken thirteen years of my life away and cost thousands of pounds. I'd been in rehab, been busted and nearly died, but it was not until this moment that I was ready to walk away from this bit of my life. And boy was I ready. I went straight to the hairdresser and had my long floppy locks cut off, I shaved off my moustache and started a new clean life. I've never looked back and never been tempted to take drugs again.

My life was transformed, and the main reason was because I could make decisions again. Until then, everything had been about facilitating the next fix, taking the easy short-term option to get ready cash to fund my habit so I could then go off and disappear. Now I had the confidence and clarity to take a long view, and get a proper perspective on what I really needed to make my business work and make me happy. I felt how I used to when I was a young man. It felt really good.

One day I got a phone call from John Carter (of Carters Steam Fair). 'Gerry, I'm not very well. I would really like it if you came to see me.'

I knew I should go and see him. I should have gone to see him a long time ago but I just couldn't face hospitals, not after what my mum and dad had gone through. But after he rang, I did go to see John.

It was just as bad as I'd feared, worse really. There are some people you can imagine going to an early grave – people you know who drive like maniacs, or drink too much or are real hypochondriacs, but there are others, and I would have put John at the very top of this list, who you think are immortal. He was so impressive and formidable – imagine walking into a ward and seeing this great barrel of a man reduced to a tiny shadow of himself. It was profoundly shocking. He had a rare form of cancer which the year before he seemed to have beaten, but it had come back with a vengeance and its progress was swift. With John in hospital, Anna took over running the fair and I helped as much as I could, particularly with booking the sites. But Christmas 2000 John died. The funeral took place on a beautiful crisp sunny December day, with a layer of snow covering the ground. Over 500 people came. It was a dramatic and moving occasion. John's coffin was carried to the church on one of his beloved steam engines with his three sons and two daughters walking behind. I was with Betty and my assistant Anne Owen. Afterwards we all felt shaken up and instead of going straight to the reception we stopped for a meal in a pub. At 58, John was just two years older than me. I stared into the bottom of my glass and felt my mortality.

'I've got to stop wasting time. I've got to change my life,' I said.

Betty and Anne nodded in agreement. What they didn't realise was that I meant my whole life. Starting with my marriage.

For almost two years after I gave up drugs for good, I didn't stray. I didn't want to. Part of the whole thing about taking cocaine was taking it with someone, preferably a pretty lady. Without it, I really didn't want to cheat. In fact I felt a desperate need to clean up my whole life. But strangely enough being clean didn't improve my relationship with Betty. We had been living very separate lives for many years. When the children were young in many ways it was an arrangement that worked – Betty looked after the home and family, I never had to worry about anything there, and I looked after the business. Betty always had everything she ever wanted, although as she points out that didn't include a real husband. But when the children have left home and you have separate bedrooms and don't do anything together and you don't have any of the same interests and you argue all the time, well it's not great. For a while, although my marriage was pretty empty, I was so busy with the new Cottle and Austen expanding circus empire my life felt very full.

Then I met Sally. I was at the opening of an art gallery in Charing Cross and gazing at a painting was an Amazonian blonde with the most amazing curvaceous figure. She had the air of being alone and a little vulnerable. I went over and introduced myself. It was one of those rare moments of instant attraction. I didn't know anyone there and neither did she. In fact she had just come back from four years in Australia and had lost contact with many of her friends. She was a bit lonely generally and so, I realised, was I. Sally was a fitness instructor – confident, funny, intelligent, independent and totally clean. If I had so much as looked at a drug she would have chucked me instantly. This was the first proper relationship I'd had for years and it felt amazing. I felt like a teenager again. Sally was quite young – thirty in fact, the same age as my daughter Sarah – but it didn't matter because we were interested in the same things. She wanted to start a new business and so did I. We went researching together. She had no ties and we travelled together – she came with me while I booked a whole tour of Ireland for the Chinese. On the way back the ferry was delayed and we ended up sleeping on the floor of the children's barn in the cafe. I laughed in a way I hadn't for years. I guess Sally showed me what real companionship felt like and that's a very different companionship to sharing a fix or a loveless marriage. I suddenly realised how lonely my life had been before I met her.

In June 2001 Betty received a telephone call from a 'so-called' friend.

'Betty. I'm not ringing because I want to. I really don't like doing this. But I think I owe it to you to tell you.'

'Oh God, what?'

'If it was me I'd want to know.'

'For God's sake, just tell me.'

'It's Gerry. He's got a girlfriend. He brought her to the circus last night and introduced her. In fact he's been taking her everywhere. I don't think she's a one-night wonder. In fact I think he's even introduced her to your girls. And she's young. Very young.'

The phone call left Betty devastated . . . and absolutely furious. That night when I walked in, she was waiting for me.

'Have a nice time last night with your girlfriend? Enjoy the circus, does she?'

'Who told you?'

'Never you mind who told me. How could you, you bastard? How long has this been going on?'

'About two years.'

'Two years. You bastard.'

'I think I should leave.'

'Too right. Go and don't bother coming back.'

That's cutting a long late-night conversation very short, but you get the idea. I think Betty was so hurt because this time there were no excuses – there were no drugs to blame, this was no one-night stand, this was a proper relationship and she could see that immediately. I wasn't going to give Sally up and I didn't pretend that was an option. So the next day I moved out and never went back. I think when things calmed down Betty would have liked us to get back together, but I was absolutely determined we should split. In fact I should have done it much sooner. I guess I did the typical male thing of leaving it until I was forced to make a move. But when I did move that was it, I was not going back.

Betty felt (and still feels) that she supported me through some terrible times and when her usefulness ended, I just threw her away. Well you could look at it that way. On the other hand our relationship was doing neither of us any good. There didn't seem to be much love lost on either side.

I don't feel good about what happened. I did love Betty. In fact I still love her, but we can't live together any more. In some ways she was right – when I gave up drugs, I finally had the confidence to walk away. She had been my rock, and I didn't need her any more. But is there any point in being unhappy and arguing away the rest of our lives?

2003 was the most extraordinary year for me. If I believed in astrology (which I don't, well only a little bit) my chart for that year must have had conjunctions, eclipses, moons crashing into suns and planets doing the cancan. Because circuses and I finally came to the end of the line, and my life was completely transformed.

When I gave up drugs and after John Carter died, I finally saw my life with a new clear perspective. It was suddenly patently obvious that I had to get out of the circus business.

OK, so the Moscow and Chinese were flavour of the month this year, but their popularity wouldn't last forever and all of this money we'd made so quickly would disappear just as fast – I needed to quit while I was ahead. I just had to look at the way Brian Austen had run his finances, always investing some of his profits into businesses other than circuses. To be honest it was also such grinding hard work and I wasn't getting any younger.

The real thorn in my side was the local authorities. Every year they became more of a pain. We were asked to attend site meetings for places we'd been going to for years and filling in sixty-page forms when two sides of A4 had always done before. I had to make statements about how many ethnic minorities, women and people with disabilities I employed, when we'd had all of the above employed in the circus for years in the natural course of things. They treated you with such a lack of respect. For example, Lambeth council had a new lady in charge. She wanted to meet me. I drove miles all the way across London to see her only to be told she'd forgotten and wasn't there. I was asked to come back another day. When I said I couldn't I was told that unless I met her face to face they would not let us use any of their sites. So I duly trekked back at the allotted hour to meet her. Six months later she'd moved job and I had to repeat the whole charade. And just imagine doing all this, times three circuses. That meant a lot of meetings, too many.

But it wasn't just the councils, it was the way the business was set up. Everything was done from Addlestone. That was where all three circuses spent the winter. That included 150 parked trucks. I had five people working for me in the office, plus Gerry Jr and Haze working on publicity, Tony Shuker on graphic design, and then there were thirty to forty artists, ten publicity boys and twenty foreign tent men working on each show, as well as the British managers and technical staff. That meant we employed 250 people, all of whom were my responsibility. And because it was a seven-day-a-week business where people lived and worked on the job, I never had a day off. My phone never stopped ringing. The problems could be large – like a council objecting to our posters and saying we wouldn't be allowed on site until they had been taken down – or they could be tiny – like a council official complaining about the Russians fishing in the local stream – but it was me who'd have to sort them all out. Like a cartoon character I felt like I walked around with a permanent grey cloud above my head with three routes maps drawn on it.

And much as I loved working with Brian (I would like to stress we never ever had an argument and are still great friends), I got cheesed off doing all the office work while he still seemed to have time to build up his own businesses outside the circus. And the thing that really got to me, he never answered the phone. OK, so Cricklade has the most abysmal mobile phone reception, but . . .

It was 7 March 2003. About four times a year we got the management teams of all the circuses together to discuss problems, new developments and generally knock around ideas. This was the first and most important meeting of the season. We decided to have it in Brian's office at Cricklade. I also decided Brian should chair the meeting – it's good to hear from someone else sometimes, I can talk too much. As the meeting got under way we discussed all sorts of practical issues – were this year's Hungarians as good as last year's? Should we give a discount on Thursdays? Should we put up the price of tickets by £2? Brian looked bored and at one point I looked round and he'd nodded off.

By the time the meeting ended I was pretty cheesed off. I phoned Peter Norris in my office. 'Any messages?'

'Just one. I'm afraid the council's rung. Your appeal for planning permission has been refused.'

That was the last straw. I had set my heart on developing Addlestone into an antiques centre. I had spent a quarter of a million pounds building a new road, new car park and new warehouse. The planning application itself had cost £30,000. I may as well have thrown the money straight down the drain.

That night I drove to Bristol, where Cottle and Austen's was playing. Just as I was on the point of despair a little thought crept into my mind. I was just down the road from Somerset. I stopped the car and rang Peter again. 'Can you do me a favour? Can you look in the For Sale file and see if you can find an advert for Wookey Hole?'

Six months ago Anna Carter had sent me an advert from a trade paper advertising the sale of Wookey Hole caves. It captured my imagination, especially as they came with practically a whole village. The problem was the amount of money they wanted – £6.5 million. I only had half a million in the bank. I'd filed the advert away. But on that cold March evening, staring into the abyss, desperation suddenly made everything seem a little more possible. Perhaps it was still for sale? If it was they would have been bound to have reduced the price, wouldn't they? Peter rang me back. The estate agents were Humberts. I rang them straight away. Yes, the caves were still for sale and, yes, the owners were now prepared to consider an offer closer to £6 million. That only left me £5.5 million to find. I made an appointment to go and look round the next day.

As I drove down into the narrow gorge of Wookey Hole, it felt like I was going into Sleepy Hollow. The place sent shivers down my spine. The tiny village was overshadowed by the Mendip Hills. A beautiful rushing waterfall tumbled down from a great height and black ravens called out menacingly in the tall trees. It was cold and dark, mystical and magical, but slightly creepy too. I loved it. You could feel the presence of the prehistoric men who had lived there at the beginning of time, driving their prey off the cliffs to fall to their deaths and dragging them into the caves to be stored and feasted on.

The caves themselves were spectacular – lots of weird rock formations, huge echoing chambers and bottomless dark pools. Legend has it that 300 years ago a witch lived in these caves until children started to die in Wookey village. The bishop was summoned from Wells. He went into the caves and touched the witch and she turned into the stone which is there today. I felt the place had huge potential. And even better the caves came with lots of outbuildings – a paper mill, four houses and a warehouse. There was so much room for expansion. And I fancied myself living in the middle of a village, a veritable lord of the manor. I turned to Gerry Jr who had come down with me. 'What do you think?'

'I like it.'

'Yes, I do too. I'm going to buy it.'

But how? I went to see my accountant, Ken Morgan. As you know, he had been looking after my finances for over thirty years and knew me well. Ken always has a wonderful 'can do' attitude but even his first reaction was, 'I don't know where you're going to get that kind of money from, Gerry.' But humouring me, he made an appointment to see Humberts.

They were an extremely up-market kind of estate agent. Their office was in Mayfair and owned by Nigel Talbot-Ponsonby, who had an estate of his own and dressed as if he was still out and about on it. They were very friendly until I made an offer of £4 million. Despite an instant total rejection, they let me take away the due diligence books which, too posh for plastic bags, they wrapped in brown paper and tied up with string.

I told Brian Austen about the whole Humberts fiasco. He took it quite seriously. 'I'd like to take a look at this Wookey Hole,' he said. So we jumped in one of his helicopters and flew over for another look. Brian liked it straight away.

'Look, I think this would be good for you, Gerry. How about if I buy your half of the circuses?★ I reckon they're worth £2 million, so I'll raise a million pounds.'

I accepted pretty much on the spot. So I had £1.5 million, the crucial question was whether and for how much I could sell Addlestone?

The week Addlestone went on sale we had sixty-nine enquiries, lots of them serious. Although I had bought it for so little in 1974, it was fifteen acres of prime development land within a mile of the

---

★ Brian and I had always spilt the circuses 50:50, which is unusual. Normally one partner would have a larger share. Ken Morgan says Brian and I are the only people he knows who have had this arrangement. But it worked.

M25. I had been told so many times it was worth a lot of money. I wasn't surprised when several big building companies came and looked round, but they all had the same problem – without a guarantee of planning permission, no one would buy. I was stuck. Then I found out the council actually didn't want us to sell. I'd been too well behaved. It suited them to have me there, so they weren't being very helpful. I told the local newspaper I was considering a very good offer from a rich gypsy. Suddenly the council came on side, and then I got a serious offer. Tommy Traylen was a local showman, very successful. He had over 150 big American trailers stored all over the South of England. He offered me £2.75 million. I wanted £3 million.

'Let's toss for it,' I said.

'OK. I'll throw,' he agreed.

He got out a pound coin and threw it in the air.

'Heads,' I shouted as it spun above our heads. It landed on the ground.

He moved his foot, we peered down. It was heads. I'd just won a quarter of a million pounds on the toss of a coin.

So I had sold my business and I had sold my home, but I still hadn't bought Wookey. I was still £1.5 million short of the asking price and they were refusing to come any lower. Meanwhile the circus moved out of Addlestone and into Brian's headquarters at Cricklade. It was an incredibly sad time. My loyal office, Anne Owen, Peter Norris and Peter Featherstone, all moved down to Cricklade. I felt I was letting them down, they never really believed I would do it – in fact they all still believe I'm going to start a new circus any time now. Paul Archer, who had come to me as a young boy in the 70s and had worked his way up to become manager of the Moscow, said, 'You sell me like I am an old Scammell truck.' This was the third time I'd sold him: once to Martin Lacey (and snatched him back) and twice to Brian.

For the thirty years we had lived at Addlestone it had been not just our home, but home for many of the people who travelled with us, some of them had lived there for thirty years too. With Tommy the showman about to take possession, every day saw another wagon pull out of the yard and more tearful goodbyes. Betty moved to Warwick to be close to her sisters. I moved back in. Except for my daughter Sarah who was still living in her mobile home on site, I was suddenly on my own. It was so quiet. I was no longer the head of my own little tribe. And the day Brian officially took over the circuses the phone literally stopped ringing. Just like that.

It was a strange time, but I wasn't worried. I didn't know how, but I knew things would work out. For the first time in my life I found the inner peace to just sit and wait. Six years earlier, still on drugs, I would have been running round like a headless chicken, making stupid decisions, trying to force things. Then it was always rush, rush, rush. Cocaine makes you feel like you never have enough time, you have to get money, you have to get a fix. You're scared to stop in case everything comes collapsing down. Instead I used the time to plan my next move.

What I needed was a loan. I arranged a meeting with two bankers from an Irish bank. They came down to Wookey from London and were complete, well what word rhymes with bankers? They had no interest in my plans for the place but all they wanted was to talk about their great drinking exploits and be taken to the pub. They didn't even have the courtesy to get back to me.

'Why don't you just ask your own bank?' Ken asked.

'It can't be that easy.'

'Well you never know,' he replied.

So I went to see my bank manager at Barclays. To my amazement he agreed straight away. 'You've been with us thirty years and you've been an excellent customer.'

That same week, the first week in September 2003, the owners of Wookey came back and accepted a lower offer. I had bought my caves.

There was one other thing that had to be sorted. I had split up with Betty but I had not moved in with Sally. Something was stopping me. We had been going out for over two years and our relationship had got to that point where we needed to take it forwards. But I really wasn't sure I wanted Sally to come with me to Wookey. I was really

really fond of her, but she was twenty-five years younger than me. She said it didn't matter, and I knew it didn't at the time, but what about later on? And then there was Anna.

As you may have gathered, I had always adored Anna Carter and we had stayed close after John's death. One weekend that summer I took Sally along to meet her. It was strange the two of them being in the same room, I had the feeling I might be going home with the wrong woman. Anna was my age, in the same sort of business, had five children and was of course totally gorgeous. The next week I went to see her without Sally. And the week after that I took her out to dinner.

'Gerry, I know you are going out with another woman. I won't go out with you if you are going out with someone else. Don't mess me about. Think about it, you've got two weeks.'

I didn't have to think about it, I knew what I had to do. The day after I signed the deal with Wookey, on 7 September, I went to see Sally and told her I could never see her again. She was absolutely devastated. It was one of the hardest things I've ever had to do.

By the end of that first week of September I had totally changed my life and changed it for the better.

❧

Wookey has surpassed all my expectations (and everybody else's, I think). We managed to increase the number of visitors to Wookey by 25,000 in the first year and 35,000 on top of that last year. Turnover has increased by more than forty per cent because we've completely overhauled the cafés and the shop. So business is good, and more importantly relatively predictable. It's given me a stable income but also plenty of opportunities to have fun.

I've been able to try out lots of ideas – Wookey now has a magical fairy garden, a wizard theatre, a teddy bear museum and a big play barn. The best idea was Anna's. Right at the very beginning she suggested we make a dinosaur park in the gorge. It does have that damp prehistoric feeling about it. We bought a job lot of giant fibreglass dinosaurs from an amusement park outside Lowestoft. It took eight articulated lorries to transport them the hundreds of miles back to Wookey and we had to chop off some of their heads to fit under the motorway bridges, but a bit of glue and they are as good as new. The locals got a bit of a shock, though, when in the middle of a parish meeting a fleet of headless monsters came rumbling past in the fading evening light.

Wookey also offers lots of scope for great one-offs. We did a special midnight Halloween trip through the caves, a Dr Who exhibition to tie in with the series relaunch, a Santa's grotto and a bunny festival for Easter. I've been able to put all my publicity skills to use. My first act was to request the return of the legendary bones of the witch of Wookey, currently on show in Wells Museum. My fight to reclaim the witch got me on to *GMTV*. Then our dalek was kidnapped and a ransom note sent. It was found a week later on top of Glastonbury Tor and had to be rescued. I appeared on *Richard and Judy* appealing for information. During the bunny fest, two of the rabbits got married. They were dressed in top hat and tails and white dress and veil. We had rose petal confetti and carrot cake for after. (It was a bit awkward when the press asked the name of the vicar's parish, but moving swiftly on . . .) The RSPCA helped us enormously by complaining we were being cruel to the bunnies by dressing them up. We were in the national newspapers defending the right of rabbits to marry.

Best of all it's a fantastic home for the family. Sarah has moved into the cottages and is head of maintenance. She is really tough and practical, she keeps the men in line. I'm so proud of her. My granddaughter Ellen has settled down in the local school and has her ponies up the road. She's a great rider, the Fossett genes are very much in evidence. Polly is running the teddy bear shop and her two children – Whistle and Beau – love the freedom that living in Wookey gives them. Whistle especially likes performing in the wizard shows in the summer. When I got a marriage license for the caves in January 2005, Polly and Jeff were the first couple to get married in them. It was a very special day. April and Ingo still travel with the circus, but always come back to Wookey at the end of the season. So with their children Harley and Maddox, all my grandchildren have a great time running around together in the holidays.

Gerry Jr, well he's a very different kettle of fish. Like me as a young man, he likes the bright city lights. I can't see him anywhere but London. He's working with Mark Borkowski, getting a great PR apprenticeship, and enjoying life to the full. The pressure was on when I was young to settle down, it's just what everyone did. But I think Gerry Jr is much better just having a good time.

Anna continues to run Carters Steam Fair and is fiercely independent. We pick each other's brains for ideas and support each other. I respect her independence, the strength she has shown taking over the business since John died and how she keeps her family together. She has been so helpful to me with Wookey, and I hope I have managed to help her as well. It's great to be with someone who likes doing the same things. Of course Anna is bright, funny and extremely sexy as well. She's cheeky and I like that. Yes, we are still very much together and I hope she will move to Wookey soon.

I have never been so content. In fact I don't think I've known what contentment was until now. I've had extreme highs, as well as extreme lows, but I've never before been able just to sit and enjoy the life I've built for myself. It could be that I'm getting old, or it could be that I made two very good decisions – buying Wookey and getting together with Anna. Today, I can actually sit and spend a whole afternoon reading the Sunday papers without feeling guilty. Something unheard of for me. That's not to say I don't still have my ambitions, it's just that they have changed. Now I want to own the biggest and best attraction in Britain. Hopefully it won't be such a bumpy ride . . .

Afterword

Confessions of a Showman?

The number of times people have said to me over the years, 'You should write a book.' I have always wanted to. For a start I've wanted to chronicle the changing world of the circus, especially as I think there is a serious prospect that the whole travelling Big Top way of life could disappear forever in this country very soon. The animals have already gone for good.

Also, let's be honest, there's a bit of ego in there as well. The idea of leaving a record of my life for my children and grandchildren, well that's very appealing, isn't it?

But now I've got to an age and stage in my life where it feels right to put my memories to paper. Sixty, with my bad habits finally behind me, I feel a real need to be honest. This book has given me the opportunity to confess my sins, put them down and hopefully draw a line under them and move on. I've been forced to examine the demons I spent most of my life successfully ignoring. It has been the hardest, most disciplined personal challenge I have ever had. It has been a kind of therapy.

Writing this book has made me realise how much my behaviour must have hurt Betty and the family. I just hope they have not been too affected by my bad and sometimes totally stupid behaviour, and that they can forgive me. Perhaps it will serve as a warning to my children not to waste their lives in the same way. I am so proud of my beautiful girls performing in our circus, looking just like their mum. It is now eight years since I stopped taking cocaine and I can now honestly say I will never go back.

Even though Betty and I live separate lives, as a family we are all very close. My kids all love Wookey Hole and I believe they will keep it as a family home. I don't think they will continue with the travelling circus life. They all say they have seen the hard work and the heartache I have been through, and now they have nice houses at Wookey it is more difficult to go off on the road again.

Why do we, the British, have to kill what we create? Philip Astley is acknowledged worldwide as having created the circus, yet we are the only country that treats circus as a lost cause. Throughout the world circus shows go on producing strong family entertainment, so I think circus is safe outside the UK. To survive in Britain, I see the future of circus as becoming theatre and arena based, if only because local authorities and health and safety inspectors are making the lives of the travelling circus unbearable. Certainly the transformation of the Circus of Horrors from a tent show to a theatre show has been very successful and the fact that it is still as popular as ever after ten years gives me hope.

Then of course there is Cirque du Soleil. I love them, but they have moved circus into a dimension which I am not sure many people like myself who came from a traditional background could adapt to.

So will I go back to circus? Do I miss it?

I really believe I have settled down forever at Wookey Hole, but my all-consuming passion for circus remains. I keep dreaming up ideas for new shows. People are able to talk me out of them because my head knows I shouldn't take the risk, but still my heart pines. Why I love it, God knows. I sat and watched a show the other day that I had seen a good few times before and I totally enjoyed all two hours of it.

But this is the real beauty of Wookey. For twenty-five years I have dreamed of starting my own circus school and now the mill building at Wookey provides the perfect space. When I had my travelling circus school in the mid 80s, I really enjoyed the enthusiasm of the young people and teaching them. Out of thirty kids it produced twelve very good performers who are still in the business, including my son-in-law Willie. The idea is for Willie to audition and work with thirty local children between twelve and eighteen, build their confidence and team spirit and put on circus shows here at weekends and school holidays. I'm sure Sarah, Polly and April will also get involved, as well as some of the grandchildren. If I could train a new generation of circus artists, children like me who come from outside the circus community, offer them the same opportunities my children had, maybe I can help to keep circus alive in this country and my family working in the circus they love. Perhaps one day someone I help will go on to set up Britain's own answer to Cirque du Soleil.

When I look back I've had a great life. OK, so there have been plenty of disappointments, but none lasted for long. I have had a life full of adventure and excitement. And I've done something many people don't ever manage – I've followed my dream.

Appendix

The Shows and the People

1970

The first **Cottle & Austen's Circus** opens on Monday 6 July at Sturminster Newton, Dorset.

    with Brian Austen, Gerry Cottle, May Austen, Betty Cottle, Michael Austen.

1971

Cottle & Austen's Circus

    with Brian Austen, Gerry Cottle, May Austen, Betty Cottle, Michael Austen, Patrick Austen, John Moore & Roger.

after June: the Juggling Melvilles (Gerry & Betty Cottle); Temple Brook & Lynne (illusion, escapology); Shetland ponies; Yacarna (pythons, yogi); the Trimbells (trampoline); Austen Bros (thrills & spills on wheels); the Inaros Sisters (Julie & Baba Fossett, aerial, tight wire); El Briarno (Brian Austen, high wire); Miss Julianna (balancing cocktail, tight wire); Babette's Loveable Dogs; the Hi-Jacks (stilts); Billy Wild & the James Sisters (Western). Clowns: Toppi. Ringmaster: Mike Denning. Musical Director: Tex Whiteford.

Christmas: Circus, Zoo & Grotto at Tricorn Centre, Portsmouth

    with Brian Austen, Gerry Cottle, May Austen, Betty Cottle, Michael Austen, Patrick Austen etc as above.

First show in Guernsey for 30 years, only circus ever in Alderney.

TV: The Philpott File 'What do you expect, elephants?' (BBC TV).

1972

Cottle & Austen's 'Combined' Circus

    as above plus Anastasini (diabolo, comedy camel). Front of House: Peter Norris. Return to Guernsey, visited Jersey.

Christmas: Granby Halls, Leicester in association with Martin Lacey & James Mellor.

    with Captain Sydney Howes (lions & lionesses); Cimarro Bros (high wire); Inga-Lise (trapeze); Hi-Jacks (stilts); Peter & Salsky (Dive of Death); the Starr Sisters (Suzanna & Sue, sharp-shooters); Patrick Austen's bears; Miss Wendy's poodle revue; Shetland ponies; camels; llamas; Ray Maxim (illusions); Jack Varney (baby elephants). Clowns: Tombo, Scats, Willie. Musical Director: Tex Whiteford.

1973
Cottle & Austen's 'London Festival' Circus
with Pawnee Joe, Otaki & Co (Western Pastimes); the Comancheros (Austen Bros & family, knives, whips, ropes, riding); Prince Kheper-Re (fakir); Austen Bros (trampoline); Trio Salvador (rolling globes); Duo Lorenz (unicycling, juggling); Miss Wendy's Poodles; Ray Maxim (escapology, illusions); Kantares (Moroccan tumblers); Patrick's Black Bears; Jack Varney (baby elephants); El Briarno (high wire); High-Jacks (stilts); Gwyn Owen (trapeze); John James (juggler); Shetland ponies; Palomino horse. Joined mid-Season by Captain Sydney Howes (lions & lionesses). Clowns: Scats, Wee Willie, Wee Bean, Tombo, Buttons. Ringmaster: Chris Christian. Musical Director: Baron Marshall. General Manager: Robert D Moore.
Christmas: **Circus on Ice, Cardiff**
with Gwyn Owen (trapeze); Alun Davies (poodles); Santus Julien Troupe, Les Kansas (unicyclists, jugglers); Jack & Yvonne Unell (escapologist); Scotts' Sealions; Miss Magè & her baby elephants; Martino (handbalancer); Running Fox, Juanita & Otaki (fire-eating); Roger Hunt (barrel-jump); Billy Wild (Western); & the Hot Ice Company featuring the Ice Dollies, Andy Nairn, Lori Portugal. Choreographer: Roger Hunt. Clowns: Scats, Willie. Musical Director: Barron Marshal. Ringmaster: Chris Christian. General Manager: Robert D Moore.
TV: The Young Generation Big Top (BBC TV). Executive Producer: Michael Hurll.

1974
Cottle & Austen's Circus on Ice
with Peggy Lorenz (trapeze); Cimarro Bros (high wire); Orramic (swaypole); Los Tornadoes (unicycling juggler); Jana-Valencia (pigeons); The Zalenkas (comedy gymnasts); Captain Sydney Howes' Lions & Lionesses; Trio Salvador (rolling globes); Otaki (Red Indian fire-eater); Bill Unwin & Barbara Franklin (adagio skaters); Jean Byrom (solo skater); Andy Nairn (ice comedian); & the Hot Ice Company. Clowns: Scats, Tombo, Willie. General Manager: Robert D Moore.
after Aberdeen in July, re-formed into: **Gerry Cottle's Circus** *&* **Austen Brothers' Circus**
on return to London in the Autumn, added World-famous Charlie Cairoli clown troupe; Billy Smart's elephants presented by John Gindl; Khalil Oghaby, strongman.
Christmas: **Gerry Cottle's Circus**, Cardiff
with Rupert the Bear; the Garcia Family (Russian swing); Cimarro Bros (high wire); Hannibal (Khalil Oghaby, strongman); Captain Sydney Howes (lions & lionesses); Carlos MacManus (Royal Welsh ponies, elephants); Miss Julianna Inaros (tight wire, trapeze); Alec Halls (musical comedy); El Hakim (fakir); Los Cubanitos (high perch); Orramic (swaypole). Clowns: Doodie, Topper, Wee Bean, Uncle Alec, Chalkie. General Manager: Robert D Moore.

1975
Gerry Cottle's Circus
with Carlos & Pat MacManus (elephants, horses, zebras, llamas); Khalil Oghaby (strongman); Eve Lynn (pigeon fantasia); Orramic (swaypole); Swinging Cottrellis (handbalance); El Hakim (fakir); Miss Julianna (low wire, trapeze); The Mohawks (vaultige riders); Captain Sydney Howes (lions & lionesses); Otaki & the James Sisters (Wild West); Cimarro Bros (high wire); Harlequin (bareback riding). Clowns: Tommy Tucker, Wee Bean, Doodie, Chalkie. Ringmasters: Mike Denning, Ken MacManus. Musical Director: George Jones. General Manager: Mike Denning. Artiste booking: Billy F Arata.
Occasional wrestling promotions with Jackie Pallo.
Christmas: **Gerry Cottle's Circus**, Clapham Common

Appendix

with Carlos MacManus (elephants, Liberty horses); Santus Julien Troupe, Les Kansas (unicyclists, jugglers); Inaros Sisters (aerial); El Hakim (fakir); Cimarro Bros, Orramic (high wire, swaypole); Pierre Picton & Chitty-Chitty-Bang-Bang; Otaki & the James Sisters (Western); Khalil Oghaby (strongman); Captain Sydney Howes (lions & lionesses). Clowns: Matto, Wee Bean, Doodie. Ringmaster & General Manager: Mike Denning. Musical Director: George Jones.
Gerry Cottle's Circus, Cardiff, 2nd Christmas Unit.
TV: Seaside Special (BBC TV)
Circus children's series (BBC TV) – as Gerry Deacon's Circus.

1976
Gerry Cottle's Circus American Centenary edition
with Cimarro Bros (high wire & King Kong swaypole); Carlos & Pat MacManus (elephants, horses); Jack Varney (zebras, camel, llamas, ponies); Captain Sydney Howes (lions & lionesses); Scotts' sealions; Inaros Sisters (aerial); Babette's Loveable Dogs; Otaki & the James Sisters (Western); Al Hakim (fakir); Khalil Oghaby (strongman). Clowns: Smedley, Mario, Matto, Wee Bean, Yo-Yo & Rollo. Musical Director: George Jones. Ringmaster & General Manager: Mike Denning. Artiste booking: Billy F Arata.
extra artistes for London Autumn season Buby Ernesto & Co (clowns); Johnny Hutch's Halfwits, Herculeans (acrobats); Flying Tonitos, Señorita Manolita, Señor Jorge, Belios (flying trapeze, aerial, tight wire, parallel bar gymnasts); Santus Julien Troupe, Les Kansas (unicyclists, jugglers); Buffalo Bill Wild & Co. (Western), the Maxello Showgirls. Clowns: Rollo & Wee Bean. Singing Ringmaster: Scott King. Artiste booking: Billy F Arata.
Roundhouse autumn season
with Cimarro Bros (high wire, swaypole); Scotts' sealions; The Herculeans, Halfwits (comedy acrobats); Mlle Yolande (footjuggler); Khalil Oghaby (strongman); Mary Chipperfield's elephants & chimps presented by Christine. Clowns: Mario, Matto & Co. Singing Ringmaster: Scott King, the Maxello Showgirls. Musical Director: Darrell Farlow. Manager: Chris Barltrop.
Channel Islands Tour
with Royal Shetland ponies; Babette's Loveable Dogs; El Hakim (fakir); Nobre (rola rola); Sisters Inaros (trapeze); Khalil Oghaby (strongman); Scotts' Californian sealions; Cimarro Bros (high wire); Orramic (swaypole); Mary Chipperfield's chimpanzees presented by Miss Christine; Otaki & the James Sisters (Wild West bonanza). Clowns: Goffy, Charlie, Matto. Ringmaster & General Manager: Mike Denning. Musical Director: Darrell Farlow.
Flying Circus to Oman, Bahrain, elephants & all!
with Carlos MacManus (elephants, big & little, Royal Welsh ponies); Santus Julian Troupe, Les Kansas (unicyclists, jugglers); El Hakim (fakir); Khalil Oghaby (strongman); Nobre (rola rola); Cimarro Bros (high wire, swaypole, high-wire motorbike); Martin Lacey (lions); Inaros Sisters (trapeze, web); Billy Wild, Otaki, James Sisters (Western), the Maxello Showgirls. Clowns: Mario, Matto & Co. Ringmaster & Producer: Mike Denning. Musical Director: Darrel Farlow.
1st Circus World Championships at Clapham Common
with Flying Ramos; Flying Armors; Rock-Smith Flyers; Flying Oscas; New Dollys; Bertini Family; Boginos; Gene Mendez; Manfred Doval; Claude & Francine Collins; Atilla; Mary Chipperfield; Michael Henriquet; Carmelita Maezzamo; Katja Schumann; Philippe Gruss; The Herculeans; the Tangier Troupe. Ringmaster: Norman Barrett. Artiste booking: Roberto Germains.

Confessions of a Showman

Christmas: **Gerry Cottle's Circus**, Cardiff

with The 8 Biros, Andressetis (Risley, footjuggling & hand-to-hand acrobats); Buffalo Billy Wild & Susan (Western); Captain Hanson's chimps & parrots & sealions); the Cardinales, Miss Aura (musical clowns, contortioniste); Cimarro Bros (high-wire motorbike); Captain Sydney Howes (baby elephant, lions & lionesses); Marcus & Rosita (strongman); Nobre (rola rola). Clowns: Charlie, Rollo, Wee Bean. Ringmaster & Manager: Chris Barltrop. Musical Director: Darrell Farlow.

Gerry Cottle's Circus, Clapham Common

with The Belios, Señor Jorge, Flying Tonitos, Señorita Manolita (horizontal bars, tight wire, flying trapeze, aerial); Tanya Larrigan (high school riding); Carlos MacManus (elephants, Liberty horses); El Hakim (fakir); Khalil Oghaby (strongman); Scotts' sealions; Brian Andro (comedy wirewalker); Otaki & the James Sisters (Western); Los Gaucious (Argentinian folklore). The Maxello Showgirls. Clowns: Sonny Fossett & Jimmy Scott. Singing Ringmaster: Scott King. Musical Director: George Jones. General Manager: Mike Denning. Artiste booking: Billy F Arata & Roberto Germains.

TV: Seaside Special (BBC TV). Executive Producer: Michael Hurll.

Film: Ring Around the World

1977

Gerry Cottle's Circus Royal Silver Jubilee edition

with Binak Bros (knockabout comedy); El Hakim (fakir); Babette's Loveable Dogs; Carlos & Pat MacManus (Liberty horses, big & little, exotic animals, elephants); Captain Sydney Howes (lions & lionesses); Cimarro Bros (high wire, King Kong, Batman & Robin high-wire motorbike); Inaros Sisters (aerial); Luis Muñoz (tight wire); Otaki & the James Sisters (Western); Captain Universe (human cannonball Chris Munoz). Clowns: Sonny Fossett, Jimmy Scott, Matto & Wee Bean. Musical Director: George Jones. General Manager: Mike Denning. Ringmasters: Mike Denning, Chris Barltrop.

from July: **Blue Unit** (the larger outfit) retaining the programme above.

new **Red Unit** starring Mary Chipperfield (tigers, exotics, Liberty horses)

with Santus Julien troupe, Les Kansas (unicyclists, jugglers); Flying Cherokees; Sasha Houcke Jr (Cossack riding, horses); Miss Yolande (footjuggler); Clowns: Noe-Noe & Gary. Ringmaster & Manager: Chris Barltrop.

2nd Circus World Championships at Clapham Common

with Rock-Smith Fliers; Flying Cavarettas; Flying Ganeas; the Great Wallendas; Manfred Doval; White Devils; Mohawks; Jerry, Jimmy & Jonny; Michaela Kaiser; Bob Bramson; Kris Kremo; Victor Ponce; Sheff Amer; Ivan Karl; Samson & Delilah. Ringmaster: Norman Barrett. Artiste booking: Roberto Germains. Live TV broadcast of final by ITV Sport, Burt Lancaster offers prize for 1st televised quadruple somersault.

Christmas: **Gerry Cottle's Circus**, Clapham Common

with house acts, artistes from tenting show.

Gerry Cottle's Circus, Cardiff *starring* Mary Chipperfield (tigers, big & little, elephants, Liberty horses, llamas, monkeys, camels, zebras, giraffe)

with Samson & Delilah (strongman); Santus Troupe (unicycles); Les Kansas (jugglers); The Loonies (comedy acrobats); Mlle Yolande (footjuggler); Duo Raycol (revolving ladder); the Swinging Cottrelli's (handbalance). Clowns: Jimmy Scott & Co. Ringmaster & Manager: Chris Barltrop. Musical Director: George Jones. Artiste booking: Billy F Arata.

TV: Seaside Special (BBC TV). Executive Producer: Michael Hurll.

The Big Time (BBC TV) with Esther Rantzen.

Appendix

1978
Gerry Cottle's Circus
Blue Unit

with Carlos & Pat MacManus (Liberty horses, elephants, exotics); Babette's Loveable Dogs; Hsiung Family (Chinese acrobats); Barbara Howes (chimps); El Hakim (fakir); Swinging Cottrelli's (handbalance); Star Girls (Julie & Baba Fossett & Princess Aasha, aerial); Captain Sydney Howes (Lord of the Lions); Betty Cottle (farmyard animals); Samson & Delilah (strongman); Ben Karim Troupe (Moroccan acrobats); Hoppe's Unrideable Mules. Clowns: Sonny Fossett, Jimmy Scott, Matto, Wee Bean. Ringmaster: David Konyot. Musical Director: Mike James. General Manager: Mike Denning. Artiste booking: Billy F Arata.

Red Unit touring Scotland including Orkney, Northern England *starring* Mary Chipperfield (tigers, Liberty horses) (pre-Blackpool Tower Season)

with Tim Delbosq (mixed cage group, big & little, baby African elephants, exotics); Santus Troupe, Les Kansas, The Loonies (unicyclists, jugglers, comedy acrobats); Mlle Aimée, Miss Elisabeth (antipodiste, rope trapeze); Jill Delbosq (aerial web); Cimarro Bros (high wire, high-wire motorbike & swaypole); Zarina (Tess Motaz, ladder balance); The Swinging Cottrellis (handbalance); Long John (Neville & Pauline Campbell, stilts). Clowns: Noe-Noe & Gary. Ringmaster & Unit Manager: Chris Barltrop. Musical Director: George Jones. Artiste booking: Roberto Germains, Billy F Arata.

Appearances in Spring by Charlie Cairoli & Co on both units.

London Autumn 'Hippodrome' Season

with the Maxello Showgirls; Bouncing Renowns (trampoline); Weishoff's Chimpanzees; Carlos MacManus (Liberty horses, elephants); Otaki & the James Sisters (Western); Ossini Troupe (high wire); Captain Sydney Howes (lions & lionesses); Farmyard fantasy; Inaros Sisters, the Five Apollos, Princess Aasha (aerial); Samson & Delilah (strongman); Star Lords (three-lane flying trapeze); Hoppe's Rodeo Mules. Clowns: Sonny Fossett, Jimmy Scott, Matto, Wee Bean, Buzby. Singing Ringmaster: David Konyot. Performance Director: Keith Anderson. General Manager: Mike Denning. Musical Director: Mike James. Artistes Booking: Billy F Arata, Roberto Germains.

Visits to Iceland, Sharjah & Iran.

3rd Circus World Championships, Clapham Common, including 'America v. the World – Circus Challenge'

with Flying Terrels, Cavarettas; Flying Oslers; the Padillas; the 7 Hernandez; Marosi Troupe; Alan Alan; Mario Manzini; the Ashtons; the Rios Bros; Lothara; De Mille; Jose Luis Munoz. Ringmaster: Norman Barrett. Musical Director: Laurie Holloway. Artiste Booking: Roberto Germains.

Christmas: **Gerry Cottle's Circus**, Cardiff *starring* Tom Roberts (elephants, ponies)

with Beverley Roberts (camels); Mlle Aimée, Miss Elisabeth (footjuggler, aerial); Otto Europa (handbalance); Inaros Sisters & Princess Aasha (trapeze); Otaki & the James Sisters (Western); Peter Salsky (Dive of Death); Betty Blue's Farmyard Funtime; Hassani Troupe (tumblers). Clowns: Sonny Fossett. Ringmaster & Manager: Chris Barltrop. Musical Director: Otto Europa.

Gerry Cottle's Circus, Alexandra Palace

with Cimarro Bros (high wire, King Kong swaypole, high-wire motorbike); Samson & Delilah (strongman); Weishoffs' Chimpanzees; Nina & Fumisha (aerial); Miss Solitaire (trapeze); Paula Lee, Claudi & Shelli (illusions); Hassani Troupe (Moroccan tumblers); Carlos MacManus (Elephants, zebras, llamas, Liberty horses). Clowns: Jimmy Scott & Co. Musical Director: Mike James.

TV: Seaside Special (BBC TV). Executive Producer: Michael Hurll.

1979
Gerry Cottle's Circus played 40 towns
with Carlos & Pat MacManus (elephants, Liberty horses, exotics, farmyard animals); Al Hakim (fakir); Miss Barbara's, Weishoffs' chimpanzees; Ben Karim Troupe (Moroccan tumblers); Ron Marshall (trapeze); Captain Sydney Howes (lions & lionesses, later presented by Robert Raven); Santus Troupe, Les Kansas, The Loonies (unicycling, juggling, comedy vaulting); (later) Jean-Paul Santus & Jane Delbosq, rolling globes; Miss Elisabeth (Aimée Santus, rope trapeze); Inaros Sisters & Princess Aasha (aerial); Samson & Delilah (strongman); Otaki & the James Sisters (Western bonanza); Siegfried (Thomas Cimarro, high wire); Hoppe's Rodeo Mules. Clowns: Sonny Fossett, Jimmy Scott, Matto, Wee Bean. Ringmaster: Barry Walls, Ron Marshall. Musical Director: Barry Lloyd, Mike James. General Manager: Mike Denning.
Christmas: **Gerry Cottle's Circus**, Fulham
with Exotica; Crazy Beaver (tight wire); Manuel Goncalves (rola rola); Carlos MacManus (Liberty horses, exotics, elephants); Tamara (corde lisse); Robert Raven (lions & lionesses); Crystal Sisters (rolling globes); Miss June (high school horses); Duo Tovarich (aerial perch); Sonny Fossett (comedy car); Weishoffs' chimpanzees; Riding Machine. Clowns: Sonny Fossett, Matto, Wee Bean. Musical Director: Barry Frost.
Ice Show, Sharjah
with the Blackpool Ice Company; Roy Fransen (Dive of Death); Cimarro Bros (high wire motorbike); Samson & Delilah (strongman).

1980
Gerry Cottle's Circus
with Julien Santus family, Les Kansas, The Loonies (unicycling, juggling, comedy vaulting); Tim Delbosq (Liberty horses, elephants); Robert Raven (lions); the Philadelphia Flyers (flying trapeze); Barbara & Sydney Howes (chimps). Clowns: Sonny Fossett, Matto, Puddles. Ringmaster: Barry Walls. Musical Director: Barry Frost.

1981
Rainbow Circus, April to June
with Superkids (Sarah & April Cottle, Michael Howes, Beau Denning, trampoline, rolling globes); Neville Campbell & family (stilts inc motorbike); Ben Karim Troupe (Moroccan tumblers); Babette & Nikki King (belly dancers); Klemendore (India-Rubber man); The Swinging Cottrellis (handbalance); Witney Family (Liberty horses, exotic animals); Gerry Cottle's elephants presented by Jack & Emil Smith. Clowns: Sonny Fossett & Wee Bean. Musical Director (10-piece band): Barry Frost. Ringmaster: Gavin Telford.
Gary Glitter's Rock & Roll Circus, Reading, Oxford & Swindon only
with Gerry Cottle's Superkids, Campbell Family, the Cottrelli's, Sonny & Wee Bean, Gary Glitter & the Glitter Band. Ringmaster: Gavin Telford.
Sharjah
with Al Hakim (fakir); Melanie (snakes, crocodiles); Ivan Karl (strongman); Superkids (trampoline, rolling globes); Campbell family (stilts); Swinging Cottrelli's (handbalance). Clowns: Sonny Fossett & Willie Cottrelli.

1982 Gerry Cottle's Circus *starring* Richard Chipperfield (tigers, lions), Ocean Park, Hong Kong from 19 January until April, then Macau
with John Chipperfield (elephants); Podeszwa (Russian bars); Swinging Cottrellis (handbalance); Ivan Karl (strongman); Flying Carrolls, Michelle Duo (all-girl flying

Appendix

trapeze, aerial cradle); Gene & Eleanor Mendez (high wire); Gerry Cottle's Superkids (trampoline); Beskidy Troupe (springboard); Dive of Death. The London Showgirls. Director: Maxello. Clowns: Sonny Fossett, Colin Enos, Wee Bean. Ringmaster: Ian Dey. Musical Director: Barry Frost. Staging: Max Butler. Artiste Booking: Billy F Arata.

1982–83
The New Gerry Cottle's Circus *starring* Richard Chipperfield (leopards, pumas, panthers, jaguars), Ocean Park, Hong Kong, December to April, then Singapore & Malaysia. Returned to UK September.
with Marcel Peters (polar bears); The Santus Troupe, Les Kansas, The Loonies (unicyclists, jugglers, comedy acrobats); Sebastian (aerial); Cherifian Troupe (Moroccan tumblers); Sonya Burger (sky-walk); The Great Marco (wheel of death); Kublers' Chimpanzees; the Super Nova Space Rocket. Clowns: Sonny Fossett, Willie (Cottrelli), Wee Bean. The London Showgirls. Musical Director: Pete 'Burrell' Burow. Ringmaster: Ian Dey. Artistes booking: Billy F Arata. Staging: Max Butler.

1984
Gerry Cottle's Circus featuring the Students of the 1st British Circus School
with The Petrescu (fixed perch); The Victorias (poses plastiques); Dimitri (trapeze) The Falcons (tumblers); Miss Sheridan (hair-hang); Chris Barltrop (Chinese magician); Jeff Siviter (fakir); Bridgette Berry, Adam Blaug, Sarah Cottle, April Cottle, Juliette Cottle, Willie Ramsay, Chris Vogelsang, Lee Sheward, Andrew Watson, Gregoire Carel, Martin Vaughan, Gina Pritchard, Anthony Wisdom, Jeremy Hanlan, Nicholas Rowe, Jackie Williams, Julian James, Rodney Newman, Kate Verney, Victor Bastar, Neville Campbell Jr, Charlotte Barltrop. Clowns, continuity: Chris Halliday, Julian Wisdom, Denise Funnell. Show conceived & produced by Basil Schoultz, assisted by Marsha Cady. Musical Director: Dave Hankin. General Manager: Chris Barltrop. Artiste booking: Billy F Arata.
Christmas: **Gerry Cottle's Circus,** Clapham Common
with Carters' Steam Fair. Circus Company as above. Clowns: The Hazzard Family (Michael Balfour, Perry Balfour, Claire & Merlin, Mikey Owers, Daniel Bodel, Agatha & Pierre). Musical Director: Nik Turner (of rock band Hawkwind). Producer: Basil Schoultz. General Manager: Chris Barltrop.

1985
Gerry Cottle's Circus featuring the Students of the 1st British Circus School (referred to by Gerry as 'Pushkin's poems'), including Summer Season at the Congress Theatre, Eastbourne
with Barry Walls (later Chris 'Christof' Gregory, the Showman); Fiona Cowie (Mechanical Doll); Chris Barltrop (Chinese Mandarin); Bridgette Berry (Arabian Princess, tumbler); Tony Rossouw (Mongolian Warrior, cloudswing); Marcia Laverack (later Jackie Williams) & Andrew Watson (aerial cradle); Chris Vogelsang (juggler); Miss Sheridan (hair-hang); Roz Bee (contortionist); April & Sarah Cottle (rolling globes); Polly Cottle; Ivan Solomons & Rodney van Reenen (feet to feet trapeze); Ian Chambers (knife-throwing); Andrew Burleigh (juggler); The Falcons (tumblers); Willie Ramsay; Lizzie Ramsay; Tony Walls; Richard Walls; Steve Lucas; Victor Bastar (leader Springboard). Clowns: April Cottle & Jeff Singleton. Produced & Directed by Basil Schoultz. Musical Director: Dave Osborne, Alan Thompson. General Manager: Chris Barltrop.
Autumn changes to company, Santus Family join show.
Moscow State Circus under the Big Top at Bristol, August (under licence from The Entertainment Corporation)

with Oleg Popov & Co (clowns); Rodionov (adagio); Elena Gordeeva (piano eccentric); Dubynin (unicycles); Petunov (hoop perch); Bernardski (aerial perch); Russian swing troupe; Georgy Borodavkin (juggler); Bondarchuk (acrobatic duet); Lydia Ionova (illusioniste); Viktor Sungurov & Larissa Sungurova (barrel jumping); Musina Aerial suite (Spartacus revolving aerial perch).

Autumn, Winter **Gerry Cottle's Circus**, returns to Ocean Park, Hong Kong for the Year of the Tiger
Tiger Cubs presented to Beijing Zoo.

with Marcel Peters (tigers); Los Alamos, Brumbach Family (Western, sword & dagger); Alham Sahari & Shira (Carlos & Tina Rosaire, crocodiles & snakes), Werner Guerrero (high wire); Miss Aura (contortionist); Babette (aerial web); David Konyot & the Cardinalis (musical clowns); Russian swing from 'Student Show' with Victor Bastar; Mr Swing (fakir); Miss Sheridan (hair-hang); Ian Jones (Dive of Death); The Flying Souzas (flying trapeze & trampoline); the Trocaderos (motorcycle Globe of Death); the Maxello Showgirls; Wee Bean Ringmaster: Ian Dey. Musical Director: Dave Osborne.
Christmas: **Gerry Cottle's Circus, Camden Lock, London**

with Clarissons' Sealions; David Sherwood (Mary Chipperfield's horses, exotics); Flying Cherokees; Stars of the Future (Neville Jr, Richard, Carl & Kristian Campbell & Charlotte Barltrop, rola rola, unicycle, juggling, & aerial); Neville Sr & Pauline Campbell (stilts); Tony Rossouw (cloudswing); Rani the elephant with Robert Raven; The Williams (Jackie Williams & Andrew Watson, aerial cradle); Suzanne Chipperfield (high school riding); Ivan Karl (strongman); Andrew Burleigh (juggler); Mona Gerbola (high school). Clown: Chris 'Christof' Gregory. Musical Director: Kenny Darnell. Ringmaster & General Manager: Chris Barltrop.

1986

Gerry Cottle's Circus Irish tour
with Yasmine Smart & Dany Cesar (Liberty horses, high school, La Poste); Marcel Peters (Lions); the Rossouws (wheel of death); the Cottle Juniors (trampoline); Rani the elephant with Robert Raven; El Hakim (Barry Walls, fakir); Pam Enos' football dogs; Duo Giovanni (April Cottle & Andrew Burleigh, juggling); the Wotnots (comedy vaulting); Hong Kong Chinese Circus Co (Miss Sheridan, hair-hang, Barry Walls, Emperor, Tony Rossouw, Mongolian acrobat, Sarah Cottle, April Cottle, Juliette Cottle, Kim Rossouw, Andrew Burleigh, Ian Jones, Willie Ramsay, Charlotte Barltrop). Clowns: The Hazzards. Ringmaster: David Konyot. Musical Director: Alan Thompson. General Manager: Chris Barltrop.
Gerry Cottle's Circus back from Ireland
with Les Rossouws (wheel of death); Duo Giovanni (jugglers); El Hakim (fakir); Cottle Jrs (trampoline); Sue Lacey (tigers); Martin Lacey (lions); Robert Raven & Rani (elephant); Pam Enos (football dogs); Gerry Cottle Hong Kong Circus Company (Barry Walls, Tony Rossouw, Ian Jones, April Cottle, Sarah Cottle, Juliette Cottle, Kim Rossouw, Andrew Burleigh, Willie Ramsay, Charlotte Barltrop). Clowns: David Konyot & Co. Ringmasters: Chris Barltrop, Martin Lacey. Musical Director: Alan Thompson. General Manager: Chris Barltrop.
Christmas: **Cottle & Austen's Circus, Battersea Park, London**

with Martin Lacey (lions); Sue Lacey (tigers); Miss Chantelle (Amanda Orry, corde lisse); Aissa & Hyatt, Trio Ben Atlas (rola rola, juggler); Austens' exotics presented by Carlos Michelli; Austens' 3 elephants presented by Michael Austen; Flying Cherokees; Austens' 4 chestnut horses presented by Michael Austen; Pam Enos' footballing dogs; the Nevadas (Austen family Western act). Clowns: The Konyots. Ringmaster & Manager: Martin Lacey.

Appendix

1987
Gerry Cottle's Circus
with June Witney (ponies, high school); Leanne Witney (poodles); Duo Chantelle (aerial webs); Amanda Orry (Spiderwoman aerial); Susan Lacey (tigers); Martin Lacey (lions); the Oscas (aerial cradle); the Giovannis (juggling); Rani the elephant & Robert Raven; Pam Enos (football dogs); Apollo (strongman); Karl & Amanda Orry, Sarah Cottle, Willie Ramsay (Western); Hong Kong Chinese Circus Co. Clowns: The Konyots. Ringmaster & Manager: Martin Lacey. Musical Director: Alan Thompson.
Christmas: **Cottle & Austen's Circus**, Battersea Park, London
with The Juggling Giovannis (April & Lee Ann Witney, Michael Howes, Andrew Burleigh); Michael Austen (big & little horses); Lee Ann Witney (dogs); Bald Eagle & Chaquita (Karl & Amanda Orry, Western); the 'B' Team (high-wire motorbikes); Flying Rochelles (flying trapeze); James Clubb's mixed cage group (wolves, hyenas, leopards, lions); Amanda Orry, April Witney, the Oscas (aerial); Exotic animal parade (Indian & African elephants, horses, ponies, camel, llamas, zebras, highland cattle, eland, baby hippo, kangaroo, emu, bison); Indian & African elephants; El Jay (aerial cloudswing); the Bauers (swaypoles); the Epsom Riders (traditional jockey riders); Lacey's reindeer. Clowns: The Hazzards. Musical Director: Pete 'Burrell' Burow. Ringmaster & General Manager: Martin Lacey.

1988
Gerry Cottle's Circus
with Martin Lacey, Othmar Vohringer (lions); June Witney (big & little, high school, Martin Lacey's exotic animals); Sarah Cottle (equine); Lee Ann (poodles); Duo Chantelle (Amanda Orry & April Plant, aerial); Susan Lacey (tigers); the Cartiers (rolling globes); the Belle Stars (flying trapeze); the Juggling Giovanni; Rani the elephant with Robert Raven. Clowns: Brum, Rum & Marie. Ringmaster & Executive Director: Martin Lacey. Musical Director: Phillip Plant. Artistes booking: Glyn Picton.
The Moscow State Circus, first-ever British Big Top Tour, with The Entertainment Corporation, May to August
with The Popovs (trampoline); Nina Chuglayeva & Vladimir Burakov (Firebird aerial web); Kaminskys (Russian bar); Shatins (casting); Daniya Kaseyeva (hula hoops); Moscow Builders (perch poles); Natalaya Zhidilova & Lyubov Chirkova (strongwomen); Druzhinas (high wire); Garamovs (flying trapeze); Viktoria Geleverya (Snake Girl contortionist); Anatoly Myagkostupov & Viktor Pilipovich (jugglers); Annayevs (Cossack riders). Clown: Anatoly Marchevsky. Musical Director: Albert Tochilovsky. Ringmasters: Leonid Spektor & Chris Barltrop.
Christmas: **Cottle & Austen's Circus**, Battersea Park, London
with Jana & her Crocodiles & Snakes; James Clubb's Canadian & Himalayan Black Bears; Zulu Warriors (acrobats); Othmar Vohringer's roaring lions; The Julians, Galos (perch, revolving aerial); Alex Larenty (elephants, comedy dog); Sally Ann Duggan (Liberty horses); the Mexicanas (Austen family Western & trick riding); Luisito & Roberto Garcia (sky-gyro wheel of death); Great Sebastian (aerial mast); Michelle Dudley (aerial) Clowns: Professor Wotnot (Patrick Austen) & the Pinder Bros. Ringmaster: George Pinder. Musical Director: Mike Fontaine. General Manager: Peter Featherstone, Chris Barltrop.
Cottle & Austen's Circus, Wembley, London
with Kornek Troupe, Despol (Russian bar, springboard); The Giovannis (jugglers); Epsom Jockeys (riders); Susan Lacey (tigers); Martin Lacey (lions); Flying Rodleighs (flying trapeze); the Oscas (aerial cradle); Miss Chantelle (aerial web); Willie Ramsay (Cossack riding); Lee Ann Witney (poodles); June Witney (exotic animals); Robert Raven & Rani the Elephant. Clowns: The Konyots. Ringmaster & General Manager: Martin Lacey. Musical Director: Chris Spencer.

1989
Gerry Cottle's Circus
Lion Unit

with Ivan Karl (strongman); Supernova Rocket; Alison (revolving trapeze); Ternos, Nitwits (trampoline, comedy acrobats); Lutz Beitzel (exotic animals, Roberts Bros 6 spotted ponies); Frank Endrix (juggling unicyclist); Miss Babette's Footballing Dogs; Othmar Vohringer (lions); Flying Belle Stars (trainer Larry de Wit). Clown: Zak, Spanners. Ringmaster & Executive Director: Martin Lacey. Musical Director: Chris Spencer.

Tiger Unit

with Hugo Zamoratte (The Man in the Bottle contortionist); Sue Lacey (tigers); Michelle Inaros (aerial); Alex Larenty (elephants, comedy dog Rags); Alexander Fenech (sword-swallower); Sally Anne Duggan (Liberty horses); Juggling Melvilles (April Cottle, Vera & John Fossett, jugglers early Season); Epsom Riders (Sarah Cottle & Willie Ramsay, jockey riders); Karl & Amanda Orry (Western with Julie Austen); Wheel of Death (Garcia Bros, later Van Dare Bros); Alain & Mona Santus (unicycling, aerial moon, juggling with April Cottle). Clowns: Karl Orry, later Hazzard Bros). Ringmaster, illusions & Tour Director: Chris Barltrop. Musical Director: David Lobban.

Christmas: **Gerry Cottle's Circus**, Grand Hall, Wembley Centre

with Alison Sebastian (aerial); Satin (aerial duo); Hugo Zamoratte (Man in the Bottle contortionist); Clarissons' sealions, horses, zebras, dogs; Alex Larenty (elephants, comedy dog); Ivan Karl (strongman); Epsom Riders (vaultige riding); Frank Endrix (juggling unicyclist); Gomari Troupe (Moroccan tumblers); Supernova (aerial rocket); James Sisters' Wild West Bonanza. Clowns: The Hazzard Family. Ringmaster: Martin Lacey. Musical Director: Chris Spencer. Artiste booking: Billy F Arata.

Gerry Cottle's Circus, Brislington, Bristol

with Sue Lacey (tigers); Chantelle (corde lisse); Lutz Beitzel (exotics); Ben Atlas (rola rola); the Ternos, Nitwits (trampoline, comedy vaulting); the Belle Stars (flying trapeze); Babette's Footballing Dogs; the Swinging Cottrelli's (handbalance); Rani the elephant & Robert Raven; Sally Ann Duggan (Liberty horses). Clowns: Willi, Zak, Wee Bean. Ringmaster & Manager: Chris Barltrop. Musical Director: Pete 'Burrell' Burow.

Gerry Cottle's Circus, Derngate Theatre, Northampton

with Epsom Riders (jockey riding); Alex Larenty (elephants, comedy dog); Clarissons' sealions; the Oscas (aerial cradle); the Salvadors, Walencias (rolling globes, doves); Flying Ramos (flying trapeze); Hugo Zamoratte (Man in the Bottle contortionist); the Rodogels (springboard). Clowns: Spanners & Zak. Ringmaster & Manager: Martin Lacey. Musical Director: Chris Spencer.

1990
Gerry Cottle's Circus
Lion Unit

with The Belle Stars (flying trapeze); De Wits (aerial cradle); Lacey's lions; Ivan Karl (strongman); & programme as previous year. Ringmaster & General Manager: Martin Lacey.

Tiger Unit, Holland, England inc Isle of Wight

with Sue Lacey (tigers); Polly Cottle (aerial rope); Sarah Cottle (ponies); the Faltinis (unicycling, juggling, Western); the Salvadors (rolling globes, pigeons); Brenner family (clowning, rola rola); Epsom Riders (jockey riding); the Venturas (aerial perch, dental act); Alex Larenty (elephants); Supernova (aerial rocket); Coty Teuteberg (comedy car); Hugo Zamoratte (The Man in the Bottle contortionist). Clowns: Charlie, Fips & Co.

Appendix

Ringmaster & Manager: Chris Barltrop. Musical Director: Pete 'Burrell' Burow.
Christmas: **Gerry Cottle's Circus**, Wembley & Longest Limo
   with Didier Pasquette (high wire); Martin Lacey (lions); Danielle (aerial rope); Brenner Bros (double rola rola); the Royals (jugglers); Babette's Footballing Dogs; Sarah Cottle (ballerina riding); Fips (plate-spinning); Marcel Peters (elephants); the Faltinis (unicyclists); the Oscas (aerial cradle); Wild West Spectacle (Sarah Cottle, Liberty horses, Coyote, cloudswing, Arizonas, whips, knives, ropes, fire, Muchachos, bows & arrows, Coyote Riders, vaultige). Clowns: Charlie, Fips & Co. Ringmaster: Martin Lacey. Musical Director: Chris Spencer.
TV: Flog It (BBC TV) – antiques programme, much-repeated.

1991
Gerry Cottle's Circus
   with Lutz Beitzel (exotics); the Royals (jugglers); Sarah Cottle (Liberty horses, ballerina on horseback); Ivan Karl (strongman); Babette's Footballing Dogs; Jindra Faltiny (aerial straps); Martin Lacey (lions); Captain Apollo (Ferenc 'Ocsi' Tabak, human cannonball); Faltini Troupe (unicycling); Coyote (Willie Ramsay, cloudswing); Marcel Peters (Indian elephants & Bully the African elephant); the Comancheros (Western); Coyote Riders (Willie Ramsay & Sarah Cottle, vaultige); the Oscas (aerial cradle); Spanish Web. Clowns: Zak & Ozone. Ringmaster & Manager: Martin Lacey. Musical Director: Pete 'Burrell' Burow.
Continental Circus Berlin
   with the Lesters (juggling); June Witney (Liberty ponies); Robert Foxall (aerial rings); Duo Galos, the Julians (revolving cradle, aerial perch); Rani the elephant & Eddie Singer; Hammich Bros (Moroccan tumblers); Lee Ann (poodles); Rob Alton (BMX flatland); the Colorados (Western); Antaeus (escapologist); the Witney Family (bareback riders). Clown: Tito. Director, General Manager & Ringmaster: Chris Barltrop.
Christmas: **Gerry Cottle's Circus** and Gigantic Indoor Funfair, *starring* Jeremy Beadle as Ringmaster, Wembley Halls 1, 2 & 3
   with Sabu (solo trapeze); The Alegrias (wheel of death); Laci (boy wonder juggler); Sarah Cottle (Liberty horses, Shetland ponies); Epsom Riders (jockey riding); Kenya Boys (acrobats); Hoppe's Unrideable Mules; Jana (crocodiles, snakes); 5 Endresz (musical clowns); the Maxello Showgirls. Performance Director: Martin Lacey. Musical Director: Pete 'Burrell' Burow. Artiste booking: Laci Endresz, David Barnes, Tip Top Entertainments.
Continental Circus Berlin, Pickett's Lock, Edmonton
   with Lutz Beitzel (exotics); Marcel Peters (tigers, Indian & African elephants); the Oscas (aerial cradle); the Witney family (ponies, poodles, high school, bareback riding); the Comancheros (Robert Fossett family, Western); Miss Rebecca (corde lisse); Robert Foxall (Roman rings); Rob Alton (BMX flatland); Captain Apollo (Ferenc 'Ocsi' Tabak, Human Cannonball); Ivan Karl (strongman); Clowns: Duo Lumiros, Ozone. Ringmaster: Antar. Musical Director: Kenny Darnell.
TV: The Red Nose of Courage (BBC TV) – satire with The Comic Strip.

1992
Gerry Cottle's Circus
   with Marcel Peters (exotics, elephants); the Faltinis (juggling, unicycling); the Oscas (aerial cradle); Babette's Footballing Dogs; Martin Lacey's Royal Bengal tigers; Captain Apollo (human cannonball); Sarah Cottle (Liberty horses); Epsom Riders (jockey riding); Los Comancheros (Western). Clowns: Fips & Beau. Ringmaster, Director & General Manager: Martin Lacey. Musical Director: Peter 'Burrell' Burow.

Continental Circus Berlin

with Gela Fossett (footjuggling); Menzah Bros (Moroccan tumblers); Witney family (ponies, poodles, vaultige riding); Robert Foxall (Roman rings); Rob Alton (BMX flatland); the Galos, Julians (perch poles, revolving perch); Rani the elephant & Eddie 'Adi' Singer; the Rodionovs (adagio); the Colorados (Western). Joined by Polly Cottle & Charlotte Barltrop (aerial) in summer holidays. Clowns: The Konyots. Director, General Manager & Ringmaster: Chris Barltrop.

Christmas: **Gerry Cottle's Circus** and Gigantic Indoor Funfair, *starring* Jeremy Beadle as Ringmaster, Wembley Halls 1, 2 & 3

with Mary Chipperfield (Liberty horses, tigers); Comanche (antipodiste); Rob Alton (BMX flatland rider); Yanika (hula hoops); Robert Foxall (Roman rings); Mighty Miklos (strongman); Los Garcias (aerial cradle); Babette's Footballing Dogs; Joan Rosaire & Goldy the Wonder Horse 'presented by' Jeremy Beadle; Philip Hanson (African elephants); The Rodionovs (adagio); Menzah Brothers (Moroccan acrobats); the Hi-Jacks (stilts); Willie Ramsay (vaultige rider); Hoffmans' African elephants with Philip Hansen; the Riding Machine with Rebecca Barltrop, the Maxello Showgirls. Clowns: Baby D, Dingle Fingle, Beau, Little Andrew. Musical Director: Kelvin Parker. Directed by Max Butler. Performance Director: Chris Barltrop. Event Manager: Malcolm Cannon. Artistes booking: Michael Cohen, MPC (Mr Beadle), David Barnes, Tip Top Entertainments (artistes).

TV: The Low Down (BBC TV) – focussing on Juliette 'Polly' Cottle.

1993

Gerry Cottle's Carnival with the **Zincalli Gypsy Circus**

with Sarah Cottle (Liberty horses); Rebecca Austen (foot juggling); Jeff Jay, Duo Jay (comedy trampoline, aerial cradle); Willie Ramsay (cloudswing); Babette's Footballing Dogs; the Black Mambas (Afrobatics); Azella (Rebecca Austen, 'dazzling designs'); Al Hakim (fakir); Romanic Revelries (Gypsy fire, knives, ropes, whips) & the Zincalli Riders. Clowns: Beau & Jojo. Ringmaster: Barry Walls. Musical director: David Europa. Manager: Malcolm Cannon.

Palace of Varieties

with the Magical Melvilles (Sarah Cottle & Willie Ramsay, illusions); Barry Walls (fakir); Duo Jay (aerial cradle); Rebecca Austen (spinning sphere); Black Mambas (acrobats).

Cottle Sisters Circus opened July in Paignton

As for Zincalli Gypsy Circus above.

Christmas: **Gerry Cottle's Daredevil Circus**, Wembley

with Jeff Jay; Suzanne Chipperfield (high school); Tonia (aerial moon); Johnny Roberts' elephants; Azella (Becky Austen, dazzling designs); Hungarian Hercules (strongman); the Bauers (swaypoles, high-wire motorbike); the Skating Luisitos (roller-skaters); the Black Mambas (Afrobats); Didier Pasquette (high wire); Romanic Revelries & the Zincalli Riders. Clowns: Philip Walker & Ro-Ro. Singing Ring-mistress: Emma James. Musical Director: Nigel Hogg. Manager: Malcolm Cannon. Artistes booking: Tip Top.

TV: Beadle's Daredevils (ITV) Producer Nigel Lithgow.

1994

Cottle Sisters Circus

with Jeff Jay, Duo Jay (comedy trampoline, aerial cradle); The Mayers (giant Space Wheel); Sarah Cottle (solo Liberty horse, high school riding); Rebecca Austen (footjuggling); the Black Mambas (Afrobatics); Trio Anjei (casting aerial cradle); The Skating Luisitos (Luisito Garcia & Polly Cottle); Romanic Revelries (Gypsy fire,

Appendix

knives, ropes, whips) & the Zincalli Riders; Delia du Sol (girl in a bottle contortionist). Clown: Tito. Musical Director: David Europa. Manager: Sarah Ramsay.

1995
The Moscow State Circus presented by the European Entertainment Corporation
with The Algini (Russian bar); Elena & Lioudvig Chtchoukine (aerial straps); Elena Iniakina (hula hoops, also illusions with Svetlana Iniakina & Anatoli Pelechak); clowns Liouk & Valla); Anna Baidina (Rag Doll contortionist); Galina & Victor Pilipovich (jugglers); Goussein & Gasan Khamdoulaev (high wire); The Brousnikine (flying trapeze); Yaroslav Viter (pierrot juggler); Svetlana & Elena Iniakina & Co (flying hats); The Baidini (perch poles); & comedy acrobatics from the Company. Ringmasters: Julie Austen & Chris Barltrop. General Manager: Chris Barltrop. Musical Director: Ian Riley. Producer: Natalia Makovskaia.
Cottle Sisters Circus
with Sarah Cottle (Liberty horses); April Cottle & JoséCristos (jugglers); Jazz & Molly Mop (comedy dog); Jeff Jay (comedy trampoline); Jungle Fantasy, Limbo dance Afrobats (Bernard Machal, Ally Masoud, Ishaka Isack, & Guy Rawlings as Kong); Becky Austen (footjuggling); Simon Mamba & Sellam Ouahabi (handbalancers); Sellam Ouahabi (rope swinging); Thomas Ramsay & Ingo Dock (cloudswing); Willie Ramsay & Jeff Jay (wheel of death); Delia du Sol (the Girl in the Bottle); Gerry Cottle Jr (in school holidays, Diabolo). Clowns: Titto & Totto. Musical Directors: David & Shane Europa.
The Circus of Horrors, initial production Glastonbury
with Undead Ringmaster Dr Haze; Sarah Cottle (Macabra); Polly Cottle (Regan); April Cottle (Pandemonia); Ingo Dock (Scud); Thomas Ramsay (Drog); Willie Ramsay & Sellam Ouahabi (Jesuit priests); Simon M, Mossmu M, Leroy M, Rocky M, Tanga M (Pygmy warriors); Delia du Sol (The Twister); Sinbad (fakir); Jeff Jay (Sakad); Yana Rodionova (Cat Girl); Alexia, Pandomo (vampires); Brian Trimnell (Jake Minustwo). Music: The X Factor (Tony Quintini, QTR, Kase, keyboards, Andy Higgins, bass, Ricki Danger, drums, Billy the Fish (Sub Zero), sound, sum Kiwi chick, lights.
The Circus of Horrors, redirected by Pierrot Bidon
at Brighton joined by Johnny Brenner & Georgia Howarth (the Phantom & his Wench); Steve Beast, keyboards; Dog Championi, drums; Pete Mundini, lights.
at Crystal Palace joined by Kenny Darnell, keyboards; Hugh Sadler, sound.

1996
The Moscow State Circus as above.
Cottle Sisters Circus as 1995.
The Circus of Horrors
Manchester 14 & 15 February, special guest Dani Behr
Festival Tour Bradford, Leeds, Stockton, Edinburgh, joined by The Prince of Pain (fakir); Michelle Sherie (the girl in the bottle); Lyn Daniels (transsexual); Alexia (vampire); Moog (assassin); Kiss My Axe (warriors); Gerry Cottle Jr (Comatose); Andy Louder, lights; Neil X, sound.
Clapham Common & Chelsea Bridge joined by Tony Walls (Mongolian Laughing Boy); Mad Michelle (Naked).

1997
Gerry Cottle's Circus presented by Tony Hopkins
with Novikova (illusions); the Marinhos (high wire); Nathalie (low wire); Charlie & partner; Duo Amadeo; Jana Roberts (hula hoops); Sally Ann Roncescu (Liberty

horses); Ionut Roncescu (comedy dog); Wolodos Troupe (parallel bar gymnasts); Karoly Donnert Jr (juggler); Martiny Clowns; Elastics Fantastics; Team Chicago (tumblers). Clowns: Mathieu & David. Host & speaker: Jan Saad. Musical Director: Nigel Hogg.

The Moscow State Circus as above.

The Circus of Horrors

  Munich plus Mad Michelle (Naked Girl in the Bottle).

  South America plus Seb Vittorini (Wasp Boy); Gela Fossett (Erotica); Todger, GTR; Simon France, lights.

  The Roundhouse, London for 17 weeks! with Misha Real, Alex Sutch (Naked Girl in the Bottle); Barry Walls (Mad Monk); The Psycho String Trio; Eddie Muir, lights; Basil Schoultz, bungee trainer.

1998

Gerry Cottle's Circus presented by Tony Hopkins

  with Karoly Donnert (comedy dog, juggling); Los Pedros (rag doll contortionist); Rebecca Austen (spinning sphere); Entcho (handbalance); Guy Saad (Liberty horses); Peter & Pepi Sandow (comedy taxi); Rob Alton (flatland BMX); The Rivelinos (musical clowns); the Ayalas (high wire); Ignatov (bareback riders). Ringmistress: Jan Saad.

  In October, a second unit also featured Kenya Boys (acrobats); Henry Ayala (clown); Garbo (robotic breakdancer); Peter & Pepi Sandow (Ghostbusters).

The Moscow State Circus presented by the European Entertainment Corporation

  with Karina Grigorieva (contortionist); The Guriyanov (springboard, Russian swing); Irina Pilipovich (trapeze); Mik & Mak (clowns); Sedov & Zoubarev (comedy hot-air balloon); Goussein Khamdoulaev & Evguenia Pilipovich (high wire); Popazov (silver arrow revolving balance); Eskine (aerial bars). Ringmasters: Victor Pilipovich & Chris Barltrop. Director & General Manager: Chris Barltrop. Musical Director: David Hale, Eddie Hankin. Choreographer: Natalia Makovskaia.

Cottle & Austen Electric Circus

  with Petre & Irina Baltadjiev (aerial & hair-hang); Yana Rodionova (hula hoops); Gerry Cottle Jr (diabolos); Nyvikova (illusions); Polly Cottle (aerial silks); Flying Ciobanu (flying trapeze); Jeff Jay (comedy trampoline, giant Space Wheel); Kenya Boys (Afrobatics); Misha Reale (cloudswing, giant Space Wheel). Clowns: Fips & Beau, Phillip (Whimmy) & Roberta Walker. Singing Ringmistress: Emma James. Musical Director: Nigel Hogg. Director: Rob Goodwin. Tour Manager: Beau Denning. Artiste booking: Laci Endresz & David Barnes, Tip Top Entertainments.

Circus of Horrors, Holland, Glastonbury, Galway, Stockton, Edinburgh, Glasgow, Leeds

  with Dr Haze; Sarah Cottle (Macabra); Polly Cottle (Regan); April Cottle (Pandemonia); Ingo Dock (Scud); Frances Richardson (Nun); Irina Baltadjiev (Mercia III); Peter Baltadjiev (Vlad); Dugany, Muhag, Germoi (Pygmy Warriors); Tony Walls (Mongolian laughing boy & warrior); Seb Vittorini (Wasp Boy); Misha Real, Claudette Rams (naked girl in bottle, cloudswing); Eddie Mony (streaker); Pityu (Demon Dwarf); Brian Trimnell (Jake Minustwo); Yana Rodionova (hula hoop girl); Jan-Erik Brenner (psycho clown); Gela Fossett (Erotica); Willie Ramsay (1st Jesuit priest); Sellam Ouahabi (2nd Jesuit priest); Gerry Cottle Jr (Comatose). Music: The X Factor (Drew Blood, GTR; Kase, Keyboards; Andy Higgins, Bass; Dog Championi, Drums; Andy Louder, sound; Eddie van de Muir, lights).

Circus Ethiopia by arrangement with Reinhard Bieschell, Swizerland, visiting Brighton Festival, Edinburgh Festival, Glasgow, Leeds, Warwick Arts Centre.

TV: Prince of Wales' Trust Royal Gala Performance (ITV) – featuring Circus of Horrors.

Appendix

1999

The Moscow State Circus as above.
Cottle & Austen Electric Circus as above.
Circus of Horrors festivals, Roundhouse, as above.

2000

The Moscow State Circus as above.
The Chinese State Circus, by arrangement with Phillip & Carol Gandey
Zheng Zhou Troupe. '15-on-a-Bike' Tour
Tenting tour UK, & Winter Tour 2000–2001 UK & Ireland.
Artistic Director for China Performing Arts Agency: Mr Tian Run Min. General
Manager for EEC Ltd: Larry de Wit.
Cottle & Austen Electric Circus as above.
Circus of Horrors Roundhouse, special guest on final night Screaming Lord Sutch
joined by Barry Walls (Baby Boy); Amy Misbehave (Sword Swallower); Nicci
Christian (Satanica); Masu 88 (Tennis Racket Man).
Circus of Horrors Theatre Tour
joined by Silvana Maimone (gypsy queen); Carrie Harvey (bearded lady); Kirsty
Ballingall (bride of Wasp Boy); Cody Christian (Maxx); Amba & Saren Janchivdorj
(Gemini Twins); Marrow (voodoo king); James McCliskey (hoopla king); Dave Patton,
sound; Rob Mander, lighting designer.
Circus of Horrors Japan Fuji Rock Festival:
joined by Todd Christian (Todrick Testicles); Haja Matajaki, sound.
TV: Trouble at the Top (BBC2) – business documentary featuring EEC Ltd & the
Chinese State Circus.

2001

The Moscow State Circus, presented by the European Entertainment Corporation,
Tenting & Bristol Christmas Season
with Uzeyer Novrouzov (freestanding ladder, first year only); The Panov family
(footjuggling); The Flying Akhtyamovs (flying trapeze, first year only, then The Eskins,
aerial bars); Goussein Khamdoulaev (high wire); The Rubtsov troupe (fast-track tram-
poline); The Averiouchkines (clowns); Serguei Ibanov (strongman, first year only);
Bougrova Sisters (rola rola); Olga Demidova & Oxana Shapyrina (aerial perch, contor-
tionistes). Ringmasters: Ilya Tetruashvili, Sergey Bakulin. Musical Director: Eddie
Harkin. General Manager: Paul Archer. Producer: Tatiana Kokhanova.
The Chinese State Circus, by arrangement with Phillip & Carol Gandey
Zheng Zhou Troupe as above. Tenting Tour & 2001–2002 Theatres Tour.
Artistic Director for CPAA. Mr Tian Run Min. General Manager: Larry de Wit.
Cottle & Austen Electric Circus
with Titto Lester (clown); Yana Rodionova (hula hoops); Irina Baltadjieva (hair-
hang); Nymkova (illusions); Karina Grigorieva (contortionist); Flying Ciobanu (flying
trapeze); Jayde Hanson & Co (Western); Domingo Morales (cloudswing); Kenya Boys
(Afrobatics); Morales Bros (giant Space-Wheel); The Baltadjievs (aerial). Dancers.
Singing Ringmistress: Emma James. Musical Director: Nigel Hogg. General Manager:
Beau Denning. Directed by Rob Goodwin.
Circus of Horrors 2nd UK Theatre Tour, Holland, Ireland
joined by Gary Stretch; Sub Zero, sound.
Christmas: The Roundhouse, London
Cottle & Austen Electric Circus, matinees
with Igor & Slavi (handbalance); Petr & Irena Baltadjiev (bolas, hair-hang, double
corde lisse); Yana Rodionova (hula hoops); Polly Cottle (aerial silks); the Ciobanu (flying

trapeze); Jeff Jay (comedy trampoline); Nyvikova (illusions); April Cottle (juggling); Jayde Hanson (ropes & whips); Sarah Cottle (sword & dagger balance, spinning cube); Kenya Boys (Afrobatics); Willie Ramsay, Jeff Jay (Space Wheel). Clowns: Beau Denning, Todd Christian. Singing Ringmistress: Emma James. Musical Director: Nigel Hogg.
Circus of Horrors, evenings
TV: Cheers for Charlie (BBC) – presenter Charlie Dimmock learns flying trapeze with Cottle & Austen Circus.

2002

The Moscow State Circus, presented by the European Entertainment Corporation, as above
Tenting & 2002–03 Theatre Tour
Theatre tour, *some acts omitted & adding* Maksim Rubtsov (juggling); Andrey Averi-ouchkine Jr (juggling on drums); Irina Tcherkassova (firebird trapeze); Ekaterina Rubtsova (hula hoop).
The Chinese State Circus, by arrangement with Phillip & Carol Gandey
Chang Chun Troupe. 'Unicyclist-on-a-Ball' Tour.
Tenting & Winter 2002–03 Theatre Tour,
Artistic Director for CPAA: Mr Tian Run Min. General Manager: Larry de Wit.
Cottle & Austen Electric Circus Big Top Rock
  with Pityu (world's smallest man, rola rola); Kenya Boys (acrobats, mast); Iona (contortionist); Tugs (aerial straps); the Crazy Crew (comedy, juggling); Yana Rodionova & Andreea Mihut (hula hoops); Jayde Hanson (Western); Igor & Slavi Makarovi (handbalance); the Flying Jantsans (flying trapeze); dancers. Clown: Titto. Singing Ringmasters: Emma James & Joe Fury. MD: Nigel Hogg. Manager: Beau Denning. Directed by Rob Goodwin. Artistes booking: Tip Top.
Circus of Horrors, back in a Big Top, Stockton, Edinburgh, Bristol, & 3rd UK Theatre Tour
  joined by Frances Richardson (sometimes Regan); the Skating Aratas; Thomas Black-heart (Blackheart the Barbarian); Hig Hire, sound.
TV: Ant and Dec's Saturday Night Takeaway (ITV) – Ant & Dec experience the Circus of Horrors.

2003

The Moscow State Circus, presented by the European Entertainment Corporation, tenting as above.
The Chinese State Circus, by arrangement with Phillip & Carol Gandey
Chang Chun Troupe as above.
Tenting Tour & Winter 2003–04 Theatre Tour.
Artistic Director for CPAA: Mr Tian Run Min. General Manager: Larry de Wit.
Cottle & Austen Electric Circus as above.
Circus of Horrors Theatre Tour UK & Ireland
  joined by Karina Grigorieva (Twisted Sister); Tarn Aitken (Warrior); Steve McGrill, drums.

2004

Wookey Hole
Circus of Horrors Theatre Tour
  changes Jeff and Polly Jay; Ellen Ramsay; Regan either Frances Richardson or Karina Grigorieva or Yana Rodionova; Ounga (Twisted Sister); Captain Dan (Demon Dwarf); Kevin Armstrong, keyboards; Per Astompt, guitar.

Appendix

2005
Wookey Hole
Circus of Horrors Theatre Tour
joined by Karl, Jane and Jan-Erik Brenner; Tatyana Ghrongi (hula hoops); Leslie Gardiner (German wheel); Claire Chaotic (Pandemonia). Music: The Interceptors from Hell (Kevin Armstrong, keyboards, Per Astompt, guitar, Tommy Tucker, guitar, Greg James, drums. Lighting designers: Big Bob Robinson, Pauli Hunger, Ginger Christian.
TV: Richard & Judy (BBC2) – featuring Gary Stretch from the Circus of Horrors.

2006
Wookey Hole
Circus of Horrors Theatre Tour as above.
including Karl and Jane Brenner.

TV items listed are for main credits only, not including news programmes.
Appendix compiled by Chris Barltrop.

Acknowledgements

My thanks to Helen – for her hard work, patience and the free therapy . . .

My appreciation goes to all my family – who have stood loyally by me, even in my very very bad days.

And to the extended family of the circus, just too many to mention over the years, including the backroom boys and girls and their families that have always kept 'the show on the road'.

Special thanks must go to my hard working personal assistants over the years. Especially to Anne Owen, who spent eighteen years on the front line. She's now semi-retired to spend time with her grandchildren in Manchester, but I believe still waiting for the call to say we are going back on the road again. To Louise Prior, who has joined me here at Wookey Hole.

I would specially like to mention Malcolm Clay. Malcolm has not only been my solicitor for over thirty years, but a great personal friend.

Malcolm is dedicated to the travelling show business. He has been Secretary to the Circus Proprietors' Association for over thirty years now, acting with government departments over transport, health and safety, work permits, constant rules and regulations, and most importantly, the winter quarters for show people. He works tremendously long hours, often for little reward; some people think he is a helpline.

The circus industry has had so much paperwork chucked at it, especially in the last ten years, without his input and experience I would have given up years ago.

I can be the showman, but the circus industry needs people like Malcolm now more than ever.

I would like to place on record what a marvellous job the following have done over the years recording and keeping alive the tradition and spirit of the British circus: Don Stacey – the circus editor of *World's Fair* for over thirty years; David Jamieson – the publisher and editor of *King Pole*; and Daniel Potier and Fin Costello – the renowned circus photographers.

Whatever happened between us over the years, without the Gandys, Roberts, Fossetts, Paulos and other hardworking British circus families, circus would not be still on the roads in Britain today. A special thanks to Laci Endresz and Reinhard Bischel who have recommended many of the top circus acts that we have engaged the last twenty years.

I must mention my special friends, Glyn Picton and Malcolm Cannon who have helped me through very difficult times, and my friends in the States, Ron and Arlene Morris.

I would like to thank everyone who helped Helen in her research for the book, particularly Betty, whose memory of those important key moments and conversations was so often better than my own. Also Sarah and April, my sister Jane, Julie Fossett, and Patrick Austen, Brian Austen, Dr Haze, Michael Hurll, Mark Borkowski, Tony Shuker, Peter Featherstone, David Barnes and John Smith.

Everyone at Vision for their unfailing enthusiasm, especially Charlotte Cole for her amazing attention to detail.

Finally Chris Barltrop, for his magnificent work on the appendix.

Helen would also like me to thank her husband Benjamin Knowles without whose support, both moral and financial(!), this book would have not been possible.

And finally Alison George, who started the whole ball rolling.